# COLLECTED TRANSLATIONS

*Also by Edwin Morgan from Carcanet*

Selected Poems
Collected Poems
Sweeping Out the Dark

(translator)
Edmond Rostand: *Cyrano de Bergerac*

# EDWIN MORGAN

*Collected Translations*

CARCANET

First published in Great Britain in 1996 by
Carcanet Press Limited
402-406 Corn Exchange Buildings
Manchester M4 3BY

A CIP catalogue record for this book
is available from the British Library.
ISBN 1 85754 253 3

The publisher acknowledges financial assistance
from the Arts Council of England.

Set in 10pt Palatino by Bryan Williamson, Frome
Printed and bound in England by SRP Ltd, Exeter

– Habar bar?
– Bar!

## ACKNOWLEDGEMENTS

The author and publisher gratefully acknowledge permission from the following to publish these translations, and are obliged to Judit Pocsik at Artisjus, Budapest, for her help:

Editions Gallimard, Paris for poems by Pierre Albert-Birot, Jean Genet, Guillevic, Henri Michaux and Jacques Prévert; Reed Books Ltd for permission to reprint poems by Bertolt Brecht; the author for poems by Haroldo de Campos; the Fondo de Cultura Economica (Mexico D.F.) for poems by Luis Cernuda; Suhrkamp Verlag for poems by Hans Magnus Enzensberger from *Verteidigung der Wölfe: Gedichte* © Suhrkamp Verlag Frankfurt am Main 1957; the author for poems by Ágnes Gergely; the author for poems by Eugen Gomringer; © 1985 Hermann Luchterhand GmbH & Co. KG Darmstadt und Neuwied, now Luchterhand Literaturverlag GmbH, Munich, for poems by Ernst Jandl; the author for poems by László Kálnoky; Mr Ferenc Csaplár, Director of the Kassák Literature Museum for poems by Lajos Kassák; William Peter Kosmas, Esq. 77 Rodney Court, 6/8 Maida Vale, London W9 1T, for 'Asesinato', 'Ciudad Sin Sueño', 'Casida del Ilanto', 'Casida de la Rosa', 'Casida de las Palomas Oscuras', 'Gacela de la Huida', 'Gacela de la Raíz Amarga', 'Canción de la Muerte Pequeña' by Federico García Lorca © Herederos de Federico García Lorca, all rights reserved; translations copyright © Edwin Morgan and Herederos de Federico García Lorca, all rights reserved; Arnoldo Mondadori Editore, Milan for poems by Eugenio Montale and Salvatore Quasimodo; the author for poems by Ottó Orbán; his executor for poems by Miklós Radnóti; © 1955 Suhrkamp Verlag, Frankfurt am Main for 'Einsamkeit' by Rainer Maria Rilke; the author for poems by Dezsö Tandori; his executor for poems by Mihály Váci; his executor for poems by István Vas; his executors for poems by Sándor Weöres.

All reasonable steps have been taken to contact copyright holders. The publisher would be interested to hear from any not acknowledged here.

CONTENTS

Preface                                          xxi

*Poems from Eugenio Montale* (1959)
Preface                                            3
Sarcophagi I-IV                                    6
'Often I've met the wrong...'                      8
Mediterranean: 'Age-old are you...'                9
Mediterranean: 'Rugged, elemental...'              9
Sirocco                                           10
Tramontana                                        11
Arsenio                                           11
Lindau                                            13
Dora Markus I-II                                  13
Motet: 'At crack of dawn...'                      15
Motet: '...well then, let be.'                    16
The customs-officers' house                       16
Low Tide                                          17
Eastbourne                                        18
New stanzas                                       19
Tidings from Mt Amiata                            20
The storm                                         22
A window at Fiesole                               22
The black trout                                   23
The eel                                           23
Brief testament                                   24

*Sovpoems* (1961)
Introduction                                      27
Boris Pasternak:
    Sevastopol 1905                               32
    To a friend                                   33
    Spring (1944)                                 33
    Night                                         34
Marina Tsvetayeva:
    'O tears in the world's eyes'                 36
Vladimir Mayakovsky:
    Ay, but can ye?                               37
    Whit mair?                                    37
    Wi the haill voice                            38

Nikolai Tikhonov:
  The boat     41
  'Frozen heather...'     42
Bertolt Brecht:
  The plum-tree     43
  Those who deprive the table of meat     43
  A worker reads...     44
  The landscape of exile     44
  Conversations rowing     45
  1940     45
  On watering the garden     46
Pablo Neruda:
  Eastern funeral     46
  Universal song: 'Heights of Macchu Picchu'     47
  Universal song: 'Let the rail-splitter awake!'     49
Leonid Martynov:
  'Poems are not composed...'     51
  The leaves     51
  'I thought I had risen...'     52
  'Evening came on...'     52
Yevgeny Yevtushenko:
  The partisans' graves     53
  The angries     54

*Sándor Weöres: Selected Poems* (1970)
Introduction     59
Eternal moment     63
The first couple     63
The underwater city     65
To die     66
Wedding choir     66
The colonnade of teeth     68
Whisper in the dark     69
The scarlet pall     70
Clouds     71
The lost parasol     72
Moon and farmstead     82
Orpheus killed     82
Queen Tatavane     83
In the window-square     87
Rayflower     88
Terra Sigillata     89

| | |
|---|---|
| In Memoriam Gyula Juhász | 91 |
| Signs | 92 |
| Internus | 93 |
| Mountain landscape | 96 |
| The secret country | 97 |
| Difficult hour | 98 |
| Coolie | 99 |
| Monkeyland | 100 |

from *Wi the Haill Voice: 25 Poems by Vladimir Mayakovsky* (1972)

| | |
|---|---|
| Introduction | 105 |
| Forcryinoutloud! | 114 |
| Fiddle-ma-fidgin | 115 |
| War declarit | 116 |
| Hymn to a Jeddart-justicer | 117 |
| To the bourgeoisie | 119 |
| The ballad o the rid cadie | 119 |
| A richt respeck for cuddies | 120 |
| Vladimir's ferlie | 122 |
| Respeck for a lassie | 125 |
| Mandment No.2 to the Army o the Arts | 126 |
| Mayakonferensky's anectidote | 129 |
| I'm aff | 131 |
| Versailles | 133 |
| A fareweel | 137 |
| The Atlantic | 137 |
| Brooklyn Brig | 142 |
| Goavy-dick! | 146 |
| Eupatoria | 149 |
| May Day | 150 |
| Anent the deeference o tastes | 151 |
| Awa wi it! | 152 |
| Comrade Teenager! | 154 |

*Fifty Renascence Love-Poems* (1975)

| | |
|---|---|
| Introduction | 159 |
| Francesco Petrarca: | |
|     'I see no place...' | 164 |
|     'Pale beauty! and a smile...' | 164 |
|     'The woods are wild...' | 165 |
|     'The eyes that drew from me...' | 165 |
|     'Great is my envy of you...' | 166 |

Maurice Scève:
   'That beauty which enriched...'         166
   'Some are the skilful poets...'       167
   'Suddenly dazzled by lightning...'    167
   'Twice now has the moon's...'     167
   'Excellent painter...'       168
   'To see, to hear, to speak...'    168
   'Flowers in evening hidden...'   168
   'My face, anguish...'       169
   'Say that desire...'        169
   'When I saw in the blue...'    169
   'To speak, or not...'       170
   'I look for restful night...'    170
   'The soaring thought...'     170
   'Within the shadow...'     171
   'Wherever you have gone...'   171
   'See how when shivering winter...'  171
   'Closely and still more closely...'  172
   'Here alone I lie...'      172
   'Wanderer: drowned body...'   172
   'See the clear day...'     173
   'Gone languid now...'     173
   'Pierced as my spirit is...'   173
   'Every length and breadth...'   174
   'Almost beside myself...'    174
   'At that happy centre...'    174
   'When (but O how seldom!)...'  175
   'When death has stripped off...'  175
   'Nothing, or little more...'   175
   'Perhaps you wonder...'    176
   'Such blessed fire...'     176
Garcilaso de la Vega:
   'One moment my hope...'    176
   'Your face is written...'     177
   'Rough are the roads...'     177
   'Sweet gifts, by me...'     178
   'While there is still...'     178
   'I came to a valley...'     178
Torquato Tasso:
   'To what joys...'        179
   'So far from you...'      179
   'No flowers by these shores...'  180

'Most perfect kiss...'                          180
'What were the dews...'                          180
'Silent the forests...'                          181
'Tarquinia, if your studious eyes...'            181
Giambattista Marino:
'My hidden treasure...'                          181
'That pair of gleaming snakes...'                182

from *Rites of Passage* (1976)
Introductory Note                                185
Andrei Voznesensky:
  Autumn in Sigulda                              186
  Parabolic ballad                               188
  Autodigression                                 189
  The first ice                                  190
  Foggy street                                   190
  Goya                                           191
  Wings                                          192
  Earth                                          193
  New Year letter                                194
  Italian garage                                 194
  Selling watermelons                            195
  Rublyov Road                                   196
  New York airport at night                      197
  Bella Akhmadulina                              199
  Violets                                        200
Yevgeny Yevtushenko:
  Stalin's heirs                                 201
Boris Pasternak:
  'My shame, my shame...'                        204
  The approach of winter                         204
  'O had I known...'                             205
  Verses on Pushkin: Third Variation             206
  Daybreak                                       206
  March                                          207
  The wedding party                              208
  Winter night                                   209
  from The Waves                                 210
  'It's an ill thing...'                         210
Yevgeny Vinokurov:
  The nightingale                                212

Salvatore Quasimodo:
  Man of my time 212
  'The rain is with us again...' 213
  Instead of a madrigal 213
  My country is Italy 214
  Thanatos Athanatos 215
  Letter to my mother 215
  Road in Agrigentum 216
  Now that the day breaks 217
  On the boughs of the willows 217
  Snow 218
  From the rock-fortress at Upper Bergamo 218
  Elegy 219
  Lament for the south 219
  'Visible, invisible...' 220
  The soldiers cry at night 220
  To the new moon 221
Guillevic:
  The skerry 222
Eugenio Montale:
  Blow and counterblow 225
William Shakespeare:
  The hell's-handsel o Leddy Macbeth 227
Giacomo Leopardi:
  The broom 229
  To himself 237
  Infinity 237
  The calm after the storm 238
  Village Saturday 239
  Holiday evening 241
  The solitary life 242
Anglo-Saxon Poems:
  The ruin 245
  The seafarer 246
  The wanderer 249
  Seven riddles 252
Friedrich Hölderlin:
  The Rhine 256
Federico García Lorca:
  Murder 262
  Sleepless city 262
  Casida of weeping 264

| | |
|---|---|
| Casida of the rose | 264 |
| Casida of the dark doves | 265 |
| Gacela of the flight | 265 |
| Gacela of the bitter root | 266 |
| Song of the little death | 267 |
| Luis Cernuda: | |
| A Glasgow cemetery | 268 |
| Leonid Martynov: | |
| You must live! | 269 |
| The eternal way | 269 |
| The sheepskin coat | 270 |
| 'Along the beach...' | 270 |
| Fact | 271 |
| 'Outside...' | 271 |
| The green ray | 272 |
| Jacques Prévert: | |
| Procession | 272 |
| Henri Michaux: | |
| 'You though...' | 273 |
| 'Huge voice...' | 274 |
| Voices | 276 |
| Landscapes | 277 |
| Labyrinth | 277 |
| 'Carry me off...' | 277 |
| Rest in Misery | 278 |
| The future | 278 |
| Robert Rozhdestvensky: | |
| History | 280 |
| Bertolt Brecht: | |
| 'When the times darken...' | 282 |
| The return | 283 |
| Hans Magnus Enzensberger: | |
| Economic miracle | 283 |
| Drowsing | 284 |
| In the reader for upper forms | 285 |
| Cicada | 285 |
| Advice to Sisyphus | 286 |
| Haroldo de Campos: | |
| Transient servitude | 286 |
| Eugen Gomringer: | |
| Untracked | 293 |
| Maybe | 293 |

From deep to deep 294
Words are shadows 295
From occasion 295
The Book of Hours (II) 296
Yury Pankratov:
Slow song 301
Edgard Braga:
'One fly...' 302
'white horses...' 302
'in my glove of gold...' 303
'living...' 303
'ballad ballad...' 304
'isle...' 304
'one poor...' 304
'white swallow...' 305
'yes yes...' 305

*Platen: Selected Poems* (1978)
Note 308
The pilgrim at St Yuste 309
Vesuvius in December 1830 309
'Love is my betrayer...' 310
A sigh in winter 310
'And I started up sharp in the night...' 311
'Fain would I live in safest freedom...' 311
Tristan 312
'Whitely the lily wavers...' 313
To a woodbine tendril 313
'The new shoots scatter their scent far away...' 314
'Truest of sages are you to me...' 314
'Forfairn's my hert...' 314
'Time and space, torment...' 315
'Who has ever held life in his hand...' 315
'At least to be at peace...' 316
Venetian Sonnets 317

from *Sweeping Out the Dark* (1994)
Claudian:
On the old man of Verona 325
Michelangelo Buonarroti:
'In me is daith...' 326
Giacomo Leopardi:
The aesome blackie 326

Flinder 328
Tae his sel 329
Aleksandr Pushkin:
Autumn 330
'Corbie tae corbie...' 333
Vladimir Solovyov:
The wintry loch o Saimaa 334
Aleksandr Blok:
'Nicht, causey...' 335
Velimir Khlebnikov:
Gaffin-cantrip 335
Ha-oo! 336
Coarse talk 336
Vladimir Mayakovsky:
For all that 337
Eugenio Montale:
Boats on the Marne 338
Wind in the Crescent 339
Xenia II(5) 339
Attila József:
Attila József 340
Heart-innocent 341
Mother 341
Meditative 342
Unemployed 343
Keep going! 343
My mother 344
'It isn't me you hear...' 345
Ode 345
'On the pavement...' 349
'I open the door...' 349
'Everything's old...' 350
They'd love me 351
My mother washing clothes a wreath 351
Dead landscape 352
The woodcutter 353
Blighty numbers 354
March 1937 355
Epitaph for a Spanish farm-hand 356
Elegy 356
Profit 358
'Freight trains shunt...' 359

xv

Night in the suburbs                                       360
'Well, in the end...'                                      362
In light, white clothes                                    363
Gennady Aigi:
    Mozart: Cassation I                                    364
    A note: apophatic                                      365
    Lake and bird                                          365
    Field: height of winter                                366
    KRCH-80                                                366
    Sending roses                                          367
    Suburban house                                         367
    The birches rustle                                     368
    Once more: places in the forest                        369
Ezra Pound:
    Lament of the frontier guard: a restruction            370

*Uncollected Poems* (1937-1996)
Endre Ady:
    I am breaking new waters                               373
    Long live the victor                                   373
    'Give me those eyes of yours...'                       374
    A stroll in the country                                375
    A graceful message of dismissal                        376
    In the boat of meditation                              377
Pierre Albert-Birot:
    'The poet salutes...'                                  378
    'Everything goes at the coming...'                     379
Guillaume Apollinaire:
    The Mirabeau Bridge                                    379
    Time to come                                           380
    The parting                                            381
    The pretty redhead                                     381
Anna Akhmatova:
    'How lovely here!...'                                  383
Rosalía de Castro:
    'When wind is hard...'                                 383
    '"I in my bed..."'                                     384
    'The spring does not flow...'                          384
    'Crows were cawing...'                                 385
    'Justice of men!...'                                   385
    'The atmosphere is incandescent...'                    386
    'Hour after hour...'                                   387

'– I love you . . .'                                    387
'Now that the frost . . .'                              387
'I do not even know . . .'                              388
'From the deep measure . . .'                           388
The bells                                               388
St Columba:
  The Maker on High                                     389
Jean Genet:
  from The Fisherman of the Suquet                      393
Ágnes Gergely:
  Crazed man in concentration-camp                      395
*The Greek Anthology*: 26 poems                         396
Heinrich Heine:
  Hoo the warld wags                                    402
  Whaur?                                                403
  'I see ye like a flooer . . .'                        403
  'The stane wi its runes . . .'                        403
  'Yonder's a lanely fir-tree . . .'                    404
  'Whit wey is my hert . . .'                           404
Vera Inber:
  from The Pulkovo Meridian                             405
Ernst Jandl:
  16 yearth                                             406
  'you were a good girl . . .'                          407
László Kálnoky:
  What am I?                                            408
  Flame and darkness                                    409
  The possible variations                              409
  The fatties at the baths                              410
Lajos Kassák:
  Abandoned objects                                     411
  Young horseman                                        417
  I am with you                                         418
  'At evening we dip . . .'                             418
  'Trees arch . . .'                                    419
Velimir Khlebnikov:
  Dragon train                                          423
  'Once more, once more . . .'                          426
  'Song of the lips . . .'                              427
  'When horses die . . .'                               427
Michelangelo Buonarroti:
  Three sonnets                                         427

Night 429
Nikolai Nekrasov:
  The poor wanderer's song 429
Pablo Neruda:
  Ode: boy with hare 430
  Ode: to my socks 432
Ottó Orbán:
  The ladies of bygone days 434
  Gaiety and good heart 437
  To be poor 438
  Chile 438
  Report on the poem 439
  The apparition 440
Jacques Prévert:
  Dunce 441
Aleksandr Pushkin:
  Desire for fame 442
  Winter morning 443
  The Caucasus 444
  The avalanche 445
  The upas-tree 446
  'I loed ye...' 447
Miklós Radnóti:
  An Eskimo thinks of death 448
  Letter to my wife 449
  Forced march 450
  Picture postcards 451
Rainer Maria Rilke:
  Loneliness 452
Viktor Sosnora:
  Dolphins 452
Three Spanish ballads 453
Dezsö Tandori:
  The greeting 455
  The bush flown away 456
Marina Tsvetayeva:
  'August – asters...' 457
  The return of the chief 458
  Dialogue of Hamlet and his conscience 458
Thirteen Tuscan folk-songs 459
Fyodor Tyutchev:
  'The night sky hung...' 462

Mihály Váci:
  The most-age                             463
István Vas:
  Pest Elegy                               464
Paul Verlaine:
  Strains of forgetfulness – VIII          466
Théophile de Viau:
  Ode                                      467
Andrei Voznesensky:
  from The Ditch                           467
Sándor Weöres:
  Homeward bound                           469
  For my mother                            471
  De profundis                             473
  Self-portrait                            475
  'Eternal darkness clings...'             475
  Ars poetica                              476
  The old ones                             476
  Le Journal                               478
Pedro Xisto:
  Seaweed                                  483
Yevgeny Yevtushenko:
  'Poetry smoulders...'                    483
  Incantation                              485

Index of poets                             487

This collection includes the complete text of *Poems from Eugenio Montale, Sovpoems, Weöres: Selected Poems, Fifty Renascence Love-Poems*, and *Platen: Selected Poems*; a selection (to avoid repetition) of poems from *Mayakovsky: Wi the Haill Voice, Rites of Passage*, and *Sweeping Out the Dark*; and a batch of hitherto uncollected or unpublished poems. I have left the various prefaces and introductions unchanged; they will have to fend for themselves across the years! The earliest translation is that of Verlaine's *Ariettes oubliées* (1937), the latest a version of St Columba's *Altus Prosator* (1996). In the course of six decades, one's ideas and ideals concerning translation are bound to fluctuate, and I have sometimes allowed myself more freedom than I wanted to claim in the introduction to *Rites of Passage*, but I would still regard the general principle of being a good servant to the foreign poet, rather than thanking him very much and then going on to write a new poem of one's own, a sound and (with luck) productive approach. The translations from Hungarian are something of a special case. In the late 1950s I came across a little volume of Italian translations of Attila József with a useful introduction and facing Hungarian text. The poems made an immediate and powerful impact. I got hold of a Hungarian dictionary and grammar, and began making English versions through the medium of the Italian. These were published in various magazines in the early 1960s, and were eventually brought to Hungarian notice. In 1966, on a visit to Budapest, I was encouraged by writers and editors who thought I had captured the 'feel' of József to make further translations of Hungarian poetry, which I did, and indeed with increasing fervour over the years. I was sent the poems, plus rough versions, and went through the originals as closely as I could, picking up, by dint of translating, a good deal of the language. The Hungarians, who tend to favour close translation, sensed that I tried hard not to let their poets down, and for my part I had something of a missionary desire to spread the news to the English-speaking world that there were major poets writing in Magyar. Without my feeling of eager identification with these poets, particularly József and Weöres, the method would not have worked. My thanks are due to Miklós Vajda and other helpers at the *New Hungarian Quarterly* (now the *Hungarian Quarterly*), and to the late George Cushing, for providing me with both material and incentive.

E.M.

# POEMS FROM EUGENIO MONTALE

## (1959)

The present selection of Eugenio Montale's poems is made from his three principal volumes, *Ossi di Seppia* (1925), *Le Occasioni* (1939), and *Le Bufera* (1956). It has been chosen to give a fair representation of his range, although stress has been laid on the first two volumes.

Montale's poetry is not easy; but neither is it so private in its references as to demand a running biographical commentary, nor so 'hermetic' in its style as to repel those who seek substance. With a few exceptions, the poems overlap on recognizable contexts of human experience, and even when they seem not to overlap very far, they attract us by that peculiar kind of genuineness which gives us keen pleasure long before we can account for its provenance.

The 'world' of Montale is a distinctive place, sometimes beautiful, sometimes frightening and desolate. We move into it gradually as the imagery of sense-impressions from poem to poem builds up a strongly felt atmosphere which in the end can be seen to pervade the whole verse: a shimmer, a play of light on water and on crumbling walls, a whiff of camphor, a face glancing in a mirror, a weathercock whirling, the rumble of distant trains, shoes squeaking on shingle, cries of children, windows flashing, chilly seaside pavilions, the thunder of the sea, the hiss of the rain, an accordion being played in the twilight....

> finché goccia trepido
> il cielo, fuma il suolo che s'abbevera,
> tutto d'accanto ti sciaborda, sbattono
> le tende molli, un frúscio immenso rade
> la terra, giú s'afflosciano stridendo
> le lanterne di carta sulle strade.

Absorbing this atmosphere is a step in comprehension, because one begins to grasp not only the tone of a particular poem (the excitement of 'Tramontana', the cold harshness of 'Eastbourne') but also the signature of the author's style, his 'hand', his way of putting things, his symbolic use of the physical and the sensuous. It has often been pointed out how closely Montale's imagery is rooted in the landscape of his native Ligurian coast (he was born in Genoa in 1896), and how well this suits the 'inner landscape' of his mental experience. As Mario Praz puts it: 'the Cinque Terra, whose wretched inhabitants wage a constant war against the elements, save every grain of fertile soil from disastrous land-slides, and grow scanty vineyards among cruel rocks . . . a narrow strip of waste land in one of the most enchanting regions of the world, the Riviera' (in *T.S. Eliot, A Symposium* . . . Poetry London, 1948).

Onto this harsh coast are thrown the cuttle-bones ('ossi di sep-pia') of another world: relics of a living creature, evidence from a mysterious, submarine, nearly inscrutable life: beautiful but strange objects, like the poems themselves. There is no cuneiform on these stark pelagic potsherds. How can we read them? What message is sent? In one sombre comment, using a different image, Montale seems to despair of communication:

> la preghiera è supplizio e non ancora
> tra le rocce che sorgono t'è giunta
> la bottiglia dal mare. L'onda, vuota,
> si rompe sulla punta, a Finisterre.

Modern poetry might well be described as a 'MS found in a bottle', but Montale is speaking more particularly of his own feel-ing of isolation, a theme to which he often reverts, and which is compounded almost equally of a desire and a fear to be swept up in the exhilarating but confusing flux of twentieth-century experi-ence. Uprooting ('Scirocco'), exile ('Dora Markus'), and absence ('La casa dei doganieri') are painful, yet nothing is more remark-able in other poems than the author's instinctive (and life-giving) yearning for abandon, change, and movement, expressed in evocations of the great natural forces of the wind and the sea.

> Ritorna piú forte
> vento di settentrione che rendi care
> le catene e suggelli le spore del possibile!

He rightly describes himself in 'Mediterraneo' as 'transfixed' and 'perplexed', an observer and a searcher, but as soon as he hears the waves, those voices make him 'drunk' and wildly dis-turbed with delight and hope –

> You loosen with your song the knots within me.
> And now your frenzy soars among the stars.

Some critics have spoken of Montale's 'pessimism', or at best his 'stoicism'. It may seem that the public contemporary world is little reflected in his work. Yet apart from making such obvious references as the poem 'La primavera hitleriana', Montale by his

4

non-cooperation, by his very withdrawnness, clearly indicated the sort of commitment he endorsed in the days of Fascism. His frustrations are a mirror of the European malaise of those years, however they may also have been motivated by elements in his personal psychology. Nor is frustration, or stoicism, the whole story. The 'struggling life ascending' in 'Arsenio', the 'thread of pity' in 'Notizie dall'Amiata', the 'stubborn hope' in 'Piccolo testamento' are all gathered up and incoronated into something more positive in 'L'anguilla', which in both form and content traces the indefatigable creative drive of life. This may be only one of Montale's moments of revelation, one of his 'occasions', but it is necessary to bear it in mind, and to place against the picture of a bottle bobbing at the mercy of the tides and perhaps empty, the purposeful and meaningful image of the migrating eel.

In these translations I have tried to reproduce as much of Montale's texture – verbal and emotional – as I could, within a framework as close to the Italian verse as the nature of English will allow. The sound-effects in rhyme, assonance, alliteration, and onomatopoeia, to say nothing of rhythm, are so subtly manipulated in the original as to defy an exact point-to-point correspondence; but I have not avoided the attempt to take care of them, even if sometimes under the principle of 'equivalence of effect'. Fortunately for the translator into English, Montale's music is strong and often dissonant rather than Petrarchan and vowel-melting. Grammatical cruxes (doubtful appositions, shadowy interrogatives, ambiguous pronouns) have usually been solved by plumping for one reading, unless it seemed important that the ambiguity should be retained. The translator, who has to understand the poem, is frequently tempted to clarify it in his translation, and this is why some translated poems look as if they had been written by a rather clever child. I hope I have managed to escape this, and to keep something of the 'tang' of my author, though in many other ways the versions of such a formidable poet must confess their imperfections.

For help and encouragement of various kinds, I would like to thank Professor D.J. Gordon, Dr Luigi Meneghello, Mr Ian Fletcher and Mr D.S. Carne-Ross.

Acknowledgements are due to the following in respect of translations previously published: *Partisan Review*, the BBC, and to the poet for permission to reprint.

## SARCOPHAGI I

Where will those curls be blown, and the young heads go
Of girls with shouldered pitchers overflowing,
Girls whose step is as light as it is sure?
Deep down a valley is opening
For their beauty in vain: shadow
Spills from trellises of vine
And the clusters droop in their swinging.
The sun pacing the sky,
The half-seen hill-slopes, lose
Their colours: in this soft-springing
Minute, nature is blinded
And steals through her happy creatures
As life, a mother indeed at whose dear will
Lightly all are dancing.
A world asleep or a world in old self-praise
Of its uninterrupted existence, who can say?
But give it, O passer-by,
The best twig that your orchard brings to birth.
Pass by: this valley is opening
Not to the mere succession of darkness and light.
It is far from here you must be led out by life.
Rest here, and refuge? No, you carry too much death.
Great gyres are yours, where you with your stars must go.
– And so goodbye, young curly-heads; goodbye so:
Going with your shouldered pitchers overflowing.

*[Sarcofaghi I]*

## SARCOPHAGI II

Step now with greater care:
At a stone's throw from here
A far rarer scene
Is being prepared for your gaze.
The door of a little temple,
Rusted, is closed for ever.
A great light lies
Down on the grassy threshold.

6

Here will never resound
Men's steps again, or a mourning feigned and cold.
Only a lean dog watches, stretched on the ground.
He will not stir, not stir
All through this hour that stares with sultry face.
Above the roof a kingly
Cloud looks out to space.

*[Sarcofaghi II]*


## SARCOPHAGI III

The fire that crackles faintly
In the grate is burning green
And a gloom charges the air
Over a flickering world. An old man sleeps
By the firedog, tired, sunk
Deep in the sleep of the forsaken.
Cavernous glimmerings fall
In a dream of bronze; O sleeper, never waken
From your forsakenness! And you who go by,
Softly go by; but first
Add here a branch to feed
The flame in the hearth and a ripe
Pine-cone to fill the basket
Thrown in the corner: it spills
To the earth its provisions kept
For the last journey of all.

*[Sarcofaghi III]*


## SARCOPHAGI IV

But where shall we look for the grave
Of the faithful friend and the lover;
Grave of the boy and the beggar;
Where shall we find a haven
For these, who embrace the embers

7

Left by the far-off blaze:
Are they reconciled? – O for a sign, a figure
Light as a toy on the glaze
Of the urn! Turn from the hushed and stony crowd
To those abandoned slabs
That sometimes disconcert
More with the symbol cut
For laughter and lament
Surging as twins together.
The labourer sees it on his way to work; he's poor,
His blind blood throbs and drives in him, to endure.
Search in this place for some primordial frieze
Able in its long memorial to win
The rough soul into ways
Of exile's gentlest ground:
Some trifling thing: a sunflower's open face
And rabbits dancing lightly round and round...

*[Sarcofaghi IV]*


OFTEN I'VE MET THE WRONG OF
THE WORLD IN MY WALK

Often I've met the wrong of the world in my walk:
There by the strangled brook with its guttural song,
There with the puckering of the thirsty tongue
Of a parched leaf, there by the horse that fell and shook.

Little I knew but what I saw in a rune,
A vision of the divine Unconcern:
There by the statue in the drowsy sun
At noon, and the cloud, and the heaven-climbing hawk.

*['Spesso il male di vivere ho incontrato']*

from MEDITERRANEAN

Age-old are you, and drunk am I with the voice
That mounts from all your mouths when they are swinging
Open like green bells rung and bluffly lunging
Back and loosely dissolving.
I lived beside you, in summers long ago –
You remember? – there was my home,
The land where the sun bakes and where the air
Grows thick with its mosquito-clouds. And now
I am turned to stone before you, as I used to be,
O sea, but I cannot believe
As I used to believe, that I merit the admonitions
You gravely breathe. You first made me know
That the puny agitations
Of my heart were only momentary motions
In yours; that there lay at the base
Of my life your terrifying law: to be as various
As vast, yet fixed in place:
And so to slough off all my filth and burden
As you do, throwing on the shore with seaweed
And starfish and cork the useless
Trash and dregs that lagged in your abyss.

*[Mediterraneo: 'Antico...']*


from MEDITERRANEAN

Rugged, elemental, is how I would have had myself –
Whirled about like your pebblestones,
Bitten hard by the salt;
A splinter cast from time, a witness of the power
Of one uncaring, unrelenting will.
The truth was different: I was a man transfixed,
Watching in myself, and in others,
The swift seethings of life – a man perplexed,
Tardy to act when no act is destroyed.
I wanted to find the evil
That gnaws and rots the earth, the tiny lever
Twisted awry that brings
The structure of things to a halt; and I saw all

The events of every minute
About to fly from their bonds in disorder, and fall.
The track of one path taken, I had still
The other soliciting my heart; perhaps
I needed the curtness of the knife,
The mind that is set and decides.
I needed other texts –
And all I had was on your thundering page.
But there is nothing I can regret: once more
You loosen with your song the knots within me.
And now your frenzy soars among the stars.

[Mediterraneo: 'Avrei voluto...']

SIROCCO

Hungry sirocco breath
On the pale scorched green of the soil
Burning!
While up above, in a sky
Smudged with a faint shining
A flake of cloud will sail
And float off like a wraith.
Hours of perplexity, shiverings
Of a life that runs like water
Through the fingers: possibilities
Unproved, visions, invisibilities,
Tumults of all the sickly
Wavering things of the world:
O arid aisles of air
I now drift,
An agave clinging in a cleft
Of the cliff,
Shunning, like the arms of seaweed, the sea
Which arches awful jaws and jars the rocks:
And in this ferment
Of all substances, with the tight-shut buds of my thoughts
Unable to burst any more, I feel the garment
Of my immobility laid on me today like a torment.

[Scirocco]

## TRAMONTANA

And now the anxious ripples have raced out
Their last circle upon the lake of my heart,
And the vast sizzling of the world, the blight
And the dying things, depart.
Today one will of steel sweeps through the vault,
Uproots the bushes, lashes back the palms,
And ploughs along the cringing sea
Huge furrows with their crests of spray.
All shapes of matter are tortured in the clamour
And rut of the elements; one single moan and roar
Rises from lacerated lives: all things are wrenched
By the hour as it flies: across the arching sky
I see – is it leaves, or birds? all flown, all gone.
And you that are tossed relentlessly in the scud
Of the plunging runaway blast
And draw to your breast your arms in bud
With flowers no sun has yet unclasped:
How hostile now, to your sense,
Those spirits that fly high in their thick flocks
Over the violent earth!
Today, my subtle life, it is your earth,
Your roots that are your friends.


## ARSENIO

Tiny tornadoes lift the dust in the air
Till it eddies over the roofs and the empty spaces
Deserted by all except the vizored horses
That sniff the ground, transfixed, while in their faces
The windows glitter from the great hotels.
Down on the front, you go along by the waves
This day of rain,
This day of sun, with the refrain (sparkling
To confuse its moderation,
Its fine close net of hours) the castanets
Set clashing.

11

It's the sign of another zodiac you must steer for.
You must go down to a horizon overhung
By the lead-grey waterspout towering above depths
Less rootless than itself: a salty whirlwind
Spiralling up in the masterless chaos of weather
To the clouds: you must go where your footsteps
Squeak on the shingle and in the knotted tangle
Of the seaweed stumble: and that may be the instant
That time has so long lain in wait for, to save you
From the end of your journey, a link in the midst of
A chain, motionless progress, oh delirious
Memory, Arsenio, of marmoreality . . .

Listen! through the palm-trees comes a springing tremor
Of violins, quenched when the roll of thunder
With its beaten sheet-metal shatters the playing;
The storm is soft under Sirius, as the star
Of the dog-days is disgorged into the azure
Of heaven and far far off seems the evening
That is so near: if lightning comes to lance it
It branches out like a precious tree, through
Brilliant showers and dewy sprays: the distant
Gypsy drum is boom and silence too.

And down into the heart of darkness you go.
Steeply it descends, making midday a night
Of blazing globes put swinging to the sea,
And far out where a single shadow holds
Both sky and water, and a few boats blow,
Flaring acetylene unfolds –
                                    until
The sky drips quivering, the soil steams as it drinks,
And you and the world around you are flooded and swirled
With the limp flapping of awnings and the gigantic sheets
Of whispering rain and the blown-down sodden shapes
Of paper lanterns scraping through the streets.

Here then are the drenched mats and rushes, and you
Yourself a reed among them, a reed that drags
Its roots where it goes, clinging and never freed,
You, trembling with life and yearning sent
Towards an emptiness ringing with broken lament,

The arch of that age-old wave that whirls you about
Becoming your gulf and vault; and here once more
Is everything that can recapture you – street and porch
And walls and mirrors – all that turns you to stone
Among the frozen lonely many dead,
And if one gesture can touch you, or if one
Word can become your friend, this is perhaps
A sign, in one spontaneous hour, Arsenio,
Of a struggling life ascending now through yours
And wind-borne with the ashes of the stars.


LINDAU

Brought by the swallow,
These blades of grass; he wants no grim blowclocks.
But at night by the dykes, the sluggish waters hollow
And obliterate rocks.
Every moment the smoking torches father
Some shadow that glides off over the lifeless banks.
Within the square saraband-dancers gather,
Swaying to the paddle-steamers' chugs and clanks.


DORA MARKUS I

The wooden bridge was the place:
At Porto Corsini leading to the open sea
And men as if transfixed, remote, casting
Or hauling nets. Your face,
Your gesture, urged my eye to the farther shore,
To the unseen; you pointed to your real land.
And then we followed the canal, right to the docks
And the city shining in scales of soot; we crossed
The sunken plain where spring was lying drowned,
A motionless season with no recolletion.

And here where life is old
And webbed in a shimmer of delicate
Oriental anxieties,
A shining played on your words as a rainbow webs
The mullet's dying scales.

Your disquiet is imaged now in my mind
Like birds in their restless migrations through storm and night
Striking the lighthouse glass:
Even your gentleness is a storm, it whirls,
Whirls out of our sight,
And rocks to sleep more rarely than the tides.
How do you endure, exhausted – how do you persist
Locked in that lake
Of your indifferent heart? Perhaps you are saved
By an amulet you keep beside your lipstick,
Your powder, your nail-file: a white ivory mouse;
And this is how you exist!

DORA MARKUS II

By now in your country of Carinthia
With its myrtles in bloom, and its pools,
You are on the bank gazing down
Where the shy carp are nibbling
Or you look over the lime-trees
Across those bristling spires
Into the blaze of evening
And waters aflame with awnings
Of boarding-houses and piers.

The twilight rolls and steals
Through the dank vale and brings
With its purring engines no more
Than the geese muttering home.
The tiles of a white interior
Tell to the blackened mirror
That saw you in other days
A story of sublime mistakes

And this has been engraved
Where nothing is erased.

Your legend, Dora, is drawn! –
Painted already in those glances
Of highborn whiskered scions
Decadent in their frames of gold;
And returning with the tardy cry
Of a tawdry accordion
When it's late and the night advances.

There your legend is written.
The bay-leaf is still green
In kitchens; the voice still speaks;
Far off is Ravenna; beliefs
Are fierce and strong with death.
What does it want from you,
Your legend? Not to be bartered
Are voice and legend and fate . . .
It is late, and the night advances.


(MOTET)

At crack of dawn, at the time
When abruptly with rumbling voice
The railway recalls to me here
The men shut in its trains
In hard tunnelled ground
With the light sliced and flashed
From the waters and the skies;

At crack of dark, at the time
When the graver that scrawls deep
In the desk bites and strains
With a new fury, and the sound
Of the watchman's step draws near:
At dawn and dark, pauses that are human still!
– Patiently thread them together with your eyes.

*[Mottetto: 'Al primo chiaro . . .']*

15

(MOTET)

. . . well then, let be. The cornet blows to the leaf,
A colloquy with the swarms of the oak grove.
Twilight glows on the shell in whose smooth cave
A painted volcano sends up happy smoke.

The coin, set here in lava like a gem,
Gleams like lava on the table and keeps down
These meagre papers. Life that seemed immense
Is briefer than your handkerchief in proof.

*[Mottetto: '. . . ma cosí sia']*


THE CUSTOM-OFFICERS' HOUSE

You don't recall the house of the customs-men
Crazily leaning high up on the cliff:
How it has waited for you, stark and stiff,
Since your thoughts swarmed into it, and then
Paused in unquiet there that night!

Libeccio's breath has lashed the ancient walls
For years; silent is your laughter, your delight;
The compass's mad random needle strays;
The calculation of the dice is false.
You don't recall; other times rise, deface
This memory; a thread is still unwinding.

I hold an end of it yet; but now the building
Recedes, and on its rooftop the smoke-blown
Weathercock pitilessly whirls and darkens.
I hold a thread; but you are left alone
And absent is your breathing from this darkness.

O that hunted horizon, where the light
Twinkles sometimes as the tanker passes!
Is this the way? (Again the breaker climbs

16

The sloping rock, again its swarms divide...)
You don't recall this house, here in my evening.
– Who stays I cannot tell, nor who is leaving.

*[La casa dei doganieri]*

LOW TIDE

Evenings alive with cries, the garden swing
Flashing in the arbour of those days
And a dark veil of mist hardly hiding
The sea's fixed face.

All past, all gone. Rapid slanting flights
Cross the wall now, and the crumbling, the fall
Of all things without respite is a confusion
Burdening the steep bank, burdening the rock
That first bore you on the ocean.

Now I am brought with the light breath of spring
A ghostly eddying
Of the drowned swallowed times and lives; and at evening,
Dusky convolvulus, only your memory
Twines, and wards off time.

It climbs on the parapet, on the tunnel in the distance
Where the slow slow train crawls into its lair.
Then comes a sudden gathering on the hillsides,
The flock of the moon, invisibly browsing there.

*[Bassa marea]*

EASTBOURNE

'God Save the King' comes blaring from the brass
Of the pavilion band perched up on its stilts
Which feebly sieve the sea as it pours in
To erase the tracks
Left damply by the horses' hoofs in this
Coastline of sand.

I am cold; the wind attacks;
But a glare fires the panes
And the cliffs shine like mica
In its white stare.

*Bank Holiday* . . . It brings back the long surf,
The wave of my life,
Crawling too softly up the sloping shores.
It is late. The crashing music wavers out,
Comes to a quiet close.

Here come the half-men, the maimed, in their wheel-chairs,
Their only companions are those long-eared dogs,
The silent children, and the greybeards. (Who knows
But tomorrow it will all seem a dream?)
                                    And here
You also come, imprisoned voice, spirit
Unshackled, bewildered, dazed,
Voice of my blood, lost once and now regained
In my twilight days.

As a hotel's revolving door is turned,
All flashing leaves and facets –
Another picks up the signal and flashes back –
So am I twirled in a roundabout that traps
And sweeps up everything it whirls; and I
(Listening still – 'My country!') know your breathing,
And I get up, and the day grows, rank and high.

Everything will appear empty: even the power
That clenches together the living and the dead
Like ores in a vein, and binds the rocks and trees,
And from you, through you, unfolds. The holiday

Is pitiless. The band
Throws back its bursts of sound, and an undefended
Tenderness spreads out at the coming of darkness.

Evil's victorious... The wheel never stays.

You were not ignorant of this, light-in-darkness.

Now in this region of the burning ray
Where at the first peal of bells you left, nothing
Is left but the bitter hearth-ash that was once
*Bank Holiday*.

.

NEW STANZAS

Now with a gesture you put out the last
Glowings of tobacco in the crystal dish,
And now the smoke in a slow spiral winds,
Climbs to the ceiling
And hovers over the blank gaze of the chessmen,
The knights and bishops; and now ring after ring
Mounts up, more living than the clinging
Rings on your fingers.

Vanished the fata morgana, the bridges of mirage,
Towers flung to the clouds –
At the first puff, gone; the smoke is shaken,
A window opens unseen. But look down there:
Phantom multitudes of a different world,
Throngs of men to whom this incense of yours
Is nothing, a chessboard world whose very meaning
Is yours to compose.

There was a time when I doubted what you knew:
Maybe as the game unfolded on that square
You moved elsewhere – though now it lours at your door:
The frenzy of extinction is not calmed
At a cheap price, if the flash of your eyes is brief,
But cries for other fires, beyond the smokescreen

The god of chance throws thickly up for you
When he is on your side.

Today I know what you want; I hear the stroke
Of Martinella, and the hoarse bell sends
Its fear to chill the ivory spines in a light
As ghostly as the snow-glare. But to endure:
To win the reward of a lonely vigil: this still
Belongs to whoever with you can cast, strong
Against the burning-glass that blinds the pawns,
Your gaze of steel.

*[Nuove stanze]*


TIDINGS FROM MT AMIATA

The squib that sputters this bad weather out
Will be a murmur of beehives by late evening.
The rafters of the room
Are worm-eaten; a hint of melons
Diffuses from the boards. Softly, the smokes
That are mounting again up through a valley
Of mushrooms and gnomes towards the crystal cone
At the summit are clouding the windows over,
And I write to you from this place, from this
Far-set table, from the honeycomb cell
Of a sphere that has been cast into space –
And the covered cages, the fire and its hearth
Where the chestnuts explode, and the veins of mildew
And of nitre are the frame you will soon
Be breaking through. The life that fables you
Is still too short if it should contain you!
Yours is the icon which opens up
A ground of bright gold. Outside, there's the rain.

And yours it was to follow the crumbling edifices
Turned black by time and soot, the square-hewn
Courtyards that have as their centrepiece
The deepest of well-pits; to follow too
The clumsy flapping of the night-birds and

Down in the bottom of the pit the luminous gazing
Of the galaxy, the crossed bonds of every torture.
But the step that echoes out into the blackness
Comes from one so solitary he cannot see
Beyond this twilight of arches and folded shadows.
Too subtle is the stitching of the stars,
The eye of the belfry is closed on two o'clock,
The very creepers are themselves a darkness
Surging up and their scent is a bitter lament.
Come back north wind, tomorrow, come colder,
Break up the ancient power of the sandstone,
Scatter about the books of hours in garrets,
And let all be a still lens, a dominion, a prison
Of the undespairing sense! Come back stronger
Winds of the pole, winds that can endear
Our chains and seal the spores of latent life!
Too narrow are the paths, the clattering feet
Of the black files of donkeys kick up sparks;
Magnesium flares reply from the veiled peak.
O the trickling that runs reluctant and thin
From the gloomy cabins, time turned into water,
The long dialogue with the sorry dead, the ashes, the wind,
The wind that comes late, and death, death that is alive!

This pious duel which is surely empty
Of terms not drawn from darkness and lament –
What part of me does it bring you? Less than the amount
The watercourse has stolen from you, moving
Snugly in its sepulchral shell of cement.
An ancient tree-trunk, a mill-wheel, the world
Has no farther frontiers. A tiny city
Of straw breaks up: and at this late hour,
Appearing to link my vigil with the profound
Sleep where you lodge them, hedgehogs come out
And slake their thirst at a thread of pity.

*[Notizie dall'Amiata]*

21

## THE STORM

The rainstorm streaming down on the stiff leaves
Of the magnolia, with the long thunder-peals
Of March, and the March hails

(Sounds of crystal surprise you where you lie
In your nest of darkness; and of the gold
Gone dead on pieces of mahogany,
On edges of bound books, only a sugar-like
Grain is burning in the shell
Of your eyelids still),

The lightning-flash that glazes
Trees and walls and holds them fixed, surprised
In its momentary eternity – marble, manna,
Annihilation – which you carry engraved
Within you to your own ruin and which binds you
More to me than love, my stranger, my sister;
– Then the rough clash, the sistra shaken, the tremor
Of tambourines over the grave and its blackness,
The stamp of the fandango, and above,
Gestures thrown on the air...

                    As happened once
When you turned round and with your hand (your brow
Left clear of the loose cloud of your hair)

Saluted me – entering into the darkness.

*[La bufera]*


## A WINDOW AT FIESOLE

An unrelenting cricket penetrating
Many coats of vegetable silk –
Perfume of camphor rising, never routing
The moths that moulder piecemeal in the books –
While one small bird creeps round and up the bulk
Of the elm, and darkly snares the sun that dives
In its green swirls. Another frustrate gleam,
And O my scarlet ivies, other fires.

*[Finestra Fiesolana]*

## THE BLACK TROUT

At dusk, bent over the stream,
Graduates of Economics,
Doctors of Divinity;
The trout noses past, flicks
And flashes his ruby-red volts
Like a lock of yours untwisting
In the bath, or a sigh like steam
Rising from your office vaults.
                              (READING)

                                        *[La trota nera]*


## THE EEL

The eel, the sea siren
That leaves behind her cold Baltic waters
In order to sport in our seas,
Our river-mouths, our rivers
Which she ascends against the deep-borne tides,
From arm to arm of the streams
Narrowing from rill to rill,
Inward always, inward, on to the heart
Of stone, filtering through
The tiny channels of the mud until one day
A light struck from the chestnut-trees
Silvers a frisking in the standing pools
Of ditches running down
From the rocks of the Apennines to the Romagna;
The eel: the brand, the lash,
The shaft of Love on earth
That only our headlong gullies or the dried
Pyrenean brooks
Lead back to her teeming gardens;
The green desire that searches
For life where only drought
Clenches and the desert hardens,
The sap and spark that speak
Of a world in birth when all the world appears
Half carbonized, a buried stump-like bulk;

23

The brief rainbow, a twin
To that other iris set within your brows
Which you flash out unclouded on the crowds
Of the children of men plunged in your muds – can you doubt
It is your sister that swims in?

*[L'anguilla]*

BRIEF TESTAMENT

This thing in the dark like a marsh-light
That flits through the vault of my head,
This snail-track shining like pearl,
This crushed-glass emery-gleam –
It is not the lamp of any church or workshop
Nourished by acolyte
Whether in black or in red.
Only this iris is mine
To leave you, the memorial
Of a faith that was often invaded,
Of a hope that burned more slowly
Than a stubborn log in the fire.
Keep its powder in the mirror
When every lamp goes out
And hell's sardana is danced
And a shadow-black Lucifer swoops down on a prow
In Thames or Hudson or Seine,
Flapping his tarry wings that are half
Torn off with exertion and effort, to tell you: Now!
Hardly a heritage – nor is it a mascot
For standing up to onslaughts from monsoons
On the mere spider's thread of memory –
But it is only in ashes that a story endures,
Nothing persists except extinguished things.
It was the sign all right: the one whose luck
Is to see it can never miss you again.
Each recognizes his own: the pride
Was not an escape, the humility was not
A meanness, the ghostly flash that was struck
Down there was not the spark of a match on a box.

*[Piccolo testamento]*

# SOVPOEMS

(1961)

These translations are issued with the desire to redress a balance – to open the door slightly on a world which political (and in part linguistic) considerations have kept too remote from Western writers and readers – to show, if not throw, a few of the lifelines that have been preserved within the European tradition: lifelines which are now as perilous to refuse as they have usually been thought naive to accept.

Plenty of trite and doctrinaire verse, and plenty of bombastic and rhetorical verse, has come out of the communist world, but those who rest happily when they reach this point of discovery are deceiving themselves, since some of the finest poetry of the century – in Blok, Mayakovsky, Brecht, and Neruda, to mention only these – has also come from that world, and it is high time that people in the West began to examine this poetry and its implications for our society.

In the early days of the modern movement, poets in West and East were faced with much the same problems, challenges and oportunities, as far as the technical liberation of verse from a tired tradition was concerned. It is in the different uses made of this liberation that the crucial split between two worlds can be seen emerging. Symbolism, futurism, imagism, and surrealism, to say nothing of free verse, were available to all; but I would venture to claim that what Blok did with symbolism, what Mayakovsky did with futurism, what Neruda did with surrealism, holds a lesson for us which we don't learn from our Yeats, Stevens, Pound or Eliot. The lesson – without trying to spell it out – is related to the fact that literary movements should serve the ends of life as well as the ends of art. And this, with all respect to Pound, means something more than merely 'maintaining the cleanliness of the tools'. Clean tools can kill as well as make. If Western writers will not take this truth from a Mayakovsky, will they at least take it from Pasternak, who said: 'Much of the work of the twenties which was but stylistic experimentation has ceased to exist. The most extraordinary discoveries are made when the artist is over-whelmed by what he has to say. Then he uses the old language in his urgency and the old language is transformed from within.' The West, at some point between 1910 and 1920, decided that it could not face up to the twentieth-century implications of this truth (just as the nineteenth century had already failed to act on the advice of *either* Wordsworth or Byron, both of whom saw clearly though in different ways the need for an art that not only touched but *served* life); and it concentrated its attention on being *interesting*, rather than inspiring or relevant or useful, and aided and abetted by modern criticism it erected an impressively sophisticated but increasingly unnecessary construct – meaningful perhaps within its own verbal boundaries and mental assumptions but meaningless in relation to life itself. After a while the 'interesting' ceases to be interesting. Imagery yields to statement, ambiguity to clarity, technical sureness and literary knowledgeableness to qualities of vision and spirit and character and purpose. A poet must be seen to be a man, and the man must be seen to speak. Eliot and Mayakovsky were contemporaries, and went through the same turmoil of the modern movement in the arts, and made use of many similar technical devices and innovations; *With the Whole Voice* and *Ash Wednesday* both belong to 1930 and represent an important stage in their personal development and attitude to society; but although Mayakovsky is dead and Eliot is alive, Mayakovsky's poem still crackles with a fierce life, while Eliot's has a dying charm. Why should the poem of the young suicide represent a victory, and the poem of the Nobel Prize-winner and OM represent a defeat? The answer lies in the relation of a poet to the world he is living in.

John Peale Bishop spoke for the Western view when he wrote:

> Present evils are for men of action,
> Art has the irremediable ones.

Most of our poets from Eliot to Larkin would agree with this statement, and their writing illustrates it. To the non-bourgeois part of the world, however, there is no greater aesthetic heresy. Having mentioned Larkin, let me invite you to make another comparison: between Larkin's much-praised poem 'Church Going' and Yevtushenko's 'The Partisans' Graves'. Both poets are brought up suddenly against the facts of death and faith, in a deserted place, surrounded by graves, and each of them surprises, in Larkin's excellent phrase, 'a hunger in himself to be more serious'; but the seriousness in Yevtushenko is sharp and precise where in Larkin it is dispersed among an attendance of stock abstractions. Edith Sitwell has attacked his 'cycle-clips': what she should have attacked is his 'bored, uninformed' residue of religious sentiment, which he neither pauses to examine in itself (as Eliot at least would have done) nor tries to relate to the life of the church (or of the Church). The graves in the churchyard are to him only 'so many dead'. What does he care about who they were, how they died, what they lived or died for?

This lack of serious care, this process of glossing over and softening, this lazy draping with a false timelessness, this distancing and dissolving of conflict – what are these but a fear of statement and commitment, a form of studied self-deprecation, a desperate disbelief in the power of poetry to speak out on man and society? Do we know how this happened? Can we change the situation?

The modern movement was tested in the 1930s, found wanting during World War II, and shelved in the 1950s (though its ghostly blandishments still linger in American academic quarterlies). Nothing can quite be said to have replaced it, despite isolated efforts by (for example) Logue and Enright, or the more important Beat writers in America. But during this same period the modern movement was being more successfully absorbed by some non-bourgeois poets – often poets whose position in society might be thought to be more difficult and unpromising. Social and political pressures, however, can be better for the arts than indifferentism. The clarity, directness, and warmth of the later work of Neruda and Pasternak owe much to the need each of these poets felt to meet the demands of the time, which were demands for a poetry that could be understood, and being understood, *used* by human beings, at this point of history and beyond. It is poetry with a sense of history, and it is suffused – ironic lesson to the West – with an awareness of the individual's place in history. Pasternak had to wean himself from the complex, enigmatic verse of his early years, Neruda had to refine the floridities of an anguished surrealism. The point is that they did this, and produced a new poetry in which the influences of the modern movement remain but have subsided to an almost invisible sap, from which the grosser art-temptations of style have slipped away, and which a man may question and not be sent packing unanswered. This sinewy, speaking, history-conscious modernity – a modernity which has 'come through' – is even more striking in the poems of Brecht, which deserve close study. (It can also be seen in work by Apollinaire, MacDiarmid, and Quasimodo.)

Neruda, surveying the vast mountain-top ruins of an almost forgotten empire, asks his great question:

Stone on stone; but where was man?
Air on air: but where was man?
Time on time: but where was man?

This is not a trite moralizing on mortality. Neruda asks the question because he would like to know the answer. He asks the question because he wants you, the reader, to think about the answer. It is not so important that the full answer cannot be given (even if science should someday enable us to re-view past events) as that human imaginative attention is being turned at long last, almost by way of expiation, onto a million anonymous persons: slaves, builders, soldiers, human sacrifices – each one of whose lives, if by some miracle we could watch it unfold in all its inward hopes and fears as well as in its external shocks, would drain the blood from our faces. No wonder Neruda speaks with such affection of the

little Wyoming Museum
whose dearest treasure is
a pillow sewn with a heart.

And no wonder he recommends for the twentieth century a 'poesía sin pureza', a poetry without purity, which is willing to soil its hands with the world, to see itself as a part of general human experience and especially of human aspiration, whether that aspiration is economic and basic – for food, for peace – or at the most advanced point of human knowledge – a rocket to Venus, let us say. 'Humanism' is a word that is hard to use today without feeling self-conscious or looking over one's shoulder, but it will serve in the present context as a rough pointer to what modern Western or bourgeois poetry has most lacked and must now painfully recover. Can anyone doubt that what we need is more life, greater awareness of all forms and manifestations of life, more confidence and more curiosity about life's workings everywhere? The West as we see it now is like an old peevish starving man, sitting straight-backed in the dust and refusing the good but plain food which is set down within his reach. He refuses because he cannot believe that he is starving, or thinks that like Elijah he has God's ravens lined up waiting to bring his long-merited sustenance. But starve he will, and be sterile, and shrivel up like a Dead Sea Scroll, if he cannot take a long clear look at himself and his artistic works, and wonder how it was that Chaucer could make poetry out of the Canterbury pilgrims – or how Milton, standing at the door of the modern world, dared to end *Paradise Lost* with a comparison of the very angels of heaven to a mere cloud of mist that glides

> And gathers ground fast at the Labourers heel
> Homeward returning.

Logical positivism (i.e. philosophical negativism), political negativism (e.g. calling anti-communism a positive doctrine), organicist aesthetics (i.e. by implication 'formalist'), 'blue guitar' poetry, dodecaphony, abstract painting and sculpture, anti-plays and anti-novels have done or are doing us a certain amount of harm, however accomplished they are and however inevitable their development may seem, because taken all in all they have gradually accumulated in our society an atmosphere of cultural withdrawal: every 'advance' in formalism is a further withdrawal from human relations and confidence – it snaps another link of trust between man and man. This is not to say that the Russian artistic scene would not benefit immensely from freer experimentation, particularly in the plastic arts. What I do say is that without the one big thing that the Soviet artist does have – interest, care, and positive confidence in and for man and society – there is too little to build on, and the arts become a sort of fascinating marginal fantasy, where talent and effort (and money) are devoted to convincing a sceptical world that the materials used are more interesting than the mind that shapes them or the end it shapes them to.

Well then: experiment if you like, but love the world. If you hear the record of Kerouac reading his 'October in the Railroad Earth' you know that the answer is Yes, whatever faults the writing has; if you read Tomlinson's book *Seeing is Believing* you know that the answer must be No, whatever virtues the writing has. I hope the poems translated here may be useful in suggesting some other lines of approach. A variety of belief and experience is represented, from the revolutionary communist dedication of Mayakovsky, through the humanist-romantic Tikhonov and Martynov, the critical socialism of Pasternak, the lively personal re-dedication of Yevtushenko (at times too individualist for Russian critics), and the émigrée conscience of Tsvetayeva (who returned to Russia in 1940), to the communist humanism of Brecht and Neruda (ironical in the one and romantic in the other) who offer the broadest overlap, in their lives and literary contacts, with the non-communist world.

**Boris Pasternak**

SEVASTOPOL 1905

October. A round of strikes.
O wind! O brood of fiends!
And the tossed bristle of seas,
Of freight-black keels.
O tempest of pamphlets and broadsides!
O sleep and starlessness! O cries
Of sirens, and the locks tried
At the sixth sunrise.

From death-cells – to tempests and pamphlets.
O nights! O speech in spate!
And facing the gunbursts – the straight-set
Candles, the mutilations!

O graveyard, that day of the burying!
And fulfilling the lieutenant's oath
The nods and embraces, the clothes,
And the tear-wet faces!
O steps, crepe-draped! O singing!
And a hundred-thousand-fold choir
Talks bronze to a bronze stranger:
Swear! Let us swear!

O blizzard that batters the fables
Like elms and maples! O wind
That shatters all earthly connections
Except interjections!
You blow to the howling land:
'The unborn watch. Don't flinch,
Not one inch back! Swear this!'
'We swear! Not an inch!'

[from *Leitenant Schmidt*, I.iv]

32

TO A FRIEND

You think I don't know darkness must reach light?
You think I'm pleased to see these gleams rebuffed?
Only a monster would not prefer the delight
A million win, if an idle hundred are sloughed.

I too am measured by the five year plan.
I fall and rise as that plan draws its breath.
Only – what is it that the breastbone of a man
Conceals? What slows me like the sloth of death?

Great soviets have still one stumbling-block.
High places for high passions must be set.
The poet's place is vacant, is it not?
If it is not, look to your soviet.

*[Drugu]*


SPRING (1944)

Mark this spring with a white stone.
Sparrows clamour livelier.
I scarcely let my pencil roam,
My soul's so tranquil and so clear.

New thoughts: and so new words are claimed.
A chorus rich in harmony,
A great voice of the earth proclaims
Each liberated territory.

This native spring, this native breath
Erases farthest wintry tracks,
And the dark rings where Slav eyes wept
Go smooth in its benign attacks.

Grass everywhere's about to sprout.
Venerable Prague still dreams.
Its warrens of streets awaits the shouts
When play will fill these dumb ravines.

Moravian tales, ballads of Serbs,
Songs of the Czechs will stir up proud
This spring and shoot from snowy beds,
Tearing the tyrant's swaddling-shroud.

Life will loom in the haze of myth,
Like flourishes in gilded homes
Where walls evoke boyar and prince,
Or Basil's holy Moscow domes.

The midnight watcher, the visionary
Holds Moscow dearest of all things.
His home is centred at the very
Source from which this epoch springs.

*[Vesna]*

NIGHT

Steady advance of the darkness
Into its dissolving: and still
The airman bores into cloudland
Above the sleeping hill:

Drowned in the mists, vanished
In the great stream of his jets,
A tiny cross on that night-cloth,
A mark on shadowy sheets:

The midnight bars below him,
Cities he's never seen,
Soldiers in barracks, stokers,
The station and its train.

The wing throws out its shadow,
The whole bulk rides the clouds.
Heavenly bodies blinter,
Swarming in white crowds.

With a terrible, terrible yawing
The Milky Way creaks round
Towards some other universe
Beyond man's reach to sound.

Measureless the horizons –
Continents – fiery shires!
In boiler-rooms and basements
Men stoke sleepless fires.

From under the roofs of Paris
The eyes of Venus or Mars
Wink out to see the playbills:
What's on? The latest farce?

Someone is still awake there,
Down in that velvet haze
By the tiled roof of a garret
That has known different days.

He stares out at the planet,
As if the heavens were aware
And solicitous of the burden
Of his vigil and his care.

Work on, work on, be sleepless!
No labour scant its powers!
Live like the star and the airman,
Fight the drowsy hours!

Waking, watching, working –
Artist, never sleep.
You are eternity's hostage
Though time's dungeon is deep.

[*Noch'*]

## Marina Tsvetayeva

O tears in the world's eyes!
Weeping of anger and love!
O Czechoslovakian cries!
O Spain filled with blood!

O black mountainside
Eclipsing every flicker!
It is time – time – time
To return the pass to its maker.

I say no – I'll not be
An unperson, with bedlam face.
I say no – who'd go free
With wolves in a market-place?

I say no – I'll not howl
With the sharks of the plains.
I say no – I'll not sail
Down streams of human spines.

I don't need either ear-
Holes or a fey eye to know
That to your mad world there appears
One human answer: No!

Paris. March-May 1939

['O slezy . . .']

## Vladimir Mayakovsky

### AY, BUT CAN YE?

Wi a jaup the darg-day map's owre-pentit –
I jibbled colour frae a tea-gless;
Ashets o jellyteen presentit
To me the gret sea's camshach cheek-bleds.
A tin fish, ilka scale a mou –
I've read the cries o a new warld through't.
But you
Wi denty thrapple
Can ye wheeple
Nocturnes frae a rone-pipe flute?

[*A vy mogli by?*]


### WHIT MAIR?

Wi a douce bit sush I unsneckit
a newspaper's een...
Aa the frontiers aye reeky and bleckit
wi pouther and pain.

Naethin in this to the twinty-year laudie,
bairn o the cavaburd.
We canna dance to sic news, but naebody
dwines at its ill wurd.


jaup   splash, slap; *darg-day*   work-day; *owre-pentit*   painted over; *jibbled*
dribbled, splashed; *gless*   glass; *ashets*   dishes; *jellyteen*   gelatine; *camshach*
crooked; *cheek-bleds*   cheek-bones; *ilka*   each; *mou*   mouth; *denty*   dainty;
*thrapple*   windpipe; *wheeple*   whistle feebly; *rone-pipe*   spout for rainwater

*douce*   gentle; *sush*   rustle; *unsneckit*   opened; *reeky*   smoky; *bleckit*   blackened;
*pouther*   gunpowder; *cavaburd*   snowstorm

Lown watter scunners man's history.
Ill-willers and wars
we shed in oor undeemous trajectory
like faem the keel scaurs.

*[Nu, chto zh!]*


## WI THE HAILL VOICE

Weel-respeckit comrades o posterity!
Gin yer archeological scaffies seekin licht
on oor benichtit days come scrungein thir clairty
petrifacts, ye'll aiblins find me in yer sicht.
Wha's yon, ye'll speir. And a boffin'll be bummin
abune the bizzin skep o aa yer speirin
hoo this was wance 'some bylin-bauldit strummer,
hert-seik o aa unbylit watter-farin'.
Professor, tak aff thae bicycle-spectacles!
I'se shaw ye the age, and gie ye my ain credentials.

Aye, I'm the watter-cairt, I'm the sanitary,
mobileezit, caad up to the front.
I gaed therr frae the posy-nurseries
o Poesy – a fleery-flichtry bint.
Her wee bit gairden was as mim as its gairdner –
denty dochter, simmer cotter, loch watter, laich lauchter.
'Alone I garden all my garden,
alone I'll water it and sort it!'
Some crambo squeeters through a watterin-spoot,
some makars skoot it frae distendit cheeks.
Squirblesome Berrymans, Betjemanly squerts – hoots,
wha can untaigle the dreichs frae the dreeps!
Sic a collieshangie's no quarantinable.


*lown* calm; *scunners* disgusts; *undeemous* huge, extraordinary; *scaurs*
shears, cuts

*scaffies* scavengers; *scrungein* searching, scrabbling about; *thir* these; *clairty*
muddy, filthy; *aiblins* maybe; *bummin* holding forth; *skep* hive; *speirin*
inquiring; *bauldit* kindled; *I'se* I shall; *mim* demure; *laich* low; *crambo*
verse; *squirblesome* ingenious; *collieshangie* squabble, wrangle

Unnerneath the waas there's an endless concertinaful
o tring-trang tyandy-andy-
a-a-nnie.
Puir honour, that any stookie or bronze o me
sud glowr up frae sic rose-beds, in thir streets
whaur hoasts rack frae the thrapple o T.B.
owre hures and clap and vandals and deadbeats.
I'm fair stawed wi agitprop, ye ken.
and naethin wid be nicer – or mair profitable –
nor I sud screeve ye True Romances, hen.
But och, I've maistert mysel therr, I've stapplt
the hass o my sangs wi my ain pen.
Gie me yer ears, comrades o posterity!
The voice o the agitator, the heid-hauder-forth!
Wi a dam fur aa rintheroot poesy-froth
I'll spang owre the leirichie-larachie ballatry-
buikies. Lat the livin hear livin braith!
I'll reach ye in yon communistic hyne-awa.
I'm no some yestersingin messeniniah-gent.
My verse'll reach ye owre scaurry century-raws,
owre heids o makars – and o governments.
My verse'll reach ye, but it winna reach ye
like shots frae fidgin Cupid at the clarsach,
and no like the numismatist's dim bawbee;
licht frae a deid starn'll no be its farroch.
My verse will tyauve and brak through Grampian time
and shaw itsel – rouch, wechty, sichty, like
some aqueduct survivit sin langsyne
when Roman slave-chiels biggit brick and dyke.
Ye rug and runge through brochs o poem-buiks:
gin ye sud find airn arra-heids o rhyme
tak tent: and gie them the respeckfu luiks
ye'd gie a wappin as auld in bluid as grime.
I'm no a dab at fleechin wi douce wurds;
wee curly-haslockt lassies' earickies
gae-na reid here frae hauf-obscenities.
My pages are fechters I pit on parade,

stookie    plaster statue; *hoasts*    coughs; *stawed*    sickened; *stapplt*    stopped up;
*hass*    throat; *rintheroot*    gadabout; *spang*    leap, spring; *leirichie-larachie*
whispering, gossiping together; *scaurry*    rocky; *starn*    star; *farroch*    source of
energy; *tyauve*    struggle; *sichty*    strikingly visible; *biggit*    built; *rug and runge*
tug and rummage; *airn*    iron; *tak tent*    be careful; *haslock*    fine hair;

39

my lines are front-lines, I vizzy them lang and haurd.
Leid-solid stauns this verse, ay preparit
either to thole daith, or win daithless merit.
Prent-fundit poems rankit gruntle-to-gruntle
aim at the warld their gunnin, gantin title.
Sherp wit, the best-loo'd airm of aa,
furst in the skirl and chairge, will shaw
its caivalry in an eident frieze,
heezin rhyme's weel-whettit spears.
And aa thir battalions, airmit to the teeth,
wi twinty year o victories to rally at,
I'd gie them, doon to the jimpest, last broadsheet,
to you, the planetary proletariat.
An enemy o the mass o wurkin men
is the auldest enemy I knaw mysel.
I mind we hud to gang wi the reid flag, when
days gaed hungry and years were dour and fell.
We unsteekt aa the buiks o Marx, as here
we'd lift the shutters fur the licht o the hoose,
but och, we didna need the readin to see
whase camp to fecht in, and which wey to choose.
It wisna Hegel lernt us dialectic.
Thon brak into wur verse frae the stramash
o battle-bullets, the bourgeois rinnin hectic
frae us, or us frae them, in some sair stash.
Lat glory, like a widda, wring her hauns,
traipse to deid merches ahint ilka genius –
dee, verse o mine, dee like the swaddie, the wans
that foonert nameless in wur forays! Be-na as
the bronzes, ton-prood: I'd tapple them. Be-na
as the maurble, sleekit: I'd scuttle it. My people –
are we no wan folk? – lat's settle wi glory, in a
monument that we baith in wur deep truible
biggit thegither: socialism, unpairtable.
Posterity, track back the scum o yer wurd-leets:
plaffin through frae Lethe, sic slypes o the mou's moribundum
as 'prostitution', 'blockade', 'tuberculosis'.
For you that are hale and swanky, an orra body,

*vizzy* inspect; *gruntle* muzzle; *gantin* gaping; *eident* steady, devoted;
*heezin* raising; *jimp* thin; *stramash* tumult; *stash* encounter, fight; *foonert*
went down; *swanky* vigorous; *orra body* odd-job-man

a makar, wi the coorse tongue o a placard, sits
labberin spit frae phthisis-slaurie grund. Aye,
at the tail o the bank of time I'll pass fur a monster
fossileezed wi my antediluvian tale.
O comrade life, lat's tak the traverse faster,
the five year plan's last days are brawly taen!
Aa my bit verse hasna massed me a maik,
auld Wily Lochheid gies my hame nae plenishin.
Lea me a clean-launert shurt to my back
and to tell ye the truith, I dinna need anythin.
When I compear at H.Q. in the gleamin years to come,
I'll haud owre the crambo-gang o grafters and crafty-buits
as a bolshie'd haud up his Paurty caurd, the sum
o my hunner-volumed Paurty poetry-buiks.

*[Vo ves' golos]*


## Nikolai Tikhonov


THE BOAT

The bushes dwindled, and the pines thinned off.
Suddenly at the earth's edge we saw
A small boat, crouching in the golden splinters
Of light from a late-foundering sun.
No voice, no footprints, and no path –
Only a crooked boat and the sparkle of the ice. –
It was as if what we walked on was sky.

The ice beckoned us forward, it shone and smiled
With white enormous eyes – O face of ice!
And we came up, and would have passed, but the boat –
The boat lay so immovable at the bank,
Its twilight planks bent taut: they spoke to us
And said: 'Here is the end of the earth.'

*labberin* lapping up; *slaurie* slimy; *maik* halfpenny; *Wily Lochheid* Wylie
Lochhead (house furnishers); *compear* appear on summons

Beyond the black headland a brightness flashed,
And gold was mingled with the lead.

You wrote with your finger on the cold ice-floe –
What you wrote there neither the ice nor the sky
Nor even I can ever call to mind.
Now that floe goes far off in the sea,
Drifting off tranquilly and breathing deep
As this one evening pierced and flushed with gold
Drifts through my breast . . .

*[Lodka]*


'FROZEN HEATHER . . .'

Frozen heather, frozen heather
    Whistling with the sea-surge,
In front of you the black shore stretches
    Charred by the barrage.

Frozen heather, frozen heather
    Sad is your whistle.
Hot and acrid flakes hang heavy
    In a grey drizzle.

Brotherly heather, frozen heather
    We made you our pillows.
Warm shall you be today, heather
    With blood of my fellows.

Once you drink that blood, heather
    Draining full measure,
Then will you thaw out, frozen heather
    O frozen heather.

Finland, 1940

*['Merzly veresk . . .']*

42

**Bertolt Brecht**


THE PLUM-TREE

The back-yard has a tiny plum-tree,
It shows how small a tree can be.
Yet there it is, railed round
So no one tramps it to the ground.

It's reached its full shape, low and meagre.
O yes, it wants to grow more, it's eager
For what can't be done –
It gets too little sun.

A plum-tree no hand's ever been at
To pick a plum: it strains belief.
It is a plum-tree for all that –
We know it by the leaf.

*[Der Pflaumenbaum]*


THOSE WHO DEPRIVE THE TABLE OF MEAT

Teach men to be content with their lot.
Those who are certain to gain by the offering
Demand a spirit of sacrifice.
Those who have risen from a banquet are loquacious
Before the hungry about the good times to come.
Those who lead the State over a precipice
Call governing too onerous
For the plain man.

*[Die das Fleisch wegnehmen vom Tisch]*

## A WORKER READS, AND ASKS THESE QUESTIONS

Who built Thebes with its seven gates?
In all the books it says kings.
Did kings drag up those rocks from the quarry?
And Babylon, overthrown time after time,
who built it up again as often? What walls
in dazzling gilded Lima housed the builders?
When evening fell on the completed Wall of China,
where did the stonemasons go? Great Rome
is thick with triumphal arches. Who erected them? Who was it
the Caesars triumphed over? Had famous Byzantium
nothing but palaces, where did people live? Atlantis itself,
that legendary night the sea devoured it, heard
the drowning roaring for their slaves.

The young Alexander took India.
By himself?
Caesar hammered Gaul.
Had he not even a cook beside him?
Philip of Spain cried as his fleet
foundered. Did no one else cry?
Frederick the Second won the Seven Years War. Who
won it with him?

Someone wins on every page.
Who cooked the winners' banquet?
One great man every ten years.
Who paid the expenses?

So many statements.
So many questions.

*[Fragen eines lesenden Arbeiters]*

## THE LANDSCAPE OF EXILE

And yet I too, on that last boat,
Watched the same cheerful dawn glow through the rigging
And the greyish skins of the dolphins riding
Through the Sea of Japan.

The little gilded horse-drawn carts
And the rosy veils on the matrons' arms
In the alleys of Manila, that marked place:
These the fugitive rejoiced to see.

By the high oil derricks and thirsty gardens of Los Angeles
And the twilight gorges of California and its fruit-markets
The bearer of bad luck
Was not left cold.

*[Die Landschaft des Exils]*


CONVERSATIONS ROWING

It is evening. Two folding-boats
Glide past, with two young men in them,
Naked. Rowing side by side
They talk. Talking
They row side by side.

*[Rudern, Gespräche]*


1940

My young son asks me: Must I learn mathematics?
What is the use, I feel like saying. That two pieces
Of bread are more than one's about all you'll end up with.
My young son asks me: Must I learn French?
What is the use, I feel like saying. This State's collapsing.
And if you just rub your belly with your hand and
Groan, you'll be understood with little trouble.
My young son asks me: Must I learn history?
What is the use, I feel like saying. Learn how to stick
Your head in the earth, and maybe you'll still survive.

Yes, learn mathematics, I tell him.
Learn your French, learn your history!

45

## ON WATERING THE GARDEN

O watering of the garden, to put the green in good heart!
Spraying of thirsty trees! Give more than enough and
Never forget the shrubbery, not even
The shrub without berries, the exhausted
Niggardly bearers. And don't overlook
The weed between the flowers, it too
Knows thirst. Nor should you pour
Only on the fresh turf or only on the parched turf:
You must refresh the naked earth itself.

*[Vom Sprengen des Gartens]*


## Pablo Neruda


## EASTERN FUNERAL

A city, potters, fishermen, in the midst of these I work
by night, and in the midst of the dead that are burned
with their fruits and saffron, wound in shrouds of red:
beneath my balcony the terrible bodies go by,
shaking chains to the sound of copper flutes,
whistling a shrill thin melancholy cry
that mingles with the colour of the lolling poison-blooms
and the clamour of the dancers in their ash-white skin
and the passions and the monotonies of the tomtomming
and the smell of the smoke from newly lighted wood.

For once the road has been turned near the murky river,
their hearts drained dry or springing to greater life,
they will roll in fire – leg, foot, all flame and fire,
and a fine ash like a veil will tremble over the water,
will float there like garlands breathed on by the furnace
or like an extinguished blaze left smouldering by wayfarers
so great and strange they had kindled it on these black streams,
feasting to this ghostly crumb and lees.

*[Entierro en el este]*

UNIVERSAL SONG
(from Book II    'Heights of Macchu Picchu')

ix
Sidereal eagle, vineyard of mist.
Lost bastion, blind scimitar.
Starred swordbelt, ritual bread.
Tumbling staircase, enormous eyelid.
Triangular tunic, pollen of stone.
Granite lamp, bread of stone.
Mineral snake, rose of stone.
Buried ship, fountain of stone.
Equinoctial set-square, steam of stone.
Perfect geometry, book of stone.
Berg polished among the squalls.
Madrepore of drowned ages.
Rampart rubbed bland by fingers.
Rooftop buffeted by wings.
Mirror-clear branches, foundations in storms.
Thrones cast down by creeping stems.
Government of the glutted claw.
South-west bluster held in the waterfall.
Unmoving cataract of turquoise.
Patriarch bell of sleeping men.
Collar on the mastered snows.
Iron lying along the statues.
Cloistered tempest, ill to reach.
Puma's hands, bloody crag.
Hooded turret, snowy dialogue.
Night hung up in roots and fingers.
Window on the fog, stiffened pigeon.
Nocturnal plant, effigy of thunderclaps.
Fundamental mountain-chain, ocean ceiling.
Architecture of lost eagles.
Cord of the sky, bee of the plateau.
Bloodstained level, man-made star.
Mineral bubble, moon of quartz.
Andean snake, forehead of amaranth.
Soundless cupola, pure fatherland.
Sea's bride, cathedralled tree.
Branch of salt, black-winged cherry.
Jaws of snow, cold thundercrack.

Nipped moon, threatening stone.
Cold flood of hair, action of the atmosphere.
Crater of hands, dark cataract.
Wave of silver, direction of time.


x

Stone on stone: but where was man?
Air on air: but where was man?
Time on time: but where was man?
Were you too the shattered relic
of unfinished man, that empty eagle
that the streets of today, the footprints,
the leaves of lifeless autumns, watch
crushing the soul right into its grave?
Poor hand and foot, poor life...
Did days of the light which drifted through you
(like rain on banderillas
spilling in festival-time)
lay their dark food petal by petal
in your empty mouth?

                              Hunger, coral of man,
hunger, hidden plant, root of the woodcutters,
hunger, was it the edge of your reef
that climbed to these high and shaken towers?

You heard my question, salt of the highways,
show me the spoon; and you, architecture,
let me pick with a stick at those stony vitals,
mount all the steps of the air into vacancy,
ransack those entrails till my hand finds man.

Macchu Picchu, did you
place stone on stone, and in the foundations, a rag?
Coal upon coal, and at the bottom, a tear?
Fire on gold, and quivering in it
the great red raindrop of blood?
Deliver me the slave you buried!
Let the hard bread of the wretched
break through the soil, show me the clothes
of the serf, show me his window.

Tell me how he slept in his days on earth.
Tell me if his sleep was
harsh, gaping, hacked like a black
hole into the wall by fatigue.
The wall, the wall! And was there a weight
on his sleep from each stone floor, and was he bowed
under stone as under a moon, in that sleep?
Ancient America, drowned bride,
did your fingers too,
rising from forests to the high void of the gods,
waved over by wedding banners of light and dignity,
merging with the thunder of drums and javelins,
your fingers, did your fingers too,
those that brought over the abstract rose and the rule
of cold, the frenzied breast of the new grains,
into the very fabric of bright matter and caverns of hardness:
did you too, buried America, you too, like an eagle
hide, in the bitterest deepest bowel-pits, your hunger?

*[Canto General*: 'Alturas de Macchu Picchu'*]*

*(from Book IX – 'Let the Rail-splitter Awake!')*

vi
Peace for the twilights that are to come,
peace for the bridge, peace for the wine,
peace for the lines that seek me out
and climb up through my blood, entangling
an old song with earth, with loved things,
peace for the city in the morning
when the bread rubs its eyes, peace for
the Mississippi River, river of origins:
peace for the shirt on my brother's back,
peace on the book like a stamp of air,
peace for the huge kolkhoz of Kiev,
peace for the ashes of the dead, these dead
and these others, peace for the black
iron of Brooklyn, peace for the postman
like day from house to house, peace
for the choreographer who shouts

with a funnel to the climbing vines,
peace for my right hand, that only
wants to write Rosario:
peace for the Bolivian, taciturn
as a nugget of tin, peace
for you to get married, peace
for all the saw-mills of Bio-Bio,
peace for the lacerated heart
of guerrilla Spain, peace
for the little Wyoming Museum
whose dearest treasure is
a pillow sewn with a heart,
peace for the baker and the things he loves,

and peace for the flour: peace
for all the wheat that's still unborn,
for all the love that'll run to the groves,
peace for all the living: peace
for all lands and waters.

And me: I take my leave here,
it's home I go, in my dreams,
home to Patagonia where
the wind beats on the byres
and the ocean spits out its ice.
I am no more than a poet: I love you all,
I go wandering through the world I love:
in my country they throw miners in jail
and judges hang on generals' lips.
And yet I love to the very roots
this freezing meagre land of mine.
If I was to die a thousand times,
there is where I'd want to die;
if I was to be born a thousand times,
this is where I'd want to be born –
beside the wild araucaria,
and the blasts of the southern wind,
and the new-bought bells.
No one need think about me.
Think rather about the wide earth,
and strike the table with love.
O that no blood would return

to drench our bread, our beans,
our music: and may I have with me
the miner and the lawyer,
the little girl and the sailor
and the maker of dolls, and let us
go to the pictures, come out

and drink the reddest wine.

It is not solutions I bring.

I came here to sing
and to have you sing at my side.

['*Que despierte el leñador*']


## Leonid Martynov


Poems are not composed in a cringing position,
Nor is it possible to write them under any man's supervision,
Contempt, it's said, can act as your ignition:
No!
Poetry's dictated only by clarity of vision.

['*Iz smiren'ya . . .*']


THE LEAVES

They
Lay there
On the pathway.

And all at once
They raised a dust and were
Changing their tints and began
To whirl in a dance, like mad things.

– What are you? –
I cried to the dervishes.

– We are leaves,
Leaves, leaves, leaves, leaves! –
They started rustling in reply.
– A landscape-painter came into our dreams
But the hands that held the brushes seemed
So loath to glow with love for us – why,
We just flew away,
Flew away!

*[List'ya]*


I thought I had risen from the grave.
My name was Hercules. I was alive.
Five hundred tons: was I heavy!
Up by the roots I plucked a grove.
Lifted my hands – I reached the heavens.
I sat: the chair-back cracked and shivered.
I died . . . And here I am risen from the grave:
Height normal, weight normal – alive
Like all men. Am merry, am loving.
I never make a chair-back shiver . . .
Yet I am Hercules, just as I live.

*['Mne kazhetsya . . .']*


Evening came on.
The western ray
Grew longer, longer, slowly, slowly,
Pointing straight at the enormous city,
Eyeing it in a spooky, February way.

It got more warm,
The milder light
Stopped frowning upon all it saw.
In the end it found out how to throw
A kindlier favour on that human sight.

*['Vecherelo . . .']*

# Yevgeny Yevtushenko

THE PARTISANS' GRAVES

And so,
I am living here at Zima Station.
I get up before daybreak – I like doing this.
In a truck, on a heap of grain, destination
anywhere, I set off; climb out where I wish;
walk into the summer taiga, miss
nothing, marvel at the earth's earthy mission.
Cranberries smoulder eerily in the grass,
and fire-red rose-hips burn away, their hearts
packed with the shaggy little red-haired seeds.
Everything is a kind of voice: 'Be wiser – but guard
against the supersubtle sophistries!'
Released from absurd, idle vanity,
I surrender the hour to what is tranquil and ordered,
to a sacred, voluntary solemnity,
and I go out into a quiet glade,
to an obelisk with its star and white simplicity.
In the midst of birches, and arrayed in tangled drifts
of the wild raspberries, you sleep, partisans' graves.
A spell is cast by graves. Once come this way,
bent under burdens, your feet where the dead lie,
suddenly in sadness you will be lightened and
see into the far and the profound.
I read the names: 'Klevtsova Nastya',
'Petr Belomestnykh', 'Kuzmichov Maxim' –
and over them all the solemn legend: 'They passed
from life, dying bravely for marxism'.
I meditate upon this superscription.
Naive, just literate, the man who in that distant
nineteen-nineteen drew it with breath-held scribble,
and yet saw in it the living truth.
Marx, I am sure, was a closed book to these souls,
who reckoned God still walked about the earth,
but went and fought, and brought the bourgeois down,
and gained the name of marxists which they own...
Destroyed in the first years of their new world
they lie here, peasants of Siberia,

with crosses on their breast, but none overhead –
above them the red star of the proletariat.
And here I stand with my boots deep in dew,
suddenly older in this hour with death
and offering all my Marx-devoted debts
and yet, not every payment, it is true...
Goodbye, graves of the partisans! You have been
my help in the one way your help could be.
Goodbye! My search, my suffering lie in wait
with the world of my struggle into man's estate:
the world of birdsong, of rustling dripping leaves,
glories, solemnities that never fade,
the world where the living think about the dead
and the dead help the living from their graves.

*[Partizanskie mogily]*


THE ANGRIES

Great twentieth century: sputnik century:
what an angst is in you, what wide perplexity!
You are a good century and a century of the pit,
cannibal-century to the ideas you beget,
century of the angry young men's target.

Young men get very angry indeed.
Their eyes flash scorn for this period.
They scorn government and they scorn party,
they scorn the church and provisions of philosophy,
they scorn women – and sleep with them,
they scorn the world, its banks and tills,
they scorn, with a painful insight, the ills
that their own miserable scorn leaves them.
The twentieth century is only their stepfather.
The depth of their hate for it, O the depth of it!
The virulently seething teenage fervour
beats dark and thick along the Hudson River;
by Tiber, Seine, and Thames the same teenagers
gather like black dogs come from the same manger.
The sharp, the cross, the sulky, and the weird –

no century has seen their like before.
I see what they don't want – that's clear;
but how to grasp what they are standing for?
It can't – or can it – be a young man's credo
to scold solid and be scolded, nothing more?
Well then, here I am, in the city of Moscow
speaking to them, plainly, as man to man:
what I say is, if I am angry I am
angry only within the love I've fed on,
the love of my own land; loud, but not loud
to hail a poor unbelief. And I am glad
that I can put my trust in the truth of Lenin,
in hammer and ploughshare true to human hand.
If I get angry about this or that –
the anger is within a dignity
of knowing I address friends, knowing I fight
in a front line for a fighter's integrity.
What then is wrong with you? Is it truth you frown for?
'Mass psychosis', the medicos say with a sigh.
All over Europe the boys slouch and glower.
The boys slouch and glower through the U.S.A.

Twentieth century: great sputnik century:
tear them out of their thunderous mixed-up scenery!
Give them – no, not a cosy lassitude,
but give them faith in what is right, what is good.
A child is not an enemy. Twentieth century, you
must help them, do you hear? – you help them through!

*[Serditye]*

*SÁNDOR WEÖRES: SELECTED POEMS*

(1970)

INTRODUCTION

Sándor Weöres is a protean poet of great virtuosity, writing in all forms, from complex metre and rhyme to free verse, keenly aware of the musical and rhythmical powers which poetry shares with song and dance and ritual, and from this delighting in the means which poetry particularly offers of uniting the sophisticated and the primitive. His inventiveness sometimes creates imaginary languages, and phonetic and visual effects similar to those we have seen in many countries in recent years. Not surprisingly, he has a very 'open' view of what poetry is and can do, and has no sympathy with any socio-political prescriptiveness. Exploration and experiment are essential to his art, as he made clear during an interview in 1963:

> Yes, I think one should explore everything. Including those things which will never be accepted, not even in the distant future. We can never know, at the start of an experiment, where it will lead.... It may take decades or centuries to prove whether it was a useful experiment or a useless one. It may never be proved at all.*

Poems which are hostages to such far-off verdicts as these may very properly be difficult, or at times even obscure. A bold use of associational imagery is coupled with a wide range of mythological and anthropological reference drawn from India and China, Egypt and Africa and Polynesia; Weöres himself has admitted the influence on him of the Upanishads, the Gilgamesh epic, and the works of Lao Tse. Although he does write about familiar figures, as in the remarkable 'Orpheus Killed', he seems more often to drive farther back and out to the least known and the least appreciated, and even to those he will invent for himself, as if it was important to remind modern man, swinging in his cradle of an extraordinary technology, how far his mysterious roots crawl into lost times and places, never quite forgotten and never quite recoverable. So he writes about Adam and Eve themselves in the guise of two imaginary mythological characters, Kukszu and Szibbabi, in 'The First Couple'. The poem ends movingly with a brief, intense encapsulation of our awareness that change is

---

* Interview with László Cs. Szabó, published in *Tri-Quarterly*, Evanston, Illinois, No. 9, Spring 1967.

traumatic, and that because this is so we look back with impossible longing to early and superseded stages:

Kukszu sprawls in scalding mud,
head in silt, feet in sedge,
face turned to the sky,
sends no more blood-rain into the body of Szibbabi,
cries with sharp call, a suckling child,
waiting for the overflowing light, for the overflowing light
waiting, for the never-returning light.

In the long, rich, exotic 'Queen Tatavane', Weöres again uses a series of invented names which are all meant to evoke the strangely isolated, melting-pot anthropology of Madagascar, where the distant Malay and Polynesian voyagers unite with the near-at-hand Africans. The young queen, bound by rituals and obligations she would dearly like to be free of, must rule over her 'two nations', and justify their struggles, trying to bring something new to birth:

Pain of two nations is fire under me,
who will ever hatch the happiness of the world?

Again and again Weöres' poems acknowledge all the archetypal sources of strength, and refuse to reject the primitive. When he uses real names, the most remote analogies and reminders can touch off our responses as readily as do the imaginary figures. In 'The Secret Country', for example, the mesmeric, winding repetitions take us down into the very essence of an Underworld, though E Daj is an actual name for Hell or the Underworld in one of the Polynesian myths. The fact that few readers will be able to distinguish between the real and invented names is Weöres' way of saying that the poet, if not literally a myth-maker, is certainly a willing collaborator with the basic mythopoeic propensities of man, science or no science, history or no history.

In such a poet, it is natural that there should go with all this a deep sense of the interconnections of human and non-human life. These connections, felt more strongly by Weöres than the everyday props and ligatures of social institutions and habits, have sometimes given him a reputation for withdrawnness or pessimism that his work as a whole does not in fact show. Yet although he is obviously not writing for a mass audience, his poetry is so sinewy with energy, so ready to break out into wonder or playfulness that its 'black' qualities must be placed in that

60

broader context of abounding creative pleasure. Even the bitter 'Internus', with its unrelieved catalogue of human failings, its Baudelairean nest of disgusts, has its positives; they emerge in the cleansing, purging power of an artist's 'No!', something utterly distinct from the cynically negative positions the consciously reflective social mind might throw up:

> The panic world is baffled at my gate:
> 'Madman! Egotist! Traitor!' its words beat.
> But wait: I have a bakehouse in my head,
> you'll feed someday on this still uncooled bread.

At the end of 'Internus' the poet imagines his death as a return to the great plenum from which everything is continuously poured. In his long poem 'The Lost Parasol', an astonishingly fertile, original, and thought-provoking work, shimmering with rhyme, half-rhyme, and assonance, the process of dissolving back into a plenum is shown step by step over a period of years, entirely natural, mostly explicable, but fundamentally awesome in its revelation of nature as relentless metamorphosis. Yet the poem is human, and touching, in taking as its central object a simple red parasol, left behind in the grass by a girl in love. The slow disintegration of the parasol, blown about by wind and storm, drenched by rain, torn by rocks and branches, invaded by insects, lizards, mice, and birds, its jaunty red faded and smudged, ends with a last flying tuft of fabric poised between sea and sky, swaying in the light of the Theatrum Gloriae Dei. The two lovers have long forgotten it, but the tiny, symbolically assertive flash of scarlet silk, the one man-made thing in that teemingly non-human landscape, has become a part of the nature that they themselves can neither escape from nor forget. The poem's final image is one of joy – the poet sings exultantly like the oriole in the forest, of love, of change, of death. The poem sings out as the red parasol sang out in the grass.

Weöres has a warm intuitive sympathy which is able to work through quite different tones and structures: the visionary brooding and Blakean 'minute particulars' of 'The Lost Parasol', the epigrammatic statements of 'Terra Sigillata', the dark sardonic probing of 'In Memoriam Gyula Juhász', the amusing but cutting pidgin of 'Coolie'. In the interview already quoted, Weöres answered with a simple 'Yes' when he was asked whether he felt 'the same humility towards your fellowmen as Montaigne felt towards the illiterate gardener'. Political regimes come and go (and Weöres has persisted quietly through oppressive periods in the past), but the basic sympathies of an unpolitical poet give his work a humanity which his immense technical gifts and wide reading in no way obscure. Two of the epigrams in 'Terra Sigillata' make the point:

The Dazzling is always coming to earth to beg for mud,
while his palace in heaven, stiff with gold, sighs for his return.

The bowed-down carrier looks up: there he stands at the
 centre of the earth!
it is above his head that the sky's vault goes highest.

Both Christianity and Marxism could be read into these couplets – and also, in the first of them, something more oriental and more deeply revolutionary than either system. Like bread cast on the waters, the poems of Weöres set off into the unknown, swirling into some Jungian E Daj of the mind where it seems as natural to 'come to the earth to beg for mud' as it is, in 'Difficult Hour', to 'lay open the powers of the bodiless inner world'.

ETERNAL MOMENT

What you don't trust to stone
and decay, shape out of air.
A moment leaning out of time
arrives here and there,

guards what time squanders, keeps
the treasure tight in its grasp –
eternity itself, held
between the future and the past.

As a bather's thigh is brushed
by skimming fish – so
there are times when God
is in you, and you know:

half-remembered now
and later, like a dream.
And with a taste of eternity
this side of the tomb.

*[Örök pillanat]*


THE FIRST COUPLE

  'Get up, Kukszu,
up, Kukszu, Kukszu, get up,
take your rod and thrash the trees!'

  'I won't get up, Szibbabi, I won't get up,
my head lies heavy in scalding mud, my eyes
are shut, my face looks up to the sky,
I will not take my rod in my hand, Szibbabi, I will not get up,
I am sending blood-red rain on you,
I am staying where I am.'

  Szibbabi went off,
when she got to the lake
lifted her apron.

'Lake frog, take a rod,
thrash the trees!'

'I won't thrash, Szibbabi, I won't thrash the trees,
I live with my own true mate,
we hide from the hungry bird,
we eat big mosquitoes day after day.'

Szibbabi let her apron down,
the blood-rain overtook her.

The frog smiled tenderly and said:
    'Beyond the lake, beyond the mountains
there are twelve big-navelled gods
so fond of fruit, so fond
of mash, mash made with lard,
and they hold suckling babies in their laps,
and in their hip-bones they hold the world,
in their hip-bones both sky above and earth beneath,
and between these the water runs up and down.'

Szibbabi left
by the lake-side, to get to the mountain,
over the mountain, to get to the twelve gods.
When she'd put the lake behind her
her head broke off from her neck,
rolled back into the lake.
When she'd got to the mountain
her trunk broke off at the waist,
lay there with her two arms.
When she'd found the twelve gods
then her two legs broke off.

The twelve gods smiled tenderly and said:
    'You under the waist,
you above the legs,
you sack of skin once called Szibbabi,
let the blood-rain leave you,
may you shut as tight
as shell round ripening seed,
and when the new light spills over
let out your young, be flat again,

become a cracked and juiceless skin,
and let your young be Kukszu.'

   Kukszu sprawls in scalding mud,
head in silt, feet in sedge,
face turned to the sky,
sends no more blood-rain into the body of Szibbabi,
cries with sharp call, a suckling child,
waiting for the overflowing light, for the overflowing light
waiting, for the never-returning light.

                                                    *[Elsö emberpár]*


THE UNDERWATER CITY

Who has no crumbling smoke – who has buried
all her flowers among the sad deaf waves, afraid
of the evil and for its sake shunning the good as well:
coward-city! she stirs my heart.

Instead of the sheet of the sky
the living sheet of seaweed, covering,
moving endlessly, noiselessly, mum as a thousand mice.
Noiseless seaweed music, thinkable music, not for the ear,
bygone city music, once heard by the ear –
musicless in this place the underwater city.

This city too I will throw off, till nothing is left.
Let her swim in the abyss of my past, waving her seaweed-cover,
lamenting her flowers and her bygone music.
Her cairn of stones, like knee-pans of scrawny gods,
their hard hip-bones and rasping ribs,
is beyond anxiety: death seizes, fuses everything.
Because I cast even this coward-city off, I want no memories of
      the music either.
Even her melancholy seaweed-cover is too much for me.

And if someone comes and asks me what I have:
what have I gathered in this world among
the monotonous mechanical clatter of nights and days?

what gives me licence to spend or hoard? –
I will show him this city. Rejected infernal city!
Look now: dying stones, flowers desired,
old trembling through the seaweed – such is the underwater city.
Yet I say: this is all you can gather together.
Because there is nothing more anywhere.

*[A víz alatti város]*


## TO DIE

Eyes of mother-of-pearl, smell of quince,
voice like a bell and far-off violins
and hesitant steps hesitating, thickening,
heavy-horned twins of emptiness snickering,
sinking, cold brimming, blue wide over all!
Wide magnet blue, ploughs flashing on,
and burning thorns in naked storm,
earth-wrinkles, dropped on pitted soil,
shaking the wild sweet nest, the bright
dish flying in its steady-spread light.

*[Meghalni]*


## WEDDING CHOIR

1
Life-filled longing of the buoyant smile strains against
imminent certainty, against the radiant food-bringer.
Brooding between good and evil, it loses bright warmth in
      languor,
slips down blood-red below empty stars, into chequered
      mutilation.
But the white bird of Union flies to it, nestles there,
settles maturely, hugely, in the flashing joy of the message.

2

Flocks of bright fables rise over the spreading scarlet cinders:
dead skeleton and growing body are praised by the grey-beard.
A cart, where troubled charm and trancelike beauty warm them-
selves wound into one,
painful and shining, like plunging into sleep: close to the cauldron
is the feast of the fable.
Kingfisher-flocks fly shrieking: the cry links everything!
the ritual fire flashes: prophecy pours time in its mould.


3

The straining pillar and the dancing fire are obstinate as a
marriageable girl:
unsignalled instantaneousness, little sailing half-moons,
veiled smile and stunned gladness, fading like the colour of
flowers,
brilliant caprices that instead of hurting brim over with love.
Long the street, but a thousand lodgings on both sides harbour
saintly unity.
Seed of all things: clear dignity! and sweet the broken fortune
piercing the husk.


4

The tense wing crumples, the glimmering laughter burns out,
shadow looms, and the steady pulse of hunger beats to its
quietus.
Between good and evil, in colourless mist, a dim ripple of the
soul,
the desperate slopes and huddles of stars adrift in it.
The Shining Fish lives, a peace unbroken,
an ambergris-scented order, clothed with imperfection and
salmon-running joy.

*[Mennyekzöi kar]*

# THE COLONNADE OF TEETH

## 1

The Colonnade of Teeth, where you have entered,
red marble hall: your mouth,
white marble columns: your teeth,
and the scarlet carpet you step on: your tongue.

## 2

You can look out of any window of time
and catch sight of still another face of God.
Lean out of the time of sedge and warblers:
God caresses.
Lean out of the time of Moses and Elijah:
God haggles.
Lean out of the time of the Cross:
God's face is all blood, like Veronica's napkin.
Lean out of your own time:
God is old, bent over a book.

## 3

Head downwards, like Peter on his cross,
man hangs in the blue sky with flaring hair
and the earth trundles over the soles of his feet.
The one who sees
has sleepless eyes he cannot take from man.

## 4

No sugar left for the child:
he stuffs himself with hen-droppings and finds what's sweet.
Every clod: lightless star!
Every worm: wingless cherub!

## 5

If you make hell, plunge to the bottom:
heaven's in sight there. Everything circles round.

6

Man lays down easy roads.
The wild beast stamps a forest track.
And look at the tree: depth and height raying from it to every
        compass-point;
itself a road, to everywhere!


7

Once you emerge from the glitter of the last two columns
the cupola your hair skims is then infinity,
and a swirl of rose-leaves throws you down,
and all that lies below, your bridal bed: the whole world –
Here you can declare:
'My God, I don't believe in you!'
And the storm of rose-leaves will smile:
'But I believe in you: are you satisfied?'

*[A fogak tornáca]*


WHISPER IN THE DARK

From a well you mount up, dear child. Your head a pyre, your
arm a stream, your trunk air, your feet mud. I shall bind you, but
don't be afraid: I love you and my bonds are your freedom.

On your head I write: 'I am strong, devoted, secure, and home-
loving, like one who wants to please women.'

On your arm I write: 'I have plenty of time, I am in no hurry: I
have eternity.'

On your trunk I write: 'I am poured into everything and every-
thing pours into me: I am not fastidious, but who is there who
could defile me?'

On your feet I write: 'I have measured the darkness and my
hand troubles its depths; nothing could sink so deep that I should
not be deeper.'

You have turned to gold, dear child. Change yourself into
bread for the blind and swords for those who can see.

[*Suttogás a sötétben*]

## THE SCARLET PALL

Your first dream – the dream just cradle-born –
two rosy children in naked interlace
eating each other, biting into soft fat flesh.

Second dream: the black sacrifice to your mother.
Lifting the stone lid, and silence out of the dark.

Third dream now: in shadows of furniture, in a corner
friends hanging head downwards in the air like
blinded lamps... who knows if they're alive...

   Oh how endlessly
dream ripples out, washes in sullen folds,
clashing thread on scarlet ground: dream: star-army!
figures of lightning on the blood-red pall!
   Remember yet:
the spearlike bud bursts from man's groin,
woman's groin unfolds its flower to meet it,
and as a bow touches a fine quivering string
the bud gushes into the offered cirque of petals.
   Remember yet:
you roam over dead plateaux and rock-wrinkles,
you come upon someone buried to the chin in stone,
and both the roamer and the buried one are you yourself.
You stumble clumsily over the protruding head,
but whose is the head that takes the kick of your boots?

   All your dream,
   all mine too:
our child-dreams drink pearls at the same spring.

A heaven of lace on the rust-crusted outposts,
images on the scarlet pall! Branch-writhing dream!

Dance, dance,
swing through the distance:
what an initiation
your childtime night was!
and the cyclops-eye of the world sat on your skull,
a thousand faces flaked to the bone on your cot,
    remember yet –

Across time and space
creep, creep to me:
our savage factious hearts have common root in the earth.
    Common, what lies in wait for us.
Think: you are walking in smoke. Your eyes are bandaged.
Heat of torches hits you; you are led by the hand.
    And soon perhaps, without fear,
    you will sacrifice yourself:
the arch of your eye-covering tugs the flame inwards!
No hiding then from your blood-coloured pall!

*[A vörös palást]*


CLOUDS

In the mirror of the open window the mirror-cloud drifts facing
the cloud. Cupids melt off at its edge, the heavy centre writhes
with the lumbering bodies of monsters, a satiny blueness retracts
and spreads bitten between gaping rows of beast-fangs. A violet
coach flakes off, hurries away into the blue and quickly vanishes:
yet it is easy to imagine it galloping there out of sight: gods are sit-
ting in it, or the no-beings of non-being, or the dead we have
heard the earth thudding down on and know nothing about any
more.

The clouds drift and the mirror-clouds face them; and for any-
one watching, nature drifts face to face with thought in the
depths of his skull.

*[Felhök]*

71

# THE LOST PARASOL

I think there is much more in even the smallest creation of God,
should it only be an ant, than wise men think.
ST TERESA OF AVILA

Where metalled road invades light thinning air,
some twenty steps more and a steep gorge yawns
with its jagged crest, and the sky is rounder there,
 it is like the world's end;
nearer: bushy glade in flower,
farther: space, rough mountain folk;
 a young man called his lover
 to go up in the cool of daybreak,
they took their rest in the grass, they lay down;
the girl has left her red parasol behind.

Wood shades sunshade. Quietness all round.
What can be there, with no one to be seen?
Time pours out its measureless froth and
 the near and the far still unopened
 and midday comes and evening comes,
no midday there, no evening, eternal floods
that swim in the wind, the fog, the light, the world
and this tangle moves off into endlessness
like a gigantic shimmering silk cocoon,
skirted by wells of flame and craters of soot.

Dawn, a pearl-grey ferry, was drifting
 on its bright herd of clouds,
from the valley the first cow-bell came ringing
and the couple walked forward, head by head;
 now their souvenir clings to the shadows,
red silk, the leaves, the green light on it, filtering,
 metal frame, bone handle, button:
 separate thing from the order of men,
 it came home intact, the parasol,
its neighbours rockface and breeze, its land cold soil.

In a sun-rocked cradle which is as massive
as the very first creation itself
 the little one lies, light instrument
on the blue-grey mossy timber of a cliff,

around it the stray whistling, the eternal murmuring
of the forest, vast Turkey-oak, slim hornbeam,
briar-thickets, a thousand sloe-bushes quivering,
noble tranquil ranks of created things,
and among them only the parasol flares out:
jaunty far-off visitor whose clothes still shout.

Languidly, as if long established there,
    its new home clasps it about:
the rocks hug their squat stonecrops,
above it the curly heliotropes
    cat's-tail veronica,
wild pinks push through cage of thistles,
dragon-fly broods on secret convolvulus,
dries his gauze wings, totters out:
so life goes on here, never otherwise –
a chink in the leaves, a flash of blue-smiling skies.

The sea-lunged forest breathes at it
    like yesterday, like long ago,
mild smell of the soft nest of a girl.
    Shy green woodpecker and russet
frisky squirrel refused to sit on it,
who knows what it hides: man left it;
but a nosy hedgehog comes up to the ledge,
the prickly loafer, low of leg,
like a steam puffer patrols round the rock;
puts heart in the woodpecker tapping at his trunk.

The sun stretches out its muscular rays:
you would expect the bell of heaven to crack.
Broad world – so many small worlds find their place
in you! Through the closed parasol's hills and valleys
an oblong speck moves: an ant that drags
the headless abdomen of a locust with rapt
persistence and effort: up to the bare heights,
down to the folds, holding the load tight,
and turning back at the very end of the way,
floundering up again with the body. Who knows why?

This finger-long journey is not shorter or sillier
than Everything, and its aim is just as hidden.

Look: through the branches you can see the hillside,
there is a falcon, a spot on the clear sky,
hangs in the air like a bird of stone:
predator, hanging over from history.
Here, wolf and brown bear were once at home,
crystalline lynx lay in ambush for the innocent.
God wetted a finger, turned a page
and the world had a very different image.

A sky-splitting single-sloped precipice,
its lap a lemon-yellow corrie of sand,
far off a rosy panorama of mist,
curly hills in a ragged mauve cloud-band;
above, the couple stood; below, the sun-wheel stirred;
in the dawn-flames, so interdependent
they stood, afraid, at the very edge of fate;
boulders rolled from beneath their feet,
    they were quarrelling, tearing their hearts,
each of them deaf before the other starts.

In the tangled thicket of their young blood
the luminous world skulks off, sinks;
    shame like a rose-branch cut
        the boy to the quick:
beyond entreaty, ready to throw himself down to...
His white shirt gestured against the blue,
    at the shrubby scarp with its bindweed
        he lurched forward, forward
growing smaller and more distant – and his frightened girl
runs after him through briars, her knee's blood is a pearl.

Tall sedges lean over the gorge
and like a gemmed porch of the depths below
an army of tiny shining shields of weeds
    and a thick dark couch of green
cling round the bark of a stump that points no-
where, here their frenzy lost its rage:
they twined together, to ask why, to cry,
like the horned moon the white flash of a thigh;
a hooded boletus at their feet
fattened its spore-crammed belly, not bothering to mate.

74

The hilltop sends down
wind tasting of stone
to crochet sudden air-lace;
and the lost parasol
shivers and half lives;
in the endlessly intricate forest, in the deep maze
of its undergrowth, a breeze
lurks, but takes off at the sharp rock-fall,
pouring over that solitary wall
and across the ravine, flying light to the dale.

Zigzag mane of the thicket
wavers and swirls,
the forest depths are sighing,
a thousand tiny leaves, like birds' tails, flicker
and glint in the light like scales;
drawn up from a breeze-wakened copse
yeasty, spicy fragrances are flying;
a snapped thorn-branch stirs, drops,
catches on the soft fabric:
on the tent-like parasol the first tear is pricked.

No one is sorry –
right above it an oriole is calling,
inside it a bow-legged spider scurries
round and round the scarlet corrie
and makes off: under the metal-arched ribs
a lizard twists in search of his siesta,
he guzzles the oven-heat and like a jester
propped on both hands peeps out from the midst;
later some mice come running in and out
and the shaft has a gaudy tit perking about.

In the vault of summer skies, diamond-blue,
an ice-white lace-mist moves in a smile;
over the plain, at the foothills of heaven,
there are dark woolpacks hanging heavy
and truant cloud-lines in crumbling style;
Apollo, body stripped, striding through,
runs young, strong, and fresh,
hot oil steams on the earth's rough flesh;
in air that rocks both valley and peak,
in empty immensities – a red spot of silk.

The girl of the neglected parasol
is just as small, lost in the broad world,
a tiny insect dropped in a sea-wide flood;
        no one to talk to at all,
wrapping her own soul round her fear,
    she curls up in a curtained room,
and hears a whipped dog whining there
as if there was no misery anywhere,
    no other wound to ache in earth or heaven;
or does he howl for all the pain of men?

            Hanging on the sky's arch
                at the lower bank
                    the dusk
                    is hazy.
    The first? How many before? On the lazy
    ridge no grass or insect measures it,
    neither cuckoo nor cuckoo-spit,
the twilights turn for ever, as created.
At the rock's edge, with forever's speed
the sleek silk vanishes into foaming shade.

Night's victory, yesterday's goodbye:
huge galley in the bay of earth and sky,
floating catafalque of dead Osiris;
scarlet embers fall into saffron high-tide,
peacock of air bends his fan from the heights,
shimmering feathers are roses and night-stocks;
an organ of gold installed in space
opens up all its pipes and lips,
pencils of light-rays spring from the rifts
and stroke the hills while darkness fills their cliffs.

            On the foamy crest of foliage
        light and shade come knotted together
        like the body's pain and pleasure.
    Fading now, from its covert, the cuckoo's message,
            and the motley unison
    of piping, chattering, chirping, splashing
            prankishness and passion.
        The evening light, that turns dreams on,
    bends through the cool slow-urging trees,
gleams in the silvery homespun of twittering beaks.

Each smallest voice is poured
   delicately into the quiet;
the nightingale among thorns, like
   a plucked metal string
cast a few notes into the wind,
then uncoils one ringing thread
   floating and spinning,
then flicks it like a veil, languid,
then bunches it rippling, potent but light,
and it fades: into a bed carved out of quiet.

The western sky is drained
of the late dusk's arching marble veins,
and the lit-up, burnt-out body of the sky
   leaves a steep column of smoke,
pierced through by stars as sharp as steel:
   pearl-crest of Boötes between waving trees,
Cygnus a cross drifting lazily by,
Cassiopeia with its double dagger, the rope
of the faintly glimmering Milky Way
loosely folding dead black space away.

The valley, a deep arena, rests,
crisscrossed by shadows of slashed buttresses;
   in the cirque a buxom Venus dances,
approaches, spins round, offers riches,
dances naked, white as snow, touches
her feet upon the dew-drenched hills,
soft-bodied, plump, with shining curls,
the slippery form is merged in darkness,
avid monsters stare her through and through;
in a swoon she waves goodbye and the curtain snaps to.

Like rows of houses in an earthquake:
   great tangle of trees at the wood's edge
      stagger and shake;
a green shoot flies up into the whirlwind,
a grindstone shrieking comes from rocky ledge,
   the wilderness tosses and groans;
on the cloud-capped hilltop a thin
   lightning burns, crackles, cracks,
then the long crisped fires streaming like flax
split above the cliff, a lion's growl at their backs.

The storm flickers through the twigs,
its thousand necks turn and twist,
it wrestles with the stumbling forest,
a writhing timber in its fist,
leathery roots clutch hard,
lightning tingles in the bark,
hundreds of birds crouch and start
in nests that shake them to the heart,
the burning, clammy monster rages still,
the sky, bowed low, seethes around the hill.

Torn-off leaves whirl anywhere,
roots of a gouged beech prod the air;
the parasol has been swept off the rock,
into a bramble-bush, beside a tree-trunk,
the downpour slaps its silk,
it is all smudged now, frayed, and the ribs show.
It is indifferent to its fate – as the hilltop holds
its head without complaint in thunderbolts,
and with the sky huddles low,
and fixed by sticky clouds watches the daybreak glow.

The parasol has a new home:
the secret world in fallen leaves,
cool dark earth and mouldering grove,
pallid trailers, roots in graves,
horrors endless, puffy, ropy, cold,
centipede country, maggot metropolis;
the days swing round like catapults,
casting the full sun over it, the old
weltering moon; and the parasol sprawls
like a flaking corpse, though it never lived at all.

Autumn rustles: stuffs dead leaves in it;
winter gallops: it is all snow;
the thaw sets it free again:
earth-brown, washed-out now.
A sprouting acorn pushes,
and through the slack, loose
fabric a tiny flag
thrusts the fibres back:
green, tender tassel steers to the weathervanes;
a few more years and a tree will shade the remains.

The parasol has changed: it has left human hands;
the girl has changed too: she is the woman of a man;
once, the red sail and the steerer ran
    lightly together, roving free,
while hosts of drunkenly foaming plum-trees
tempted the wasps to stir noisily
    and deep in the girl's heart the bumble-bees
began to swarm and buzz mischievously;
since then, this wild army has been busy,
building a fortress in her woman's body.

    Both man and woman have forgotten it now,
    though it was the first witness of their linked fates:
Lombard silk and red Rhine dye,
long-travelled Indian ivory,
Pittsburgh iron, Brazilian wood, how
    many handcarts have trundled its parts,
    they have gone by rail, they have gone in boats:
a world to make it! son of a thousand hands!
yet no curio: old-world frippery;
lost: no joy in that, yet no great misery.

Branching veins draw it into the dark,
    light-unvisited mud weighs it down,
it is mere rags, dying in dribs and drabs,
it has stopped serving exotic demands
and like a bird escaping its cage-door
    takes up its great home:
the dissolving soil, the swirl of space, the rays
draw it all ways, confused, astray,
old shoreless floods map its new phase:
this is creation's first emergent day.

    Neither sun, moon, nor watch
    can measure creation's second and third days:
    the father of vegetation keeps his watch
over it, pumpkin-head, Saturn, dark face
with grey eyebrows hanging to his chin.
    Pulsing life-fluid filters in:
powdered cloth, rotten wood, rusted iron
dissolve and disappear in tangle and thorn,
and sucked up slowly by each hair-vein
it seethes alive again in the humming vortex of green.

Its handle is visible through the leaf-mould.
A brown moth settles there, perches awhile.
    By midnight it has laid
hundreds of eggs, a mass of tiny balls
placed in smooth strips, finely embroidered.
And like a biblical ancestress
she opens her wings, floats victorious,
queen fulfilled in happiness,
    not caring that dawn brings death:
God in the sky drew up my trembling crest!

The parasol no longer exists: bit by bit
    it set off into the open world,
    all changed, part after part;
even the eyes of Argus might find no trace,
    swivelling across the light,
    sliding down to the shade;
  only a single feeble fibre remains,
  poised on the top of a bramble-prickle,
  it is mere fluff, next to invisible;
flies up from the thorn-prick, jumps into the saddle

of a storm! Air-pockets toss it lily-thin,
    the mountains shift below
in stampede, buffalo trampling buffalo;
fog-blanket opens on dark forest paths,
brooks twinkling down in the shy straths,
sharp drop of the crag wall, a mine,
toy trains of tubs moving along the rails,
scattered homesteads, a town with its smoke-trails,
and overhead, the great bleak acres of silence
and below, the hill from which the tuft went flying.

Upwards, still higher up it floats:
the moon hangs close like a white fruit,
the earth is a round, tilted, blotchy shroud
    framed by blackness and void.
    Bathed in airy juices,
the fluff swings heavy like a full leather bottle,
    descends to the ground, settles:
    on a green plain, in drizzly mists,
it hovers lightly among the acacias
and probes a calf's ear as its resting-place.

A thunderstorm crashes, carries it off,
flies with it raggedly over moor and bog,
like a spool it turns, winding the fog,
    and when it is all spun onto a distaff:
low blue sea and high blue sky are combers,
    two sun discs gaze at each other
    and between the two blue shells
        a ghostly sail
        sways, tranquil,
uncaring whether it sways in air or swell.

The vapour-tulip throws back its head,
a glass-green other-worldly meadow glistens,
at the horizon a purple thorn gathers;
darkness surrounds the far-off island;
a little ray like a woman's glance flickers,
caresses its fugitive lover, glitters
as it flutters onto its drowsy son,
while a smile dawns eternity on man,
its arches bend and march on their way
between watery shores, Theatrum Gloriae Dei.

*       *       *

The red silk parasol was my song,
    sung for my only one;
this true love is the clearest spring,
    I have smoothed its mirror with my breath,
I have seen the two of us, the secret is known:
    we shall moulder into one after death.
Now I expend my life exultantly
like the oriole in the tree:
till it falls down on the old forest floor,
singing with such full throat its heart must burst and soar.

*[Az elveszített napernyö]*

81

## MOON AND FARMSTEAD

full   moon   slip   swim
wind   fog   foam   chord   hum
the   house   empty

rampant
thorn   fence
eye   blaze

moon   swim   flame
grass   chord   twang
cloud   fling

the   house   empty
door   window
fly   up

chimney   run
fog   swirl
full   moon   circle

the   house   empty

*[Hold és tanya]*


## ORPHEUS KILLED

I lie in a cold shaded courtyard, I am dead.
I am sobbing over my body, so many women, men.
Grief rolls from the drum and I start dancing. Who
killed me, why?
    I drift round the market, in palaces,
in taverns, among the flute-players, till in drink
I can say to the drunk: Look at me, I am
your hearts: engaged to death for the sake
of beggars and the blind.
    Stone I am and metal I am
on a slave's cross. The corpse is staring wide-eyed,
grief rolls from the drum and I dance. I am everything

and I am nothing: oh, look at me. I am everyone
and I am no one: stone and metal, many shapes,
on a slave's cross. Why did the priests kill me?
Did I slight their temple?
     Dismembered I lie in the wasteland,
what urn is there for my white dust? Why
did the women tear me? Do they want my dead love?

Wolves of the famished earth prowl all round me,
decay rains rolling down and I start dancing.
Cain I am and saint I am: kneel at my feet.
Leper I am and clean I am: touch me. Body
moves, weak joints crack, cold tears trickle, he
sweats, sweats. Mindless I am and wise I am,
ask no questions, understand in silence. Dead I am
and alive I am, a dumb face, I. A wax-face
sacrifice turns skyward, ringed by staring horror, grief
rolls from the drum and I dance.

     No asking back
the body stretched on the cross. I lie harvested in the wasteland,
no asking back the grain laid up in barns.
Death's drum rolls, I whirl in the dance for ever,
the song flooding the valley refreshed by my blood,
my secret endless life entangled in the groves of death.

*[A megölt Orpheus]*


## QUEEN TATAVANE

O my winged ancestors!
Green branch and dry twig you gave me
for my two empires, to plant one and to lash one.
I am small as a weasel, pure as the eastern Moon,
light-ankled as a gazelle, but not poised for flight –
my heart lies open to you, to every silent suggestion.

The Elephantstar took my fifteenth year,
the Dragonstar brought this, the sixteenth.
I am allowed three husbands by ancestral decree
and seven lovers beneath the holy jasmine-leaves.

Not for me to escape with girl-friends to the fields,
for happy laughter, goats to milk, fresh milk to drink,
instead I sit on the throne in your light year after year,
an ebony idol with the world's weight on my neck.

Negro caravans, Arab ships are my traffic and merchandise,
I pay well, though I see most as polecats and monkeys,
but even the sky rains on unchosen ground, seeds burst unchosen.
I survey the naked hosts lost in their prison,
all of them I love as if they were my children,
punishing them with the rod and if need be by the sword,
and though my heart should bleed my looks are frozen.

Wake up, my fathers and mothers! Leave the ash-filled urn,
help me while the mists crawl;
your dark little daughter pleads with you as the last queen,
waiting among the garlands of the cedar-hall.

My seat among stone lions, the man's throne empty at my side,
my brow is glowing ruby-wreathed like the dawn-clouds,
my purple-tinted fingers, my drowsy almond eyes
shine like a god's as they strike down and raise;
what you found sweet and bitter I come to, I taste.

Orange veils on my shoulders, fireflower wreaths on my dark hair,
the reedpipe cries, the eunuchs drone, the altar's set.
Come Bulak-Amba my starry bull-browed ancestor!
Come Aure-Ange my lovely holy milk-rich ancestress!

Mango, areca, piled on the altar,
the year's brimming rice, brown coconut, white copra,
all round, red flower thrown on red flower,
sweet sandalwood fumes float up into the air.

Great man-spirit with no name: eat!
Great woman-spirit with no name: eat!
Huge emptiness in the silence behind the drumbeat: eat!

I call you, my father over the foam,
my old begetter, Batan-Kenam,
you are coming in your sun-chariot, four-elephant-drawn,
through the head-waving rattlesnakes of five cosmic storms,

my soldier, ageless, coral-garlanded,
blue-shirted arms,
lance of sky's shark-bone, turtle shield,
cut-off locks of the seven dancer-stars shimmer at your belt,
your elephants lumber and stamp, tiger-herds are felled,
and you rest on your elbow at the world's end in the lee of the
    loud blue mountain –
I salute you my glittering visitor, my far-off father!

I am wrapped in my veil, I am hidden,
the welcoming hostess is timid,
I hand out half-peeled oranges on a gold dish:
look at me here, I am your own flesh,
you know I am supple and clawed like a forest cat,
you pause if you see my dark green shining eyes,
my white-hot teeth-embers,
behind, my skeleton is lace-fine, a dragon-fly:
see your one-day-old woman! one smile is all she would wish!

I summon you Aruvatene, my mother!
I call you. I am your daughter. Do you love her?
Your little one, will you be her protector?
Look, Nightqueen, at your tiny drop of dew:
the sparkling skin, the swelling breast!
You thick-starred heavenly palm-tree, I dance for you.
Blow the pipe, roll the drum,
my dance-wind skims about you, let it come!
my silver ankle-jangle chatters – from you it came!
my orange shawl flies out – you gave it my name!

But if your beautiful face goes ashy as mist
I give you my blood to drink from your ancient chalice,
turn back, I leave you in peace,
eat, drink in silence.

Come too, Andede, good grandmother,
you are as old as the wind
that snuffles in the oven-cinders.
I shall never be so old,
fugitive with blowing flowers.

Andede, good grandmother,
you are as wrinkled as the stone
that snaps off from the mountain.
I shall never be so wrinkled,
I am the rock-escaping fountain.

Andede, good grandmother,
you smile like a yellow desert place
grinding its bones, toothless sand-cascades
skirting the cosmic border.
That is not my smile,
I am the lady of two empires,
sword and bread on my lap together
under the trickle of my tears.

Andede, good grandmother,
you champ and smack like the green dragon
that swallows up the wildest moor.
But I can never be satisfied,
two nations fight to eat from my hand
and bread forever lusts after sword.

Andede, good grandmother,
perpetually decaying, never destroyed,
you are puny but sinewy, like a root in the earth,
I am the mother of everybody,
I would take them all on my lap,
I would let them all eat and sup,
but when I even raise my hand, I die.

Great man-spirit with no name: eat!
Great woman-spirit with no name: eat!
Huge emptiness in the silence behind the drumbeat: eat!

Come forward, now, great, ancient, unforgotten,
every sky-dome-breasted queen,
every lightning-dashing king!
I know that your good
is our only food,
but if misery surges again,
here I am – my blame alone,
I your shadow, your orphan,

prostrate under your cane,
beg for that bastinadoing!

For heaven's sake help me then!
Oh I am the virgin peahen
who instead of living eggs
found redhot stones between her legs
and with anxious wings spread wide
broods to hatch a void.
Pain of two nations is fire under me,
who will ever hatch the happiness of the world?

[*Tatavane Királynö*]


IN THE WINDOW-SQUARE

              In the window-square
    *a star*   clots
              on black sky
dull light forms a minute
the trees surge darkly
distant sea sings in leaves
    outside your tight-shut minutes
    your star tears you away
the infinite flows and foams through the garden
but in this room space is concentrated
drowns in angle and bay
on red slopes of the armchair
stretches transparently
on the tendril-blue neck of the ewer
flies up to stay
    your ring on the table
    inextinguishable candle
night slaps the island
hear the sea lapping
things in their deaf shells
    clotting in the window-frame
    grief hangs over a deep
you picture-book of the universe
in full-lighted age-old existence

shut now at a touch
but my eye runs over the cover
   as this star wanders
   with its light-year rays
   with its blank shoreless gaze

*[Ablak négyszögében]*


## RAYFLOWER

Rayflower
about the head
so flickery
then fled

Above the shoulders
below the chin
a lonely night-light
is carried in

In front of the chest
lace-foam flying
already the fire there
fading dying

In the swelling
of the belly
a shadow spreads
enormously

In a dark sea
no foot lingers
fearing to leave
the lucifer fingers

*[Sugárvirág]*

## TERRA SIGILLATA

*Epigrams of an ancient poet*

Useless interrogation: I know nothing. An old man fallen asleep,
I wake as a baby, and you can read your learning from my
wide blue eyes; I only glimpse it in recidivist streams.

   *

A red-fingered child pats grey cakes at the seaside,
I ask for one, he says no, not even for a real cake, no.
Well now, old prophets, what do you want from me? the twenty-
    four
sky prisms, when I look blind into hearts and read them.

   *

If you want your fortune, I'll reel off your identity, your
    expectations,
but I'm deaf to my own words – no plundering secrets.

   *

'You say you're God's offspring: why do you scrape along like
    paupers?'
'Even Zeus himself, when he takes human steps on earth,
begs bread and water, parched, starved as a tramp.'

   *

The Dazzling is always coming to earth to beg for mud,
while his palace in heaven, stiff with gold, sighs for his return.

   *

The bowed-down carrier looks up: there he stands at the centre
    of the earth!
it is above his head that the sky's vault goes highest.

   *

Beautiful the lonely pine, beautiful the bee-wreathed rose,
beautiful the white funeral, most beautiful through all – their
union.

*

The treasures of a tree! Leaves, flowers, fruits.
How freely it gives them, clinging to the elements alone.

*

The forest has modesty, the wolf hides his death in the shadows,
but a bought mourner will shrill without shame at a stranger's
burial.

*

The swindler doesn't slip up with his bogus balance-sheets when
his heart is firm,
but when bursting out crying and taking pity on the innocent.

*

Crime has majesty, virtue is holy; but what is the troubled heart
worth?
There, crime is raving drunk and virtue is a jailer.

*

The moment I slice the cocoon of my fate: my skull is the sky-
dome,
fate-shuttling stars scuttle across its arch.

## IN MEMORIAM GYULA JUHÁSZ*

Let the beasts whine at your grave my father
whine at your grave
let the beasts whine
between the byre and the blade
between the slaughterhouse and dunghill
between the clank of the chain and desolation
my mother as Hamlet said
let the old hunchbacked women whine
between the hospital and the glad rags
between the asylum and the lily-of-the-valley
between the cemetery and the frippery
and the wretches with buried ulcers
between stately doctors and strapping priests
all those paralysed by deferred release
on the far side of hope on the near side of confrontation

Let butterflies twist above the stream
Ophelia who drowned before we were born
the roseless thorn is yours
the profitless pain
the lacklustre ghost in a mourning frame
the falling on knees face in the mud
the humiliation boundless and endless
the dead body without a cross
the unredeemed sacrifice
the hopelessness that is for ever hopelessness

Let rabid dogs howl at your grave
let hollow phantoms hoot
my starry brother my bearded bride
the good is only a moment's presentiment
evil is not eternal malice
in the meantime blood flows
lacerated life cannot die
death is deathless liberty

---

\*    Hungarian poet, 1883-1937.

## SIGNS

**I**
The whole world finds room under my eyelid.
God squeezes into my head and heart.
This is what makes me heavy.
This is what makes the donkey I sit on unhappy.

**II**
Heaven's crazy-man: light: you
pouring your face on the surface of the water,
what is that girl's face you proffer
stripping from your own madness?

Great saint, having swum through this world
you came to the empty silence, endlessness,
you climbed with the void to a crystal wedding-dress:
be frank, what woman is it like?

**III**
Man, waken the secret woman in you;
woman, light up your masculine state:
for if the Invisible embraces you,
it will enter you and take you into it.

**IV**
Oh how large then is love
if it goes with us in our whirlpools?
And what large love lies waiting in us
if it can be taken into our whirlpools?

**V**
More than your heart's cloudy afflictions,
more than your mind's labour of doubt –
value your toothache more than that,
for its energies.

Words alone can answer your questions,
but each thing answers itself.

*[Jelek]*

INTERNUS

## Growing Old

My brain's gutterings unwind,
its light – that poverty of mind –
keeps drawing in its radius,
keeps glowing in still dimmer space;
with God's help, I shall hardly see
how far off the cell-wall may be.


## Self-Portrait with Dog

The man I was is dying, his gasps are faint:
the heart is like a stone that stops the throat.
The life-spark, to get its breath back, leaps out
at long last from the miserable body
into a dog, to find tranquillity.
I lay my head down on my master's foot.
I don't feel his pain, I don't remember. I don't.


## Dissolving Presence

It's not my self that interests me,
only that my death, so certain,
saves me from unwanted clowning,
though a tramped-on worm can hurt me.
Is dying going into nothing?
No more despair, no more desire.
But after-life may be no plaything?
I can endure from fire to fire.
Life and death don't interest me,
I only need that harmony
which matter cannot even bear
or reason take into its sphere.


## Double-faced

My self: though this perpetual guest
is hardly boring company,
he's a tick to bite my privacy,
without him I'd have quiet and rest.

Because he's attentive to my demon
and shapes its early hints in words
I put up with his earthy being
till evening ends, not afterwards.


*Out of the Inner Infinity*

From inward infinities I still look out
now and again, seeing through my face
clouds or the winking lights of stars in space.
My eyesight fails, that leaves me like the rest,
the outside world has shut my gates, I'm left
where there is no earth left, but only sky;
and no event, no grace and no surprise,
no surface, nothing seen, no nebulas,
only reality at peace and luminous,
boundless and measureless and nameless,
a love that's still desireless and still changeless.
The panic world is baffled at my gate:
'Madman! Egotist! Traitor!' its words beat.
But wait: I have a bakehouse in my head,
you'll feed someday on this still uncooled bread.


*The Muddy Drink is Going Down and the Bottom
of the Glass Shows Through*

After death shall I still exist?
No handcuffs then upon my wrist,
I have dissolved identity,
why wish it in eternity?
Being or non-being: nakedness
suits undying presences.


I never thought it could be so:
my body gasps for its last breath,
yet still and easy is my soul.
My life is wantless and unwanted,
a beggar going on undaunted,
even by my death unhaunted,
with losses and with gains untaunted.
Fate is too kind! I had best not
die this way, like a dying god,

a smiling victory well flaunted;
I should be pulled up by the root
with a cowardly last shout
and get the real end of a man,
not judged for what I solely am.

*Nocturne*

Bored with my being, unutterably,
boxed in male bones perpetually,
I'm given no rest from his presence,
he and I are old bed-fellows,
I can feel his warmth, his sweat,
from his hair-roots to his feet,
feel the twistings of his bowels,
his man's-stump and his milkless nipples,
the wheezing of his lung-bellows,
his heart-beats on uneasy pedals,
his gnawing and his stabbing pains,
his lusts that break the lagging reins,
his times of hunger and of thirst,
his filled-and-emptied bag of dust,
and what he feels and thinks within
I feel and think, unmoved, with him.
In beastly body-warmth I lie
stuck to a drumming rancid sty.
His daytime braying makes me sick
like his dead snoring, I can't stick
his senses' narrow window-glass,
the wooden O of his mind, a mass
of memories, symbols parroted
hand in hand and madly led.
I'm sick of dandling, pampering him,
of wiping the tarry rump of him,
of taking in his hungry cares,
of making his head utter prayers;
I've been his patient unpaid slave,
caring nothing for what I gave.
Not executioner, but guard,
I hold him close, but killing's barred:
he will die someday just the same,
die in peace or die in pain.

Each cell and seed he has, in its fervour
would go on fucking and gorging for ever,
and the pitiful keen-kindled mind
for ever have new knowledge to find,
but clenched in vice of flesh, I stiffen
in cramps of an enclosing coffin.
His life and stir are my own death,
and I fly on his final breath
into the love of God, fly back
till I'm a stitch in nothing's sack
and need no longer share my soul
or body with my self at all,
being unbounded plenitude,
the latency not understood
who taking all things into him
pours his wealth from a stintless brim.

## MOUNTAIN LANDSCAPE

Valley brook
birdsong squabble.

High quiet
home of god-faced
rocks hanging.

And higher, Nemo's song,
hilltop grindstone-squeal:
ice cracks smart.

*[Hegyi táj]*

## THE SECRET COUNTRY

One day we'll jump on a floating log, E Daj the distant is waiting
    for us,
we'll float on the log, wing-locked butterflies,
dance gently downwards through the traveller's-joy
beneath the sea, no one aware of us.

Below earth and sea there is a black lake,
motionless and mirror-sharp,
no one knows its chasms:
E Daj the distant is waiting for us,
one day we'll jump on a floating log, plunge in.

The old men say:
As long as we live,
everything we see
hangs in that mirror in the lake,
our faces, our figures
figured facing down.
The palms, the lianas, the foxes, the stars
all hang there in the mirror of the lake.

Short-lived the butterfly, but it visits the old farmhouse,
puttering about it with its whispering
wings, we hear them whispering,
we run, run into the house.
We don't speak to it, we don't speak to shadows.
It knocks at the door, knocks and knocks, breaks off, goes back
    home,
E Daj the distant is waiting for us.

The old men say:
Our faces and figures are reflected in the black lake,
no one sees its depths:
whatever is, was once in them,
whatever was once in them, falls back there,
and this is the eternal return.

The man throws his spear, bends his bow,
the woman scrapes a hole for the fire,
all look for handholds, build huts:

and this is how we live, hanging head down in the mirror of the
    lake,
one day we'll jump on a floating log, plunge in.
We can't see what lies below. E Daj the distant is waiting for us.

*[A rejtett ország]*


## DIFFICULT HOUR

Time for black prophecies is over: the Winter of History is whistling around us.

Man, with suicidal power in his limbs, poison in his blood, craziness in his head like a mad dog: nobody can see his destiny.

If he wants to scarify people to the bone with his new instruments of devastation: his only attainments are loss of the wheel and of fire, forgetfulness of speech, life on all fours.

But let him extricate himself: let him give up his myriad maggot-teeming acts of idiot self-will, his termite provision-activities for the outer world: first let him measure and order the inner world.

Familiar and ordered inner worlds outgrow individual greed, learn to rub along with one another, even to be in harmony with their outer world.

This is the old practicable way. Up till now, the bloodstained currents of history may have moved with beauty and grandeur but moved to a common death, or worse, narrowed their streams to the further agony of a relentless dehumanization.

But today some cradle rocks a fire-baby bringing divine gifts such as we hardly saw in our dreams.

And just as in bygone days they laid open the secret strength of the material world: they will begin now to lay open the powers of the bodiless inner world.

In the hands of these children the lamp of reason does not dictate, but serve: shining through subconscious life-forces and supraconscious spirit-forces alike, illuminating them and setting them to work in turn.

It was always others man conquered in the past; but – oh tremulous hope! – in the future he conquers himself, and fate subdues itself before him, and the stars.

*[Nehéz óra]*

COOLIE

Coolie cane chop.
Coolie go
      go
           only softly-softly
  Rickshaw
  Car
  Dragon-carriage
Coolie pull rickshaw.
Coolie pull car.
Coolie pull dragon-carriage.
         only softly-softly
Coolie go foot.
Coolie beard white.
Coolie sleepy.
Coolie hungry.
Coolie old.
Coolie bean poppyseed little child
big wicked man beat little Coolie.
       only softly-softly
  Rickshaw
  Car
  Dragon-carriage
Who pull rickshaw?
Who pull car?
Who pull dragon-carriage?

Suppose Coolie dead.
Coolie dead.
Coolie no-o-o-o-t know dead!
Coolie immortal
            only softly-softly

*[Kuli]*


MONKEYLAND

Oh for far-off monkeyland,
ripe monkeybread on baobabs,
and the wind strums out monkeytunes
from monkeywindow monkeybars.

Monkeyheroes rise and fight
in monkeyfield and monkeysquare,
and monkeysanatoriums
have monkeypatients crying there.

Monkeygirl monkeytaught
masters monkeyalphabet,
evil monkey pounds his thrawn
feet in monkeyprison yet.

Monkeymill is nearly made,
miles of monkeymayonnaise,
winningly unwinnable
winning monkeymind wins praise.

Monkeyking on monkeypole
harangues the crowd in monkeytongue,
monkeyheaven comes to some,
monkeyhell for those undone.

Macaque, gorilla, chimpanzee,
baboon, orangutan, each beast
reads his monkeynewssheet at
the end of each twilight repast.

100

With monkeysupper memories
the monkeyouthouse rumbles, hums,
monkeyswaddies start to march,
right turn, left turn, shoulder arms –

monkeymilitary fright
reflected in each monkeyface,
with monkeygun in monkeyfist
the monkeys' world the world we face.

*[Majomország]*

*from*
*WI THE HAILL VOICE: 25 POEMS*
*BY VLADIMIR MAYAKOVSKY*
(1972)

INTRODUCTION

Although it is now nearly half a century since the death of Vladimir Mayakovsky (1893-1930), his work still keeps a springy and accessible vitality, and his ideas and feelings about the relation of poet to society are as relevant and controversial as they ever were. He took enormous risks, throwing hostages to time in his devotion to transitory issues, and some commentators have accused him in this of a paradoxical foolishness, a perversely wilful stifling or misdirection of his admitted genius. 'He wasted his talent,' wrote Patricia Blake, 'drawing posters, and composing thousands of slogans and "agitational" jingles that urged the Soviet people to drink boiled water, put their money in the bank, and patronise state stores.'* But who is to say that these activities, which to Mayakovsky (and he was artist, editor, playwright, film-writer, as well as poet) were an important part of the cultural midwifery of the new Soviet state, can only be regarded as a 'waste of talent'? *Ex ungue leonem.* Here is one of the 'agitational jingles', written in 1920 during the civil war period, and saying roughly 'Wrangel! – out!':

> Vrangel – fon,
> Vrangelya von!
> Vrangel – vrag.
> Vrangelya v ovrag!

The marked beat, the word-play, the popular mnemonic patterning all speak Mayakovsky. The pleasure he took in writing the jingle is clear, yet it is also the useful little snap of Bolshevik polemic it is designed to be. Of course a man so strongly individual and original as Mayakovsky could not transform himself into the spokesman of a new and tough-minded social order without cost. He was entitled to say, in his late poem 'With the Full Voice' (1930), that he was 'fed up with agitprop' and had 'trampled on the throat of (his own) song', but at the same time, and equally, he is proud of the fact that he was able to mould himself in accordance with the demands of a Revolution he wholeheartedly believed in, and he claims that his verse will reach and affect posterity – *because* of the honesty of its pain and its cost, is what one might add – when life itself has moved on and the art-

* In V. Mayakovsky, *The Bedbug and Selected Poetry*, ed. P. Blake (Weidenfeld & Nicolson, 1961).

works of our struggling age are dug up like arrow-heads and antediluvian bones.

When Mayakovsky read 'With the Full Voice' in the House of the Komsomols in Moscow in March, 1930, the poem was well received, and he obviously felt encouraged at that moment that such a complexly-textured poem should have broken through the audience barrier. He commented: 'The fact that it got across to you is very very interesting. It shows that we must, without impoverishing our technique, work devotedly for the working-class reader.' In the more-proletarian-than-thou word-battles of the later 1920s, Mayakovsky was often under attack for his difficulty, or for what was regarded as the lingering bad legacy of futurist extravagance in his work, or for what seemed to some an insufficient identification with workers' problems and aspirations. Many of the attacks were unjust, and distressed him greatly; the philistines, gaining confidence and power, certainly contributed to his eventual suicide, whatever more personal causes were at work. Resilient, if not resilient enough in the end, Mayakovsky had made more than one spirited reply to his enemies. In particular, his article 'Workers and Peasants Don't Understand You' (1928) gave this interesting defence of a Soviet artist's position:

'A genuine proletarian Soviet art must be comprehensible to the broad masses. Yes or no?'
– Yes and no. Yes, but with a corrective supplied by time and propaganda. Art is not born mass art, it becomes mass art as the result of a sum of efforts: critical analysis to establish its soundness and usefulness, organised diffusion of the work through party and state channels if its usefulness is agreed, good timing of mass diffusion of the book, no clash between the question raised by a book and the maturity of the questions of the masses. The better the book, the more it outruns events.

The last sentence seems almost to show Mayakovsky as Machiavelli. At first it clinches the argument for state supervision which the previous sentence unfolded, and then by a species of double-take you find that he has left behind, after all, a classic little time-bomb from the *avant-garde*. The ambience is going to have its work cut out to catch up.

It was Mayakovsky's unenviable dilemma to feel obliged, by his own conscience, to attempt the transition from a brilliant, explosive, tormented, and largely subjective futurism to a more outward-looking, more comprehensible and more comprehensive, yet not self-compromised poetry. The polarization between those who extol the early poetry for its expressive freedom (and this includes Boris Pasternak as well as many Western critics) and those who suspiciously walk round it because futurism is pre-revolutionary and has sinister connections such as Marinetti (and many Soviet critics are still in this position), has been unfortunate. Mayakovsky's work is in fact more of a piece than is often admitted. Although his poetry became less dependent on startlingly unexpected sequences of imagery, he never gave up his belief in innovation; and conversely, Soviet critics rightly point out that even in the pre-1917 poems like *A Cloud in Trousers, I,* and *The Backbone Flute* the poet's concerns often reflect society at large although dealing with themes of personal alienation and erotic hangup. In 1918 – post-Revolution but only just – Mayakovsky wrote: 'Revolution in content is unthinkable without revolution in form.' For content he was thinking about 'socialism-anarchism', and for form 'futurism'. Nevertheless, the statement stands as a general position which he kept, with very few qualms or qualifications, even when Lenin and Lunacharsky thought otherwise. In his poem 'A Talk with the Taxman about Poetry' (1926) he still writes, in the midst of a most entertaining defence of the hard work of a professional poet: 'Poetry – all poetry! – is a journey into the unknown.' And in the long essay 'How are Verses Made?' (also 1926) he repeats: 'Innovation, innovation in materials and methods, is obligatory for every poetical composition.'* In that essay, innovation joins careful craftsmanship, a feeling for the age, the use of the spoken language, and a commitment to social struggle as one of the prerequisites for modern poetry.

But what were the innovations? There was a turning away from nature (which bored Mayakovsky) and an attempt to incorporate into verse something of the urban, industrial, and technological dynamism of the modern world – hence the importance to him of Brooklyn Bridge as a symbolic object, and hence the imaginary Wellsian workers' palace of the poem 'Versailles', with its million rooms of glass and steel so bright they hurt the eyes. There was a determination to refresh and revive language, not only in the post-Revolution sense of a newly liberated popular speech which must find its way into art (though ironically, when Mayakovsky says 'whore' or 'shit' his Soviet editors trot out a Victorian dot-

* Quoted from the translation by G.M. Hyde (Cape, 1970).

dot-dot) but also at the aesthetic level of mind-bending imagery and juxtaposition, and an acutely inventive use of word and sound in every device of onomatopoeia, alliteration, assonance and dissonance, pun and palindrome, and perhaps above all (and in the spirit of the highly inflected Russian language) morphological play and dislocation.

Mayakovsky was one of the signatories of the 1912 futurist manifesto 'A Slap in the Face of Public Taste', which said among other things:

> The past is crowded...Throw Pushkin, Dostoyevsky, Tolstoy, *et al.*, *et al.*, overboard from the Ship of Modernity...All those Maxim Gorkys, Kuprins, Bloks, Sologubs, Remizovs, Averchenkos, Chernyis, Kuzmins, Bunins, etc., etc. need only a *dacha* on a river...We look at their nothingness from the heights of skyscrapers!...*We decree* that the poets' *rights* be honored:
>
> 1) to enlarge vocabulary in its *scope* with arbitrary and derivative words (creation of new words).
>
> 2) to feel an insurmountable hatred for the language existing before them...
>
> And if *for the time being* even our lines are still marked with dirty stigmas of your "common sense" and "good taste", there tremble on them *for the first time* the summer lightnings of the New-Coming Beauty of the Self-sufficient (self-centred) Word.*

This iconoclasm was in the mood of the time and Mayakovsky went along with it. Three years later, in his own little manifesto 'A Drop of Tar', he had backpedalled sufficiently from futurism to agree that the movement was dead but at the same time he argued that its effects lived on and were now generally diffused: 'Today we are all futurists. The people are futurist.'

In fact Mayakovsky's solidity and authority seem to be shown in the fact that for all his originality and formal brilliance as a writer, he was essentially less extreme than fellow-theorists like Kruchonykh, Khlebnikov, and Kamensky, and their work remains of great interest but more narrow and obsessed. Experiments in Russia at this period included visual poetry, sound-poetry, and combinations of the two. All these experiments find some reflection in Mayakovsky's work, but it is others who take them further.

---

* Quoted from V. Markov, *Russian Futurism: A History* (MacGibbon & Kee, 1969).

With visual poetry, it is not surprising that Mayakovsky should be interested, given his own artistic leanings and his close friendship with a number of well-known artists. His revolutionary play *Mystery-Bouffe* (1918) had set designs and costumes by the suprematist painter Malevich. His long poem *About This* (1923) was illustrated by the remarkable photo-montages of his friend, the constructivist 'artist-engineer' Rodchenko. His collection of poems *For the Voice* (1923) was designed and given a stunning typographical layout in black and red by El Lissitzky – constructivist again, and as fresh and eye-catching today as if no fifty years had intervened. Mayakovsky himself, in his first book, *I*, hand-lithographed in 1913, showed his own interest in the visual possibilities of poetry, as may be seen in this translation of the opening section:

> Along the pavement of my soul
> worn out by feet
> the steps of madmen beat
> their hard-heeled sentences
> where
> cities
> are hanged and steep-
> les congeal with their twisted necks
> in the noose
> of clouds
> I go alone and shriek that on cross-
> roads
> they are cruc-
> ifying po-
> lice

Even in that early poem, we see the interaction of eye and ear – the line-breaks doing a certain amount of visual 'enacting' of the meaning but also suggesting that the poem must be read aloud in a certain way – and this looks forward to the almost paradoxical volume *For the Voice* (dominantly visual in appearance, yet with poems designed for public performance) and also the general later Mayakovskian habit of 'stepping' the lines to indicate a reader's phrasing, though again not without a degree of meaningful stimulation of the eye.

When it comes to the ear, we know from many reports and observers that Mayakovsky was a spellbinding reader, who regarded the auditorium as both challenge and reward. Something of the quality of his voice can still be heard, on what is apparently the only recording commercially available*, where he reads from 'An Extraordinary Adventure' ('Vladimir's Ferlie' in the present volume), and although the recording is so bad that the words are often hard to follow, some impression can be got of his scooping and pouncing mastery of pause and emphasis. 'Vladimir's Ferlie' is interesting to hear as well as see, because it has a hidden regular stanza-structure counterpointed by a continuous narrative-style printing with the lines broken up into irregular lengths. Only the pattern of the rhymes, caught chiefly by the ear, gives away the underlying stanzaic grid; by disguising the grid (which is nevertheless felt) the poet achieves all sorts of subtle free-verse effects that are not really *vers libre* at all.

Mayakovsky deploys aural resources inventively and lavishly, throughout his poetic career. But he never followed his friend Alexei Kruchonykh (whose work he admired and publicly defended) into *zaum*, the 'transrational' sound-poetry which involved, in effect, the creation of an imaginary language. Kruchonykh believed that *zaum* could produce 'a universal poetic language, not artificially created like Esperanto, but organically born.'† Both Kruchonykh and Mayakovsky were agreed about the immense power mysteriously inherent in language, but Kruchonykh's splendidly unWittgensteinian slogan SLOVO SHIRE SMYSLA (his capitals!)‡ – 'the word is broader than its meaning', i.e. a word contains but is not merely coextensive with its so-called meaning, and the glory is in the overlap not the template – must increasingly have seemed to Mayakovsky to burke the problems of the auditorium and of communication.

In the same way, he would accept but not imitate the experiments of his co-futurist friend Vasily Kamensky in visual poetry. Kamensky's 'ferroconcrete' poems (the name curiously prophetic of the concrete poetry of recent years) were to him a concentrated but restricting parallel to his own interest in the visual presentation of poetry as a means of increasing impact. And again, the move towards riddle and enigma in the ferroconcrete poems would hamper communication.

What gives Mayakovsky's work its peculiar character, and I think also its peculiar value, is its unusual combination of wild

* *Govoryat pisateli*, Melodiya 05592(a).
† In his manifesto *Transrational Language Declaration*, 1921.
‡ In his essay 'New Paths for the Word', 1913.

*avant-garde* leanings and flashes and something of central human concern. A grotesque and vivid comic fantasy is never lost; neither is the sense of pain, of loneliness, of longing, sometimes disguised by creative exhilaration; neither is the sense of history and the role and duty of the poet. He wrote too much, and there is in his long poems some tedious rhetoric and breast-beating. But the tribute of Boris Pasternak, describing his reaction to seeing the self-shot poet in his coffin in April 1930, stresses his remarkable significance.

> Other people by now had taken the place of those who had filled the room earlier in the day. It was quite quiet. There was scarcely anybody crying now.
>
> All at once, down under the window, I thought I saw his life, now utterly a past-tense life. It sidled away from the window up a quiet street, like Povarskaya, tree-lined. And the first person to be met there, huddling to the wall, was our country, our incredible, impossible country, for ever knocking at the centuries, now accepted in them for ever. There it was, just below me, within earshot. One could have taken its hand. The bond between them was so striking that they might have been twins . . . Of all men, he had the newness of the age climatically in his veins.*

Very Russian, and very modern, is Pasternak's verdict. The two things no longer go naturally together, but they certainly did in the years from 1910 to 1930. What is perhaps strange is that Mayakovsky still seems modern. Ezra Pound was once, like Mayakovsky, extremely active in telling people to 'make it new', yet with the passage of time Pound's work seems more and more to be being sucked back into the late Victorian romanticism it tried to burst out of. Pound, of course, although he contributed to Wyndham Lewis's vorticist, sub-futurist magazine *Blast* in 1914-15, was no futurist, and Wyndham Lewis's description of him as 'demon pantechnicon driver, busy with removal of old world into new quarters', is a telling pointer to the gulf between Pound's modernism and that of his Russian contemporaries. Mayakovsky was not looking for new quarters for an old world. He had a new world.

At the time of his death he left some verse fragments which movingly bring together the personal and public concerns of the

* *Safe Conduct* (1931), translation by Alec Brown (Elek, 1959).

poet. Usually called love poems, they are only partly that. They speak of aging, of history, of the universe; of poetry and the power of words. They even – Shakespearian touch – have a pun. 'Tragic' seems an insulting term to apply to them, and they are best left to find their own way and make their own points:

1

Loves me? loves me not? I wring
my hands
            the broken fingers drift away
like petals of roadside daisies
                    withering
plucked to tell fortunes in May
The grey my barber sees is there all right
but even if it all bursts out
                    like silver
I hope – I believe – you'll never find
shameful good sense has sold me down the river


2

Past one already
               you must be in bed
Yet I wonder
          if you too are –
I'm in no hurry
             And why should I send
express telegrams
          to wake you
             with fear


3

the sea withdraws to its deeps
the sea withdraws to its sleep
As they say the incident is cloves
the love-boat wrecked on reality
You and I are quits
And why again expose
mutual pain affront and injury

4

Past one already you must be in bed
In the dark our Galaxy like Oka's flare
I'm in no hurry and why should I send
express telegrams to wake you with fear
As they say the incident is cloves
the love-boat wrecked on reality
You and I are quits and why again expose
mutual pain affront and injury
See how still now this world is
Night has paid the sky its due of stars
in such an hour we rise we speak to eras
to history to the created universe


5

I know the force of words I know the tocsin of words
I don't mean words for plushy claques in stalls
I mean the kind that clatter coffins forward
onto their four oak legs and walk them off
Oh yes they reject you unprinted unpublished
But the cinch tightened the word bolts away
saddle-bells for centuries and trains crawl up and
snuffle the calloused hands of poetry
I know the force of words It hardly shows
more than a petal kicked by dancers' heels
But man within his soul his lips his bones...

The translations which follow are in Scots. There is in Scottish
poetry (e.g. in Dunbar, Burns, and even MacDiarmid) a vein of
fantastic satire that seems to accommodate Mayakovsky more
readily than anything in English verse, and there was also, I must
admit, an element of challenge in finding out whether the Scots
language could match the mixture of racy colloquialism and ver-
bal inventiveness in Mayakovsky's Russian. I hoped Hugh Mac-
Diarmid might be right when he claimed in 'Gairmscoile' that

> ... there's forgotten shibboleths o the Scots
> Hae keys to senses lockit to us yet
> – Coorse words that shamble thro oor minds like stots,
> Syne turn on's muckle een wi doonsin emerauds lit.

113

## FORCRYINOUTLOUD!

Forcryinoutloud!
The starns licht up – aa richt:
does that prove some loon hud to hae it?
Does it prove some loon mun want their starnhuid?
Does it prove some loon mun caa it pairls – thon strawn o spit?

And pechin at the sicht
o the fluther o midday stour
he gangs blowtherin in to God,
gangs eerily for fear he's ahint wi his veesit,
gangs snoolin and greetin,
gangs kissin the etairnal horny haun,
gangs beggin for a starn –
wan starn or he mun dee!
gangs sweerin
he canna thole sic starnless miserie!
And syne
feels a curmurrin in his wame
but pits on a calm souch aa the same
and speirs at a sowl passin by:
'It's mibbe no sae bad, sir, hey!
mibbe no sae frichtsome,
whit d'ye think?'!
Forcryinoutloud!
The starns licht up –
aa richt;
does this prove some loon hud to hae it?
Does this prove there's a law intae it,
that ilka gloamin
owre the hoose-tap
wan starn has juist gote to bleeze and blink?!

*[Poslushaite!]*

starns  stars; *loon*  fellow, bloke; *thon*  yon; *pechin*  panting; *stour*  dust;
*blowtherin*  blundering, plunging; *snoolin*  snivelling; *greetin*  crying; *thole*
bear; *syne*  then; *wame*  stomach; *calm souch*  quiet demeanour; *speirs*  asks

114

# FIDDLE-MA-FIDGIN

The fiddle near dwinnilt to naethin wi sichin and beseikin
till we a blash it burst oot greetin
sae like a wean
that the drum hud to say:
'Weel din, weel din, weel din!'
But it grew weary anaa,
weary o hearin the lang-dringin fiddly-bits,
and slunkert oot into the rid-het Kuznetsky
and daunert awa.
The baun glinkit skancelike at hoo
the fiddle was greetin its hert oot
wi nae words,
wi nae meesure,
and a stupit cymmle by its lane
stertit to bash in some coarner:
'Whit's that!
Whit's it daein?'
But yince the bombardon
(thon
bressy-snootit
sweetin-chookit tuba)
cam blowin:
'Eejut!
Dry up!
Girner!'
I gote to my feet, sprachlt
stacherin amang the crotchets,
the frichtit music-stauns aa crunkelt,
cried oot (though guid kens why):
'My Gode!'
I kest mysel on thae widden shouthers.
'D'ye ken whit, my fiddle?
The gait you're gangin's awfy like my road:
juist like you I

dwinnilt   wasted away; *sichin*   sighing; *blash*   burst; *wean*   child; *dringin*
singing slowly; *rid-het*   red-hot; *daunert*   strolled; *baun*   band; *glinkit*   glanced;
*sweetin-chookit*   sweaty-cheeked; *Eejut*   idiot; *Girner*   complainer; *sprachlt*
sprawled; *stacherin*   staggering; *crunkelt*   crumpled

yowp and yowl –
and canny prove a thing to ithers!'
Lauchtir fae the baunsmen:
'Sticky end for him!
A widden wumman for his waddin-day?
– His heid seen tae!'
But me – I dinna gie a doken.
Me – I'm no sae bad, man.
'D'ye ken whit, my fiddle?
We mun –
set up hoose thegither!
Whit d'ye say?'

*[Skripka i nemnozhko nervno]*


WAR DECLARIT

'Eenin pa-pur! Eenin pa-pur! Eenin pa-pur!
Ger-many! Au-stria! It-aly!'
And a burn o purpy bluid cam wor-
ryin through the squerr, aa black-bordit and drubbly.

Café stramash heezit a bluidy snoot
aa purpified wi skraich o beasts' jaw-banes:
'Poosion the rinnin Rhine wi bluid! Shoot
cannon-thunner owre thae Roman stanes!'

Sherp bayonets laceratit the lift,
the starns grat doon like sievins o grain,
and peety, trampt and traisslt underfit,
squealt: 'Ach, lea me alane, alane, alane!'

Generals o bronze on their glintin plinth
implorit: 'Lowse us, and we'se be therr afore ye!'
Kisses o depairtin caivalry scliffit ahint.
Fitsloggers fidged for the butchin-glory.

*bordit* bordered; *drubbly* muddy; *stramash* uproar; *heezit* hoisted;
*thae* those; *lift* sky; *starns* stars; *traisslt* trod down; *scliffit* shuffled;
*fidged* itched, fidgeted

116

The hiddle and dream o the city began to grue
to the eerie gaffin-gowlin o the guns.
Fae the west the rid snaws fluther through,
toothrife flesh and fell o mithers' sons.

Squad eftir squad swalls oot the squerr,
veins on their broo swall ragein like hards.
'Wait till we dicht, dicht wur dirks owre therr –
on the sleekit hures o Vienna's boulevards!'

The newsboys burst their lungs wi 'Pa-pur! Pa-pur!
Ger-many! Au-stria! It-aly!'
And the burn o purpy bluid cam wor-
ryin, worrying through the nicht, black-bordit and drubbly.

*[Voina ob'yavlena]*


## HYMN TO A JEDDART-JUSTICER

The convicks sail the Rid Sea, pechin,
oarin the galley through,
rairin abune the shackle-nicherin
a sang o their hame – Peru.

Peru-folk, yowlin o Peru – their Paradise,
the burdies, the jiggin, the tarts,
the croons o orange-flooers ticed
wi the baobab heavenwarts.

Bananas, ananas! Sic a tass o pleesures!
Wine in the bosie o the jaur...
Till the judges tuk Peru, like Caesars,
– guid kens for why, or fae whaur!


*hiddle* hidden workings; *grue* shudder; *gowlin* howling, growling; *hards*
porridge-scum; *dicht* wipe; *sleekit* smooth and sly;

*Jeddart-Justicer* prejudging judge; *pechin* panting; *rairin* roaring; *abune*
above; *nicherin* whinnying; *tass* mass; *bosie* bosom

And the burdies and the jiggin and the she-Peruvians
were aa umbeset by decreets.
The een o the judge are twin tin-cannikins
skancin in a midden. He treats

a blue-and-orange peacock to a luik,
a fish-cauld, lenten glaff –
the grand renbow on the tail o the peacock
like winkie groosit aff!

And nixt to Peru, fleein owre the prairie
are thae wee hummin-burdies:
the judge claucht wan puir colibri
and shaved it to the hurdies.

And nae strath noo has burnin bens
wi fierce volcanic lowe.
The judge tuk up his strathfu pen:
'Nae Smokin in the Howe.'

My verse anaa in puir Peru
's unlawfu: penalty, torture.
The judge said: 'Ye'll no sell sic a brew
o liquor in this quarter.'

The equator grues as the shackles ring.
Peru's loast wings and folk . . .
aa bar the judges, harsk, thrawn, mingein,
cooerin in the laws' cope.

D'ye see the peety o the man o Peru?
Aff-loof they gied him to the galleys.
And the burdies and the jiggin, Peru, me, you –
the judges shak aa wi their malice.

*[Gimn sud'e]*

*groosit* shivered; *thae* those; *claucht* caught; *hurdies* hips; *lowe* fire;
*grues* shudders; *thrawn* obstinate, perverse; *mingein* wretched; *aff-loof*
offhand

118

## TO THE BOURGEOISIE

Stick in, douce folk. – Pineaipple, feesant's breist:
stuff till ye boke, for thon is your last feast.

['Yesh' ananasy...']


## THE BALLAD O THE RID CADIE

Wance upon a time there lived a Cadet laddie.
And this Cadet laddie had a wee rid cadie.

Forby this bit cadie he'd colleckit fae somebody
the Cadet had fient a rid corpuscle in his body.

He thocht he heard a revo – wheesht though – LUTION, rid and
    bluidy!
The wee Cadet was ready wi his bluid-rid cadie.

Like grumphies in claver lived the haill Cadet caboodle,
the Cadet and his cadaddy and his grampacadoodle.

But up whupt a rouchlin outstrapolous blad o
wind and rippit thon cadie to a shadda.

Cadieless Cadet, black-heidit and shoddy!
The rid wowfs cam and had him wi their toddy.

Aabody kens thae wowfs was no ill-deedie!
But they gowpt him cuffs an aa, like maws at a haddie.

Sae, gin ye pley at politics, my laddie and my leddy,
mind o the ballad o the wee rid cadie.

[Skazka o krasnoi shapochke]


*douce*  good, respectable; *boke*  vomit; *thon*  yon

*cadie*  cap; *grumphies*  pigs; *blad*  blow; *wowfs*  wolves; *thae*  those; *maws*
seagulls; *haddie*  haddock; *gin*  if

119

## A RICHT RESPECK FOR CUDDIES

Horse-cluifs clantert
giein their patter:
crippity
crappity
croupity
crunt.

Bleezed in the blafferts,
wi ice-shoggly bauchles,
the street birled and stachert.
The cuddy cam clunk,
cloitit doon doup-scud,
and wheech
but the muckle-mou'd moochers werna lang
in makin theirsels thrang,
gawpus eftir gawpus, aa gaw-hawin
alang the Kuznetsky in their bell-bottom breeks.
'Aw, see the cuddy's doon!'
'Aw, it's doon, see the cuddy!'
And aa Kuznetsky gaffit.
Aa but me.
I didna jyne the collieshangie.
I cam and kest
a gliff intil
the cuddy's ee...

The street's owrewhammelt
in its ain breenges...

I cam and I saw
the muckle draps that scrammelt
doon the cratur's niz-bit
to coorie in its haffits...

*cuddy* horse; *cluif* hoof; *clantert* clumped along as on clogs; *crunt* quick heavy blow; *bleezed* hit; *blafferts* blows, gusts; *shoggly* shaky; *bauchles* old shoes; *birled* spun; *stachert* staggered; *cloitit* fell heavily; *doup-scud* falling with a thump on the buttocks; *thrang* numerous; *gawpus* gaper; *gaffit* guffawed; *collieshangie* uproar, squabble; *gliff* glance; *breenges* bursts, rushes; *coorie* nestle; *haffits* mane

And oh but the haill
clamjamfry o craturly
cares cam spillin and splairgein
fae my hert wi a reeshle!
'Ned, Ned, dinna greet!
Listen to me, Ned –
ye think thae buggers are the saut o the erd?
My chiel,
neds are we aa, to be honest wi ye;
nae man's unnedlike, in his ain wey.'
Aweel, it micht be
the beast was an auld yin
and had nae need of a fyke like me,
or was my thochts a wheen coorse for a cuddy?

Onywey
Ned
gied a loup whaur he liggit,
stoitert to his feet,
gied a nicher
and the flisk
o his tail doon the street.
My chestnut chiel!
Back hame to his stable
lauchin like a pownie
staunin by the stable-waa
feelin in his banes able
to dree the darg and the dowie
for the life that's worth it aa.

*[Khoroshee otnoshenie k loshadyam]*

---

*clamjamfry* mob; *reeshle* rustle; *greet* cry; *thae* those; *erd* earth; *fyke*
fusspot; *wheen* little; *liggit* lay; *nicher* whinny; *flisk* move restlessly;
*dree* endure; *darg* (day's) work; *dowie* sad(ness)

## VLADIMIR'S FERLIE

An unco thing that involvit the makar at his simmer
ludgin, the Rumyantsev hoosie, Mt Akula, Pushkino,
eichteen mile alang the Yaroslavl railway.


Twal-dizzen-sun-pooer gloamin-bang,
July ablow the wheels o simmer,
the lift skimmerin
the het day lang –
and on his hoalidays the rhymer.
Pushkino's braes swalled up to meet
the humphy back o Mount Akula;
the clachan sprachlt
at their feet,
and curlt its dry bark-thackit hool. A
hole
gantit ayont the clachan and
withoot a word o a lie, richt in
yon hole the sun wid jouk, and land
hooly and quate at ilka nichtin.
Syne
on the morn's morn
up it flees,
bluid-rid again, to drook the warld.
Day eftir day!
Aweel, thae ploys
began
to get me
fair ensnarled,
and wance I gote my dander up –
aathing richt fleggit and bumbazed –
I cried oot to the sun's face:
'Hup!
Ye're toastit eneuch, auld tarloch-taes!'
I cried oot to the sun:
'Auld truggs!


*ferlie* wonder; *unco* strange; *makar* poet; *twal* twelve; *ablow* below;
*lift* sky; *skimmerin* shimmering; *clachan* village; *sprachlt* sprawled; *hool*
shell, covering; *gantit* gaped; *jouk* duck; *hooly* gently; *quate* quiet; *syne*
then; *drook* drench; *thae* those; *fleggit* frightened; *tarloch-taes* lazybones;
*truggs* lazy worker

ay lowtherin work-shy in the cloods –
and me here, pentin posters, the juggs
roon my hass, aa weathers and moods!'
I cried oot to the sun:
'Bide a bit!
Listen, my gowdy-pow, why nut gie
this senseless settin a by,
and sit
wi me
here for a cup o tea!'
– Whit have I done?
I'm loast, I'm sunk!
It's comin towards me,
its nainsel,
on shanks's lowe
wi nae begunk –
across thae fields it shairly mun quell
wi its fiery stoggin: the sun! And me,
I want naethin but to hide my trimmlin,
I mak a wee retreat. But its ee
's in the gairden noo: and noo it's thrimmlin
richt through
the gairden.
Body o the sun!
It burst door, winnock, and winnock-frame:
it brasht and breeshlt
till it wan
its pech, it spak fae the pit o its wame:
'Thon bleeze has never been retrackit
sae faur as this sin I was makkit!
Ye caad me, poet?
Whaur's yir trackie?
I like my jeelie guid and tacky.'
My een were greetin wi the heat –
it nearly druv me mental but –
I muttert: 'Samovar –'
and 'Seat –

*lowtherin* loitering; *juggs* iron collar; *hass* neck; *gowdy-pow* golden head;
*lowe* fire; *begunk* trickery; *thae* those; *stoggin* stab, thrust; *thrimmlin*
threading; *winnock* window; *pech* pant; *wame* stomach; *thon* yon; *trackie*
teapot; *greetin* crying

starn, sit ye doon, sir,
will ye nut?'
What deil had gied my harn a wrinch
to bawl at him unblate?
Struck dumb,
perched on the coarner o the binch,
fearin the worst was yit to come,
I'm – O, but an unco and preclair
licht cam streamin fae the sun
till
bit by bit
I forgot my fear,
fund my tongue, cam oot o my shill:
I talk to'm
aboot this and that;
near deaved, says I, wi my agitprop,
and the sun says:
'Grantit,
but ye mun tak
a lang clear sicht, and the deavin'll stop!
D'ye think it's easy
for me to shine?
Wid ye try it, eh?
Juist try up therr! –
Gang furrit in
yon eident line –
gang furrit shinin gowd and shair!'
And sae we cracked till it was daurk
– I mean, until it wid ha been,
for the nicht cudny find us.
Nor c-
ud we be mair thick, freen wi freen.
And I loupt up
to gie his shouther
a free and freenly dunt, and he,
the sun himsel, said:
'Weel, dear brither,
there's something jynes baith you and me.
Makar, let's tak

---

*starn*  star; *harn*  brain; *unblate*  freely; *unco*  strange; *fund*  found; *deaved*
deafened; *furrit*  forward; *eident*  attentive; *cracked*  talked; *makar*  poet

a luik
and a sang
owre this dour warld o fents and scartins.
My sunlicht'll be doon in a spang
wi yours
in makarlike exhortins.'
Twa-barrelt solar
gun: kerrrumpy!
Nicht's murky jyle-waas crummle-o.
Ming-mang o licht and rhymer's stumpy,
shine on and never stummle-o!
And gin the sun
sud weary or
the nicht be sweir
and want to snore
in a lang lie –
my licht'll soar
wi aa its micht and answer for
anither ringin
day to daw.
To shine ay and shine aawhere, shine
to the end o endmaist days –
that's aa!
This is the sun's
slogan – and mine!

*[Neobychainoe priklyuchenie . . . ]*


RESPECK FOR A LASSIE

I says to mysel in the gloamin,
why for no? Is she no fair on?
It's that dark naebody'll see
what naebody'll ken.
I leanit owre the lassie, juist,
and juist
as I
was leanin owre

*fents*   rags; *scartins*   scrapings; *spang*   bound, spring; *stumpy*   pen; *sweir*   loath

I says to her
(I michta been her faither then):
'The craig o passion's stey,
my dear,
I beg ye stay away,
my dear,
I beg ye stay away.'

*[Otnoshenie k baryshne]*


## MANDMENT NO.2 TO THE ARMY O THE ARTS

That means you –
sleekit baritone-craturs
fae the days o Adam
ginnlin yet,
ginnlin sowls in thae dunnies cried theaytres
wi yir arias o Romeos and Juliets.

That means you –
penters, or is it *peintres*,
like weel-girst gawcy cuddies,
ay nibblin and nicherin, the delicht o Russia,
studio-duddrons,
auld-style draigons
at the limnin o wee flooers and bodies.

That means you –
cooerin wi the mystical leafletfuls,
yir broos aa runklt like plewland –
futuristicos
imaginisticos
acmeisticos
trachlt in moosewabs o crambo-doodlin.


*stey*   steep

*sleekit*   smooth and sly; *ginnlin*   tickling, catching; *thae*   those; *dunnies*   dens, dungeons, dumps; *girst*   pastured; *gawcy*   plump; *cuddies*   horses; *nicherin*  whinnying; *duddrons*   sluggards

126

That means you –
chyngin the weel-kaimed
hair-dos to draiglety-locks,
patents to bauchles –
proletcult-chiels
pansin wi patches
yon coatie o Pushkin that taks aa the knocks.

That means you –
hoolachan-hoochin, chanter-chunterin,
giein yirsels like mad folk
or daein a bit o sin hidlins,
wi yir ain spaedom o a future as chunky
as wan huge academical meal-poke.

Wha's tellin ye?
I am –
genius or nae genius,
castin aff my whigmaleeries,
a worker wi the Rosta-charlies,
I'm tellin ye –
afore they tak their gun-butts to expel ye:
Gie it a barley!

A barley!
Bury it.
Splew
on the rhymies,
and on the arias,
and on the rose-buss,
and on aa the ither drumloorachies
fae the arts' arsenals.
Wha's fidgin to ken
hoo – 'The poor, dear man!
O how he could love
and what unhappiness was his...'?
It's skeely makars,

*bauchles* old shoes; *pansin* dressing; *knocks* clocks; *hoolachan* swarming;
*hidlins* secretly; *spaedom* prognostication; *Rosta* Russian Telegraph Agency;
*fidgin* itching, fidgeting; *skeely* skilful; *makars* poets

no langhaired dran-drans
that's necessar noo to us.

Listen!
The morungeous locomotives!
Their maen's blawn in through cracks and flair:
'Gie's coals fae the Don's pits!
Smiddy-men,
engine-biggers to the depot therr!'

Heidwatters o ilka river
hae cairried the gap-ribbit steamers
that gowl through the docks: 'Gie here
some ile fae Baku's refeenries!'

And aa the time we clish and clash,
seekin to trap some secret sense,
'Gie us unkent forms!' – the fasht
voice o things waffs its lament.

Whaur noo are the fules
wad staun afore the 'maestros', hingin on their mou
for whatever micht devaul on a gawkin crood?
My freens,
gie us an unkent art – art that'll move
this
great republic granin up fae its drumly groove.

[*Prikaz No. 2 armii iskusstv*]

---

*morungeous* bad-tempered; *flair* floor; *bigger* builder; *gowl* howl, growl;
*fasht* troubled; *devaul* fall; *granin* groaning; *drumly* muddy

## MAYAKONFERENSKY'S ANECTIDOTE

Nicht haurdly gane: day loups up:
and ilka morn loup wi't
folk to CENTGEN
folk to GENCOM
folk to COMPOLIT
folk to POLITCENT –
hooses skail, offices fill,
till wow! the papers rin like watter,
and if ye seek some matter –
tak hauf a hunnert –
aye, the maist important –
the boys wi the pens are gane like whittricks
to committees and cognostins and burroos and statistics.

It is mysel:
'Can I no hae an interview, an audition?
The name on the knock's Tammas Fugit, ye ken –'
'Comrade Ivan 'vanich is at a session
of the Union of KINPROP and KULTADMIN.'
I stummle up a hunner sterrs.
The licht's kinna dim.
Yince mair:
'They say, come back in an hour.
They are all in session, in conference:
subject, purchase of ink-bottles from
GOVCENTCOOP-ink-bottle-shop.'

Eftir an oor –
fient a scriever-chiel,
fient a scriever-lassie –
juist hee-haw.
Ablow 22, they're aa
awa to a session o the KOMSOMO'.

Up I sclim till the nicht's abune me,
tapmaist storey, tapmaist o seeven.

---

*skail*  empty, scatter; *whittricks*  weasels; *cognostins*  conferences; *burroos*
offices; *knock*  clock; *scriever-chiel*  clerk; *hee-haw*  nothing; *ablow*  below;
*sclim*  climb; *abune*  above

'Can I no see Comrade Ivan 'vanich noo?'
'No, not even
now. In session, in conference, on committee
A and B and C and D and E and F and G and H. Pity!'

Fair scunnert,
in on their sederunt
I breenge like an avalanche, disparplin
my fremit aiths on ilka haun,
when glowff! –
folk cut in hauf, sittin aroon –
bluidy cantrips o auld Mahoun!
And whaur, whaur's their ither hauf?

'It's the slashers!
They're deid!'
I'm ramfeezelt noo, I rair and I bawl,
I'm no concos-mancos wi that grugous sicht.
But a wee wee voice, a wee prignickity
voice o a scriever-cum-key-skelper: 'All
the people you see are at *two* conferences; indeed,
they have daily
to attend twenty;
and thus, willy-nilly,
and quite literally,
they must tear themselves apart to appear.
Boots to belt – elsewhere.
Belt and above – in here.'

I canny sleep for waumlin thochts.
Nicht's haurdly gane.
Day loups. I see't aa plain:
'Oh for
yin mair
sederunt to convene
to congree to conclude

---

scunnert disgusted; *sederunt* meeting; *breenge* burst, rush; *disparplin* scattering;
*fremit* strange; *aiths* oaths; *cantrips* magic tricks; *ramfeezelt* confused and
exhausted; *rair* roar; *concos-mancos* compos mentis, sane; *grugous* horrible;
*scriever-cum-key-skelper* shorthand-typist; *waumlin* rolling uneasily

to comblasticastraflocate sans avizandum
ilka sederunt and tap-table-tandem!'

I'M AFF

Ticket –
                sneck.
                        Cheek –
                                    peck.
The whussle blaws,
                        we've breenged awa
whaur
            thae warld-troddlin wemen
                                        traik
like a herring-drave in their hose-net.
                                            Caa
the-day
            wur weirdie-heidit guest,
but gie fair focus
                    to the morn's-morn's pow:
a toon
            and a mou
                        are beslaistered at best
by the selsame
                    telltale cosmetical lowe.
The gay linties
                rin to this faur-aff airt.
Paris has naethin
                    the girner gets!
Paris –
            Place de l'Etoile –
                                saired


*avizandum*   judicial consideration

*sneck*   punch (a ticket); *breenged*   burst, rushed; *thae*   those; *pow*   head;
*beslaistered*   daubed; *lowe*   fire; *linties*   linnets; *airt*   direction; *girner*
one who complains fretfully; *saired*   served

by sic starns,
                    its Estelles, its vedettes!
Gang whusslin,
                    skirr and skaig
                                        and slash
through Liége
                    and roon by Brussels toon.
But it's Brussels,
                    Paris,
                                Liége
                                        that fash
and slash the hert
                    o the Russkatoon.
Gin this
            was a sledge
                        to pit my cares on,
my feet in snaw
                    like a page o the papers...
a whusslin
            fae the steppes o Kherson
to cairry me
            wi the snaw-capers...
– The wee lowes in the loanin,
the gloamin,
                the faur road:
the hert stounds wi its longin,
in the breist
            a sair load.
Och, but yin mair,
                            yin mair
dance, mair feck o versin!
Och, but yin mair,
                            yin mair
crack o rhymes, Mayakpherson!
Och, but yin mair,
                            yin mair
mony mair nor yin therr...
– Folk
        fae ilka kintra and clime,

*starns* stars; *skirr* scurry; *slash* walk roughly through mud and rain;
*fash* trouble; *lowes* fires; *loanin* lane; *feck* abundance; *crack* talk

eidently *cultive*-in their *jardin*, 'll
say,
        when they see me
                        doiter and dwine:
Thon yin's bluid's
                in a fell brangle!

[Yedu]

## VERSAILLES

This is the road,
                aye.
                        Whit coontless Louies
hae banged alang it to the palace-yetts,
jossichin
            their twinty stane
                            o moolies
amang the silks
                o their gildit chariots!
And it was by here,
                    fliskin the jynts
o his ain hurdies,
                    the Marseillaise in his ears,
his croon kaput,
                his breeks tint,
the Capet
        gaed fae Paris
                        in a breese.
Noo
    Paris
        taks its pleesure on it,
caurs flee by
            in a glintin stream...
wee hures,
            landlords fu o grace and the gear o't,
Americans,

---

*eidently* attentively; *doiter* totter; *dwine* waste away; *Thon* yon; *brangle* tangle

*jossichin* shaking violently; *moolies* crumbling flesh (lit. earth); *fliskin* moving
restlessly; *hurdies* hips; *tint* lost; *breese* hurry

133

                    and me.
Versailles.
                    A blash o eloquence:
'Bygode thae deid-yins done theirsels weel!'
Palaces
            wi thoosans o buts and thoosans o bens
and a bed
            and a brod
                        in ilka shiel!
Ye canny bigg
            like this
                        again –
no if ye staw
            a haill life for it.
And see
            ahint the palace,
                        scattert like rain,
juist to mak shair
            that their air
                        had a surfeit
o douceness and nae foof:
                        lochans and foontains,
                                    and mair
lochans wi foontains wi –
                        losh! –
                                    bronze taeds.
Aa roon,
            for gentle kittlin
                        o genteel *moeurs*,
the loans
            are hoatchin wi stooky shades:
Apollos aawhere,
            and thae
                        Venus-susies
withoot their airms –
                        loads o them tae.
And further on,
            the ludgins
                        for their Pompadusas –

*blash* burst; *brod* table; *shiel* hut; *bigg* build; *staw* stole; *douceness* goodness,
respectability; *foof* stink; *taeds* toads; *kittlin* tickling; *loans* lanes; *hoatchin*
swarming; *stooky* plaster statue

134

the Muckle Trianon
                    and the *Petit*.
Here's whaur
                    Pompadoris
                                   was taen for her douche, and she's
beddit here
                    in the wee Pompadorchester suite.
I mind me o life –
                    och, but whit's new, whit's new?
Sic 'beauty' –
                    luik hoo it teases mense and sense awa!
Is it no like gaein
                    plap
                            intae a Benois
wattercolour,
                    or amang the bit verses o Akhmatova?
I watched it aa,
                    I fund the feel o things.
Aa yon grand
                    beautiosity, and yet
what drew me
                    maist of aa
                                was the grim dint
on a smaa table-tap
                            o Marie-Antoinette's.
Thon wadge
                    was druv in
                                by the bayonets
o the revolution,
                    to a dance and a sang,
when
        the queen-quyne
                            was steery-fyked alang
by sansculottes
                    to the widdy steps.
I luik
        at it aa –
                    enviable vistas and blinks!
The gairdens enviable,

*mense* respect; *fund* found; *thon* yon; *quyne* girl; *steery-fyked* rushed in a riot;
*widdy* gallows

                    sae deep in roses!
O for sic
            culture noo –
                    siclike, but distinct,
biggit to the new virr
                    and breenge o the machine!
Aff
    to the museums
                    wi thae royal closes
and single-ends!
            Lat's see
                    the gless and steel
o a workers' palace,
                    wi a million rooms to fill,
sae bricht
        it hurts the een.
For the edification
                    of aa
                    that hae still
                            nae lack
o coupons or cunyie,
                    aa the kings that hae still –
                            their braith,
the sun lolloped doon
                    fae the blue guillotine wi a swack
like the Antoinette's heid,
                    bluid-gowd
                            on thon stane back-claith.
The thrang o chestnits
                    and lime-trees
                            was soomin adrift,
wee leafs toused
            to the ghaist o a fleece.
In the bodiless nichtcap
                    o gloamin,
                            the lift
pu'd up
        Versailles' museum-sheets.

                                        [Versal']


*biggit* built; *virr* energy; *breenge* burst, rush; *cunyie* money; *thon* yon; *thrang*
numerous; *soomin* swimming; *toused* ruffled; *lift* sky

## A FAREWEEL

The caur's here,
                    the last franc's been chynged.
– Whit time dae we set aff for Marseilles? –
Paris
        rins alangside
                        to keep me in rynge
o aa
        the unpossible bonnyness o its face.
Watter
            o pairtin,
                        come to my een,
split
        the hert
                    o the sentimentalist!
It's Paris I wad choose
                        to live
                            and dee in –
gin there was nae sic warld
                        as Moscow
                                to miss.

                                        [*Proshchan'e*]


## THE ATLANTIC

Spain blins the ee
                    wi its white stane,
its waas staun
                like teeth on a saw.
Till twal,
            the steamer lined its wame
wi coals,
            and drank fresh watter an aa.
The steamer's
                airn-ticht snoot

*gin* if

*twal* twelve; *wame* stomach; *airn-ticht* iron-tight

137

                         gied a trimmle
and at wan o'clock
wi a snort,
               up-anchort
                         and oot o the dock.
Europe
         began to hiddle and dwinnle.
Sloggs
         o watter
                   rin by the sides,
huge-boukit,
               like anno-domini.
Burdies in the cloods,
                       fishes in the tides,
but aa roon –
               watter's drummlin me.
It's swoochin and wallochin
                             fae thon athletic
breist,
         whiles workin eidently,
whiles
         fu as a puggy:
                         the Atlantic
Sea.
'O to jink up t' th' Sahara –
brithers, richt into my barra . . .
Brak oot, spit doon,
steamer's ablow.
I want it – droont,
I want it – I dinna, though.
Gang dry up-by –
fish-soup mun byle.
Ach, d'we need fowk? –
owre skinny for a denner.
Aaricht,
         sail on the gowks,
I'll no touch a finger . . .'
Soun o the waves

*hiddle* hidden workings; *dwinnle* waste away; *boukit* bulked, bodied; *drummlin*
confusing; *thon* yon; *eidently* attentively; *fu as a puggy* very drunk; *ablow* below
*denner* dinner; *gowks* fools

                        maks deck-hauns eerie:
stounin them
                wi their bairnhuid,
                                or the voice o their dearie.
But me:
        I'd raither
                unwrap the flags yince mair.
It's brocht us
                its trauch-trattle,
                                its ramfoozlin rair.
Suddenly
            the watter's
                    gane lown and gless-clear,
wi fient a doot left
                    for ony hert here.
And then,
            wow –
                    and the deil kens fae whit airt –
the wattery
            Revcom
                    loups oot o the deeps.
And a guaird o draps –
                    watter-partisans – sterts
up,
    heich,
            heich up fae the rummlin streams,
in a hurl to heaven,
                    syne in its doonfaa sweeps
skelpin the purpie o the faem to smithereens.
Again
        the watters are soldert into wan,
till a wave's
            commandit
                    to buller up aheid,
and the huge
            clood-hoodit wave
                            spangs doon,
skailin

*trauch-trattle* monotonous chatter; *ramfoozlin* disturbing, maddening; *rair* roar; *lown* calm; *airt* direction; *Revcom* Revolutionary Committee; *syne* then; *faem* foam; *buller* boil and bellow; *spangs* bounds, springs; *skailin* emptying, scattering

                    a shooer
                                o slogans and decreets.
And the waves
                        sweer
                                to the central widewatter-committee:
Storm-wappins'll never
                                be quaet until we've won!
Won whit?
                        This circumequatoriality
o the draps o the Soviets michty unner the sun.
The last wee waves in their peerie assemblies
are bummin
                        aboot something
                                        in the grandest style –
the ocean's
                gien them
                                a weel-washt smile
and liggs
            for this oor
                                tranced fae its tempests.
I luik owre the rail.
                        Fecht furth, my freens!
At the fit o the ladder,
                            slung therr
                                        like a bit fretwork brig,
juist whaur the oceanic undertakkin begins,
the districk wave-committee's
                                steamed up
                                            guid and thick.
And underwatter a thing's growin,
                                    strang but wary-like,
a palace
            o the skeely
                            coral-craturs,
to lichten the burden
                            for workin whale-wives,
disjaskit jock-whales
                            and garten-whale-kinder.
Noo

*peerie* small; *bummin* buzzing, droning; boasting; *liggs* lies; *skeely* skilful;
*disjaskit* exhausted

140

some hae laid doon
                        a path for the moon,
to mak it crowl
                on its kyte
                        like a lubber.
But the enemy'll
                no nip in therr –
                                it canna move
ayont
        the unwinkin
                        watchfu Atlantic ee.
Ye chitter, whiles,
                        in the skimmer o the moon-lacquer,
and whiles ye're hooin,
                        droont in the faem o wounds.
I luik –
        I luik –
                and ay I find the sea,
the samin sea,
                the neebor sea,
                        the loo'd sea.
Your gurly braith
                ay gies my ear its secrets.
Gled am I
            to owreset ye
                        in the een.
O in the braidth –
                in the act –
                        in the bluid –
                                in the speerit
my elder brither,
                my revolutionary freen!

                                *[Atlanticheskii okean]*


                            .


*kyte* paunch; *chitter* shiver; *skimmer* shimmer; *hooin* moaning; *faem* foam;
*samin* same; *loo'd* loved; *gurly* rough, growling

## BROOKLYN BRIG

Coolidge ahoy!
Can ye shout wi joy?
This makar'll no be blate
                        at namin
what's guid.
                Blush rid
                        at my praises, you s-
uperunited states-man –
                        rid
                                as the flamin
flag o Sovetsky Soyuz.
Like a cracked sanct
                        hirplin
                                to his kirk,
to some stere,
                semple
                        Culdee wig-
wam o stane,
                here
                        in the grey dwam and mirk
o gloamin
                I set fit doucely on Brooklyn Brig.
Like a conqueror
                        enterin
                                the toon he has taen,
the swanky
                ridin his cannon-rig
its giraffe-snoot cockit,
                        I'm fu wi glory, I'm fain
o life,
        I'm prood
                to sclim on Brooklyn Brig.
Like a daft penter-chiel
                        that digs an auld-maister's
madonna wi his sherp lovin een,
                                I trig-

_makar_ poet; _blate_ backward; _Sovetsky Soyuz_ Soviet Union; _hirplin_ limping;
_stere_ austere; _Culdee_ early Christian order in Scotland; _dwam_ swoon;
_doucely_ softly, freshly; _sclim_ climb

ger my sicht
            fae the airy
                        starn-thrangsters
doon
      through aa New York
                        by Brooklyn Brig.
New York,
            pechin
                  in daylang ure and stour,
pits by
      its trauchle noo,
                  and its giddy waas
shaw nane but freenly spooks
                        that skoor
the lichtit windaes
                  wi hamely-glintin claws.
Ye can juist hear
                  the grummle
                              o the rummlin El,
and up here
            there's naethin
                        bar that laich grummle
to tell
      hoo trains
                  are traipsin, clatterin fell,
like ashets in a press
                  flung thegither in a tummle.
See the shopkeeper
                  humphin his sugar fae
a mill
      that seems
                  to loup oot o the stream –
while
      masts gang furrit unner the brae
o the brig
            nae langer nor preens.
It's prood I am
                  o this

.

*starn* star; *thrangster* numerous; *pechin* panting; *ure* smog; *stour* dust;
*trauchle* drudgery; *skoor* scour; *laich* low; *ashets* dishes; *furrit* forward;
*preens* pins

143

                    wan mile o steel,
    my veesions here
                        tak vive and forcy form –
    a fecht
            for construction
                        abune flims o style,
    a strang
            trig-rivetit grid,
                        juist whit steel's for!
And if
        the feenish o the warld
                        sud come
    and chaos
            clout the planet
                        to smithereens
    and the wan thing
                        left staunin
                            in the sun
    sud be this brig spreedeaglt owre the reeky stanes –
    then,
            as a hantle
                        o puir peerie banes
    swalls
            to a curator's
                        vaudy dinosaur-chaumer,
    sae
        fae this brig
                        some faur-aff geologist yonner
    in the centuries'll
                        bigg up
                        the haill warld o oor days.
He'll say:
                'See thon
                        muckle steely paw –
    it jyned
            the prairies to the seas; fae this end
    Europe
            breenged Westwart, Westwart,
                            blawin

*abune* above; *reeky* smoky; *peerie* small; *vaudy* showy; *bigg* build; *thon* yon;
*breenged* burst, rushed

144

a flaff
            o Indian fedders
                        doon the wind.
See
        the rib therr –
                        minds me o a machine;
I wunner,
                staunin wi a steel-fit grup
in Manhattan,
                    wid the hauns rax
                                steeve and clean
to hook and rug owre
                        Brooklyn
                                by the lip?
And see
                the electric cable-strands – we ken
it's eftir
            the James Watt era,
                            that here
the radio
            hud fouth
                    o bummin
                                men;
and planes
                were fleein
                        through
                            the atmosphere.
Here,
        some folk
                fund life
                        a gairden-pairty,
ithers
        a lang-drawn
                    tuim-wame
                            granin-time.
Doon therr,
            the workless pairted
fae it,
        heid first

*rax* reach; *steeve* firm; *rug* tug; *fouth* plenty; *bummin* boasting; *fund* found;
*tuim-wame* empty stomach; *granin* groaning

into the Hudson's slime.
And noo...
noo the eemage
gaes sae clear, sae faur
it skimmers on the cable-strings
richt to the feet o the starns.
Here in my een
I can see
Mayakovsky staun –
he stauns as a makar,
the syllables jow in his harns –'
– And I'm gawpin still
like an Eskimo at an injin,
like a cleg at the neck-band
drinkin it aa in.
Brooklyn Brig –
man...
that's BIG!

*[Bruklinskii most]*


GOAVY-DICK!

Perjink and roon
like the arse o a barrel,
the moon
stood owre
Livadia Palace.
It sparplt oot-owre
the thristy warld –
erd,
sea,
Livadia – the spail o its chalice.
Noo the tsar's palace
is a workers' sanatorium.

*skimmers* shimmers; *starns* stars; *makar* poet; *jow* (i) knell, (ii) toll; *harns* brains; *injin* engine; *cleg* gadfly

*goavy-dick!* wow! *perjink* neat; *sparplt* scattered; *erd* earth; *spail* guttering

The moon's fair beside itsel,
                              up like a daftie.
Een
      gawp oot
                  fae a sonsy bap-face
at posters on palace-waas: IN THE AUDITORIUM
APPEARING TUESDAY
COMRADE MAYAKOVSKY.
Thon tyrannous laird
                        juist here,
                                    and here,
swufft through his salons
                          and billiard-haas,
but the gurr
            o Romanovs
                        in the scorer's ear,
cuein
      their baa
                mang the la-di-das
nicherin
        aboot them,
                      disny unchance me.
My spiel to the moujiks:
                        'Verse – form and content!'
– The skellat.
            The moon-siller's
                              fadin and tarnishin.
Under the Mazdas
                I
                  staun at the rostrum.
Facin me,
          folk fae Ryazan,
                            fae Tula,
sit straikin Slavonic bairds,
                              dashin
their Auld Russ lintlocks back fae their foreheads.
Their faces are frank,
                      mair open nor an ashet,
they lauch when they sud,
                          and when they sud,

*sonsy* thriving and pleasant; *nicherin* whinnying; *skellat* bell; *ashet* dish

                                        luik dooly.
Wid that the man
                wha disprizes
                                the Soviets
cud be wi me here,
                        near drunk wi gledness:
palaces
        read in,
                and no in stories!
Whit's read?
                Poetry!
                        In whase ears?
                                        Peasants'!
Nae ither kintra
                can yit maik this –
whaur else
                wid sic dreams
                                no be whims?
I
  see it aa
            as a miracle –
whit's here,
                and whit's still makable!
Luik:
        eftir my talk
                        two moujik-bodies
buirdly as elephants
                        are daunrin awa:
they sat doon
                thegither,
                                ablow the gless baa,
and the wan
                to the tither
                            made
                                this observe:
'Well, Mac, he guv us
a nice
        wee rhyme
                        in yon last bit o verse.'


*dooly* sad; *maik* match; *buirdly* well-built; *ablow* below

– And lang the Livadians
                              bizz like bees,
on their yalla loanins,
                        by the blue bit sea.

                                        *[Chudesa!]*

EUPATORIA

O for the souch o the seas
                              and the glory o
the breeze
                that waffs owre Eupatoria!
(By-ordnar kindlike
                        in its peripatorium
it kittles
            the cheek o the haill Eupatorium.)
We'se lie
            on the *plage*
                            and plouter at the sandy-pats,
broichin and bronzin
                        wi the broon Eupadandycats.
Skellochs
            and splish-splash
                                and the skraich o rollocks!
The joukin swankies,
                        the Eupajollocks!
Smeek-black broos
                    o Karaite Jews
wi their skyrie bunnets
                        and Eupataproos!
And him,
            fair pechin for as dark a skin,
puir Muscovite-
                Eupataryan!

*yalla* yellow; *loanins* lanes

*kittles* tickles; *plouter* dabble; *broichin* sweating; *skellochs* shrieks; *smeek* smoke; *skyrie* gaudy; *pechin* panting

149

Aawhere, roses
                on jimpy shanks,
and joyfu weans
                at their Eupajinkajanks!
Ilka seikness
                cries Kamerad
                                uncondeetional
to the glaury plaisters
                Eupamedeecinal.
Ilka kyte
                kests twa stane to Kilquhanity
in the rummle-and-pummle
                                o Eupatorianity.
It's a peety
                for aa the ither
                                sanatoria.
Man, there's juist nae place
                                like Eupatoria.

                                        *[Yevpatoriya]*


MAY DAY

(A wee sang for laddies and lassies)

Leafikie leafikie green!
We ken the winter's awa.
Lat's gang
                whaur the swire's as bricht's a preen,
me
        and you
                        and us an aa.

Luik at the spring, hingin
her washin owre the schaw.

*jimpy* slender; *weans* children; *glaury* muddy; *kyte* paunch

*swire* dip in hill; *preen* pin; *schaw* grove

We'se gang and rin, rinnin and singin,
ying,
        singin,
                springin an aa.


A lowe on the paper the-day!
A lowe on the sheets by the waa!
Lat's cairry a lowe mair rid nor thae –
flaggies
        and banners
                and streamers an aa.
Lauchin the spring skelps through
the streets as bricht's a baa.
We'se gang richt furrit like sojers noo –
you
    and me
            and us an aa.

*[Maiskaya pesenka]*

ANENT THE DEEFERENCE O TASTES

A cuddy,
        goavin at a camel,
                        lauchit:
'Whit
    kinna cuddy's yon,
                    aa bim-bam-bauchlt?'
The camel skrieked:
                    'Ye caa yirsel a cuddy?
Ye're naethin
            but a scrunty
                    shilpit camel!'

*ying* young; *lowe* fire; *thae* those; *furrit* forward

*cuddy* horse; *goavin* staring; *bauchlt* misshapen; *shilpit* thin, puny

151

– Ach,
      lat auld Frosty-Pow abune unscrammle
the twa puir cratures;
              *he*
                kens the brose fae the gundy.

                      *[Stikhi o raznitse vkusov]*

AWA WI IT!

Auld makars' clarsach-pluck
                was fine at shawin
war's eemage
        sae enviably braw:
lang merches –
        exploits –
            to a choir and a baun!
The lasses gawp
        at a gowd uniform.
Through smilin moothies,
           een in constellations,
hussars gang furrit
        in whiskert formations.
Prance through the fecht –
          and soon
              ye'll be vaunty
wi epaulettes
        and pips
          and the gift o hauf a county.
But dee
      if ye like
          in the on-ding o cannon –
the future's ay
        a dab haun
          at the cenotaphin.

*abune* above; *brose* porridge; *gundy* toffee

*makar* poet; *baun* band; *furrit* forward; *on-ding* attack

152

Aye,
    and even the-day
               there's some will champ
at the rhymer's bit,
        and lee
             like the faither o lees:
'Clad in beauty,
        men of beauty's stamp
carried
    their bodies...'
Braw is it?
       *Danke schön* for the harp
ye wheedlt sic braws oot o,
             wi sic ease!
War and warcraftiness
          that makars hae glorifyit
makars noo mun disludge
          till they're despisit.
War
    is yon wind
        that stinks wi hiddled corpses,
war
    is a factory
       that turns oot paupers.
It's a lair,
     and nane
        can meesure its sides.
It's glaur,
     hunger,
        typhus, and lice.
War
    shaks its moneybags
        for the rich,
but for us
     it's the castanet-chap
          o a crutch.
War's
    a mandment,
       war's
        a manifesto:

*makar* poet; *lair* grave; *glaur* mud

'Burds and wives
                    ye'll gie
                              a prosthetic caress to!'
Owre aa this planet,
                         my people, my brithers,
mak this proclaim:
                      that war sall wither.
And ony time it's necessar
                              to ding doon
                                        cliques
o governors
              or governments
                                 for the guid peace o the warld –
tak that
          in yir stride,
                          O proletarian chiel
for ye are the crier and forerider
                                    o the peace o the fauld.

                                                          *[Doloi!]*

COMRADE TEENAGER!

A thoosan years
                    God's gorbies gied
fae the kirk-steeple the jow o the Wey:
'Time eneuch when ye're a man, my lad,
juist you rin ootside and pley.
Lat the knout
                  dislade its blad,
beggars' shoulders arna shy.
Time eneuch when ye're a man, my lad,
juist you rin ootside and pley.
Lat be the murk that knaws nae gleed,
lat be the waes that gar men cry –
time eneuch when ye're a man, my lad,
juist you rin ootside and pley.'

*proclaim* proclamation; *ding doon* overthrow

*gorbies* ravens; *jow* (i) knell, (ii) toll; *dislade* unload; *blad* blow; *gleed* spark

In wan word,
                   ma mannie,
be a wee modest flooer,
smell sweet to yir mammy,
nae mair's
                   in yir pooer.
Comrade
               o the Higher Grade,
flee fae sic a masquerade!
Think o the Commune
                           that caas us furrit noo,
we mun close ranks – the auld yins,
                                    the kiddies,
                                          the men.

Comrade teenager,
                   ye arna a babby-boo;
be a bonny fechter –
                   a committit man,
                           ye ken.

*[Tovarishchu podrostku]*

*furrit* forward

# FIFTY RENASCENCE LOVE-POEMS
## (1975)

Chaucer translated Petrarch; Milton praised Marino. Yet the tradition of European love-poetry during these three centuries which Petrarch established and Marino brought to a resonant and flashy conclusion has never since the seventeenth century regained anything like the favour it once enjoyed, and the poets from that tradition who retain most interest now will tend to be those who (like Scève and Marino) most transform it. Nothing post-Renascence – whether Neoclassical, Romantic, or Modernist – has yet recreated circumstances of feeling and opinion that would be generally receptive to the calm, refined, ordered, ideal, yet neither frigid nor inhuman world of Petrarch's lyrics. 'Today,' said a *Times Literary Supplement* editorial commenting on his 600th anniversary celebrations in 1974, 'he must be among the least read of the major writers of the West.' And the editorial went on to stake out with some firmness his claim to major status as humanist and man of letters but had no very convincing case to make for him as a poet. It may well be that an immediacy of charge, if we demand it, will never again be got from Petrarch, and that a fine glaze – ah yes a truly beautiful glaze, and of the first quality! – must stand between us and him: the deadly glaze of the ideal, which he most laboured to perfect. Not that there was nothing underneath. 'So what do you say? That I invented the beautiful name of Laura to give myself something to talk about...! And that in fact there is no Laura in my mind except that poetic laurel for which evidently I have aspired with long-continued, unwearying zeal; and that concerning the living Laura, by whose person I seem to be captured, everything is manufactured; that my poems are fictitious, my sighs pretended. Well, on this head I wish it were all a joke, that it were a pretence and not a madness!' (letter to Bishop of Lombez, 21 December 1336).* But underlying realities were to be given not the clarity of reportage but a filtered, exalted, exemplary clarity, even at the risk of some removal from flesh and blood, as he interestingly commented in a letter to the Bishop of Albano in 1352: 'You command me to write in a clear style; and I have every wish to obey you in everything. But on one point we disagree. What you call

---

* *Letters from Petrarch*, selected and translated by Morris Bishop, Indiana University Press, 1966. Subsequent quotations from Petrarch's letters from this edition.

"clear" is something close to the ground; I think that the higher the style the clearer, provided it doesn't get involved in its own clouds.' This suggests that we might be prepared to find some subtlety in the style, and particularly in the tone, of this poetry, if we can suspend some of our deep-rooted antagonism to lack of verbal density. Obviously the discredited excesses, common-places, and lifeless conceits of minor Petrarchism as it later developed will never please again, but when Du Bellay wrote in his 'Contre les pétrarquistes' (1553)

> J'ay oublié l'art de Petrarquizer,
> je veulx d'Amour franchement deviser,
> sans vous flatter, et sans me deguizer –

he is not telling the whole story, even though a Petrarchist him-self. There is no clinching, undiscussable opposition between 'talking frankly about love' and writing in a clear high style but with a basis in experience, and this is true whether Petrarch's Laura and Scève's Délie existed as loved individuals and Marino's Lilla did not, since the kind of art involved is able to take care of this problem – as can be seen in the light tone of Petrarch's letter giving his assurance that Laura was woman and not idea. Pet-rarch is not too worried if Laura remains relatively undefined; his greater worry would be if his readers received no impression of what he feels in terms of – particularly – gratitude, recollection, longing, regret, absence, melancholy, all of these no doubt generalized within a long tradition of courtly love and of classical love-poetry, yet also at the same time, given that the accepted doctrine of imitation meant to Petrarch not portraitist copying sitter but son suggesting father only by 'a mysterious something' (letter to Boccaccio, 28 October 1366), coming at us with that almost covert originality and freshness which to him would seem, if he achieved it, the greatest art. But doesn't he achieve it? –

> A wood grows where one laurel once was seen.
> My adversary by a practised sleight
> draws me bewildered through the maze of green.

With Maurice Scève we may feel more at home because of the more concentrated texture of the verse, the sense of a more intel-lectual attack, the apparently more intense, troubled, and boldly speculative deploying of emotion. Yet, as I.D. McFarlane points out in his edition of *Délie*, the first and last of this sequence's 4,490 lines contain clear echoes of Petrarch which can only be intended as a tribute to the Italian poet. Despite this, however, and despite the use Scève makes of the common fund of Petrarchan and Neoplatonic themes and literary devices, the overall impression of *Délie* is extremely unPetrarchan. For one thing, the ten decasyllabic lines of the *dizain*, though reminiscent of a sonnet in general effect, seem to pack more meaning into less bulk, mainly as a result of their involuted, much less open syntax. And following to some extent from this, though it is also a question of the temperament and experience of the two poets, the Scève *dizain* permits itself (and indeed enjoys) a much greater degree of interpretative difficulty, and even obscurity, than the Petrarchan sonnet. *Dizain 118* is a good example. Yet Scève can be his own man at the other end of the scale too, occasionally showing a realism and immediacy which Petrarch would have been uneasy about, as in *Dizain 161*. In the former instance, Scève is enacting a state of mind in which not only has the lady herself almost disappeared as a physical reality, but the lover too is dissolved, like his purely physical longings, in an abyss of nescience, a gulf of oblivion: its near-mystical paradox is that the higher the lover aspires, through and beyond the physical, the deeper he sinks and drowns 'aux oblieuses rives'. By contrast, *Dizain 161* is urgent, basic, exclamatory, and clear: the jealous lover torments himself by thinking of the lady in bed with her husband, and gives his Hardyesque cry against marriage vows which may be legally binding but were certainly not made in heaven. What Scève does in these two examples is to show himself willing to leave the even, golden central area Petrarch loves to cultivate. He is not so much a man of the middle way. In addition, he is able to push his own widely varying moods into traditional Petrarchan contrast-structures (light/darkness, hope/despair, presence/absence and so on) in such a way as to renew them, and I don't mean through meeting 'sincerity' tests, which would be impossible in any case, but generally by developing, turning over, replacing images or themes that Petrarchists had deadened. In the very beautiful and joyful *Dizain 58*, the two basic contrasts of storm/calm and war/peace are finely opened out into a continuous and convergent forward movement: the warrior, having honourably won, becomes a pilgrim; the clear weather leads him up among mountain lakes, and his new joys are like an immense sheet of water flowing out into some unmapped Patinirish landscape; all is high, distant, beckoning, unknown, paradisal.

Petrarch himself had been interested in the whole of Europe, and it was fitting that his influence should be widely felt, from Scotland to Cyprus, from Portugal to Hungary. One of the best-documented fertilizations is the reintroduction and establishment of the Petrarchan sonnet form in Spain by Boscán and his friend Garcilaso de la Vega (after an earlier abortive attempt by Santillana). Boscán tells us how he was urged by the Venetian Ambassador in Granada in 1526 to try his hand at Italian-type sonnets, how hard he found the task of adaptation ('very artificial, this kind of verse, differing in many particulars from our own'), and how he was encouraged by Garcilaso, who in fact was soon to become his master in the form. There is nothing 'muy artificioso' about the sonnet in Garcilaso's hands, at any rate in the best examples. Although critics often emphasise his grace and refinement, there is an underlying strength, a deliberateness, a statement-making quality which somehow fits his short life spent more as soldier than courtier.

> All that I have I must confess I owe you.
> For you I came to life, for you I live,
> for you I'd die, and do die, after all.

He draws an unexpected power – almost a Wordsworthian rather than a Renascence effect – from the image of the lost dog in 'A la entrada de un valle', and he gives again a surprising, dark resonance to the *video meliora proboque, deteriora sequor* theme of 'Por ásperos caminos'.

The poems so far referred to, by Petrarch, Scève, and Garcilaso, have achieved their success within a regular grid structure where lines of equal length and an agreed rhyme-scheme impose on the poet a useful limitation – useful, that is, provided he is willing and able to use it, by freshly filling it out, and not lazily pacing round a pinfold of clichés. But in the examples I have translated from Tasso and Marino, the poet takes a greater freedom to draw out a different music. These madrigals, brief poems with irregular and sometimes incomplete rhyme, and irregular alternation of long and short lines, were capable of containing the most subtly concentrated and musically disposed effects of pause, emphasis, and suggestion, which in Tasso released a love-poetry of unusual delicacy and in Marino an 'occasional' poetry of striking and often bizarre virtuosity. The fact that Tasso was able to incorporate, in this art-poetry, words from popular songs, and that Marino was a famed 'performer' of spoken verse as well as a poet whom Monteverdi set to music, will help to remind us of the close association between poetry and music at this period (and Petrarch too, as we know, was in the habit of singing his own poems to some sort of lute accompaniment). But this is exceedingly tricky territory, and it is as well to insist on the music of poetry as being different from the music of music; and even when a madrigal has been positively devised to be sung (which many were not), it has secrets for the eye which the coarser sense of the ear (*pace* Pater) will blur and over-genialize. 'Soavissimo bacio' and 'Tacciono i boschi' are extremely remarkable poems for their size and unpretentiousness, and if there is such a thing as the spirit of a language they say something about Italian that must be the despair (or wild hope) of any translator. Marino's nasty little asps, trembling and twinkling prettily in the ears of Lilla, return us, though not without their own strange music, to the world of the *concetto*, half Petrarchan and half Baroque, perfectly artificial, and yet perfectly natural in that the Lillas of this world *do* sometimes show themselves through the jewellery they wear, not so much ignorant as aware of their power. *Novità*, yes; *meraviglia*, yes; but no loss of the shock of recognition.

I would like to express my special thanks to Dr Ian Fletcher for suggesting the idea of this book and for urging me to complete it.

ACKNOWLEDGEMENTS

The following texts have been used in making these translations:

Francesco Petrarca (1304-74)  *Le Rime*, ed. G. Contini, 1964.

Maurice Scève (*c.*1501-*c.*1560)  *The Délie of Maurice Scève*, ed. I.D. McFarlane, 1966.

Garcilaso de la Vega (1503-36)  *Obras completas*, ed. E.L. Rivers, 1968.

Torquato Tasso (1544-95)  *Poesie*, ed. F. Flora, 1952.

Giambattista Marino (1569-1625)  *Poesie varie*, ed. B. Croce, 1913.

Some of these translations, or earlier versions of them, have appeared in *College Courant, Colonnade, Nine, An Anthology of Medieval Lyrics* (ed. A. Flores, Random House, New York, 1962), *An Anthology of Spanish Poetry from Garcilaso to García Lorca* (ed. A. Flores, Doubleday, New York, 1961), *Lyric Poetry of the Italian Renaissance* ed. L.R. Lind, Yale University Press and Oxford University Press, 1954).

## Francesco Petrarca

I see no place I can escape to now.
Those eyes have been my enemies so long
that oh, I dread the pain may break too strong
for heart to bear, for heart's peace to allow.

I think of flight, but in my teeming brow
the rays that have been planting love along
the days and nights these fifteen years still throng,
dazzling me more than the first brilliant bough,

and now their image is so multiplied
I cannot turn where I am out of sight
of that light or a light it has supplied.

A wood grows where one laurel once was seen.
My adversary by a practised sleight
draws me bewildered through the maze of green.

['*Non veggio ove scampar . . .*']


Pale beauty! and a smile the pallor there
hung over tenderly, a veil of love
which sent such awe into my heart that above
in my face it moved and shone out everywhere.

I knew then how the saints in heaven's air
gaze on each other; what she was thinking of,
in pity, to my eyes held shape enough,
to others unseen; I cannot look elsewhere.

The most angelic glimpse, the humblest deed
of any woman deep in love, to this
would be a theme of scorn, its praise unjust.

She bent her kind sweet glance, but I could read
what fell, these silent words I could not miss:
who is it steals from me the friend I trust?

['*Quel vago impallidir . . .*']

The woods are wild and were not made for man.
Now men and weapons fill them with their fear.
I walk there free, the only terror near
being my Sun and the bright rays I scan –

her piercing Love! And I walk singing (but can
such thoughts be wise?) of her who in absence is here,
here in my eyes and heart to make me swear
I saw girls, ladies, where beech and fir trees ran!

I seem to hear her, when I hear the air,
the leaves, the branches, the complaint of birds,
or waters murmuring on through the green grass.

Never so happy, never in silence so rare,
alone in a grim forest, without light, without words –
but still too far out from my Sun I pass!

*['Per mezz'i boschi . . .']*


The eyes that drew from me such fervent praise,
the arms and hands and feet and countenance
which made me a stranger in my own romance
and set me apart from the well-trodden ways;

the gleaming golden curly hair, the rays
flashing from a smiling angel's glance
which moved the world in paradisal dance,
are grains of dust no passion now can raise.

And I live on, but in grief and self-contempt,
left here without the light I loved so much,
in a great tempest and with shrouds unkempt.

No more love songs, then, I have done with such;
my old skill now runs thin at each attempt,
and tears are heard within the harp I touch.

*['Gli occhi di ch'io parlai . . .']*

165

Great is my envy of you, earth, in your greed
folding her in invisible embrace,
denying me the look of the sweet face
where I found peace from all my strife at need!

Great is my envy of heaven which can lead
and lock within itself in avarice
that spirit from its lovely biding-place
and leave so many others here to bleed!

Great is my envy of those souls whose reward
is the gentle heaven of her company,
which I so fiercely sought beneath these skies!

Great is my envy of death whose curt hard sword
carrier her whom I call my life away;
me he disdains, and mocks me from her eyes!

['*Quanta invidia io ti porto . . .*']

## Maurice Scève

That beauty which enriched the living world
when she was born, in whom I die, yet live,
not only in my eyesight's gleaming world
has printed her most vivid line and tint
but locked my mind within such strong-charmed circle
where I admire and marvel at her miracle
that almost dead, I am wakened by her grace
into the daylight of my dark desires
to burn and burn, and (this her miracle) then
she plunges me in the abyss of darkness again.

['*Celle beaulté, qui embellit . . .*']

Some are the skilful poets of histories,
perpetuating the exalted acts of princes;
some are at home with brilliant victories,
or sharpen satires, bitterly indignant;
some too in songs make public private passions
or find delight in pleasantly recalling
follies, to hear men laugh at their diversions.
    And I? Have I then nothing for revealing?
You alone I have, and nothing I write and say
but this, to your heart, to your heart I cry and I cry.

*['Qui se delecte a bien narrer . . .']*


Suddenly dazzled by lightning in the fields
a man sees instant darkness everywhere;
then when the gradual brightness reappears
he guards his eyes against the fires of the air.
    But I, in safety perfectly instructed
by flash of your inimitable grace
which threw in shadow every joy I had had
with those most sweet yet sharply-showered rays,
no longer err in plain and daily light.
    For now to adore you is my light and life.

*['Quand l'œil aux champs . . .']*


Twice now has the moon's crescent shown
and twice again, invisible, gone down:
and twice the sun appearing has empowered
the vision of you I guard within my mind
till even my forbidden force takes heart
for these great hours, so sharply sundering us,
when life and I must live our lives apart.
    For dying in this dragging absence still
(although in you I live) gives services
as great to time as pain in absence does.

*['Ja deux Croissantz . . .']*

Excellent painter, who first showed love blind,
feeble and fickle bowman, chalk-faced child!
His arrows render lover to lover blind,
he melts their fury to the infantile,
they waste in pique, in anxiousness grow white,
more restless than the spring or autumn skies.
    So God in us: O love and discontent
his alchemy infuses in this heart! –
his gold of all delight, quick, warm, and suave,
his lead so soft and chilled, grim as the grave.

['*Bien paindre sceut...*']


To see, to hear, to speak, to touch the flesh
made up the circle of my love's desire,
and that one end all lovers hold most dear
had no being in our acquaintance, no wish.
    Ah, what has been the fruit of my restraint,
buried and sanctified by vows too chaste?
Misfortune falls on our attempted good
and I might be miscalled for doing bad
because in my good loving I soon ceased
to see her, hear her, speak, and touch her flesh.

['*Le veoir, l'ouyr, le parler...*']


Flowers in evening hidden, hidden their fairness,
everything that lives hidden in the end by time –
why sow in me these cries and tears and cares,
saying she too will be lost, she too, sometime?
    That man who set on her his eyes and thought,
whether in love and delight his soul was caught,
or whether in blind wretchedness he faltered,
daughter and heir of all the heavens would call her,
and goddess in good truth he might surmise
could he but see with one of my two eyes.

['*Si le soir pert...*']

My face, anguish to any human sight,
would have moved Scythians to melt in pity;
such tenderness as theirs might be has died,
under the hard earth's frozen canopy.
    What then will make an end of my lament,
in such frail forecast of an end as this?
With a fair show of hope upon my brows
I speak assurance to my soul and my heart,
promising myself to be set free at least
by death, the goal of those whom grief has seized.

*['Ma face, angoisse . . .']*


Say that desire, foreimaging the thing
most greatly loved, is mirror to the heart,
which always makes its glass the imaging
of her in whom my soul delights to rest:
should I obey my vain and luring will,
flying from that which follows after me still?
    As fast the stag, so fast the hunter runs
the sooner to lay his power in the nets;
as farther I, so nearer fly the pangs
of that great sweetness, Lord of bitterness.

*['Si le desir, image . . .']*


When I saw in the blue and serenity of her eyes
the air after long tempest cleared and swept,
driving at once on my desert and prize
as victor in an honourable assault
I could begin to lift my head to the heights:
ah then the lake of my new-found delights
brimmed over, and far far beyond its shores
spread into regions I had never known,
with cairns by which my pilgrim thoughts could rise
in pride and joy and dance through Paradise.

*['Quand j'apperceu . . .']*

To speak, or not, no man will disallow
who gives the rein of freedom to the will.
Yet, should it happen someone says to you,
Lady, either your lover lies forgetful
or else he draws his Délie from the moon
to show you at evasive wax and wane –
let that execrable name depart
from you to him who angles for our hurt!
    In that admirable name I would conceal
you, shining in the dark night of my soul.

['Taire, ou parler . . .']




I look for restful night, refreshing all
the harsh and the vexed hearts, to bring my peace,
but once the harsh sun goes to its dark holds
my mite of joy falls too in that abyss.
    For then that goddess, her great crescent flashing,
lights up the glooms of this terrestrial heaven,
and quickly in me this other moon arises,
dazzling the soul, the tranquillity, the centre,
and rousing in me my well-accustomed pain
makes night itself more harsh and wakeful day.

['J'attens ma paix . . .']




The soaring thought sent from my frail desires
moved me to more exalted enterprise,
stealing me away insensibly from pleasure
to turn the wondering memory from that good
wherein my soul had long been prisoner:
and there, like snow before the sun, I am dissolved,
and then my sighs leave their deep centres, rise,
lift up their voice and cry to such a height
that soul and recollection sink, and I
founder in the oblivious abyss.

['Le hault penser . . .']


170

Within the shadow of those sombre hours
when slow sleep draws its peace across the world,
as I lie buried in the curtained night
a dream comes which unchains my mind from me
and sets it down again as close to hers
that's reverenced for queenly quality.
    Yet in such sweet and quiet interview
she is so strong that I soon lose all fear,
persuaded I possess her lying there –
if only as Endymion knew the moon.

['A l'embrunir des heures . . .']


Wherever you have gone, in you I breathe;
wherever I am, there my soul lies dead.
However far you go, still you are here;
here though I seem to be, my heart has fled.
    If Nature should decry her sense outraged
to see me live in you more than in me,
the blessed power which moving soundlessly
infuses the soul within this passive frame
foreseeing it in itself still unfulfilled
extends it in you as its most perfect field.

[En toy je vis . . .']


See how when shivering winter makes his stay
the trees in the bare fields are shrivelled away,
and then when spring with his clear days comes in
green buds, leaves, flowers, and fruit again are seen,
    and trees and shrubs, hedgerows and thickets shine,
unwind their waves of gay and dancing green.
    So while your pitiless cold is bent on me
my hope stands stripped of its green flourishing;
then when I sense your soft and warming spring
my year is crowned with April, proud and clear.

['Voy que l'Hyver tremblant . . .']

Closely and still more closely I feel that knot
binding my soul to its beatitude,
so long as pain is powerless to persuade
a severing from that happy servitude.
   But no wild fever in its troubled course
swells out too strongly in intemperance,
possessing me through the great variableness
of that one hope which pricks me day and night.
   – Unimaginable deliciousness,
whose very shadow is the mind's delight!

*['Je sens le noud . . .']*


Here alone I lie, there she and he,
I on my bed of pain, on soft sheets she;
my weary flesh sprawled on rancorous nettles,
hers in its nakedness folded in his arms.
   O but (unworthy he) he touches, holds,
she suffering him: forced love's not strong,
ravished by him under this unjust bond
which human law, and not divine, has formed.
O justice in fiat to all but me: you fall
in punishment on me for others' wrong!

*['Seul avec moy . . .']*


Wanderer: drowned body in the open sea:
shuttlecock, plaything and mock of wave
and wind: bitter the gulf: waverer
buoyed on my own unfathomed misery –
   till you, O hope, upon this moment sinking
into the ignorant chaos of my brain
suddenly with her name recalled awaken
me from the profound abyss and perishing:
I prick my ears to hear that name resound;
I am dazzled, struck; I am hidden from my mind.

*[Comme corps mort . . .']*

172

See the clear day crumble down in darkness;
its brilliance lives on in its good effects.
Joy and delight are mourners of themselves,
though pleasure rages to fill tangless lives.
    Every magnificence moves to its defeat,
the lusts are brittle, follies are in the heart,
and trees that flourish a high crown of leaves,
brief splendours, crash at length in dying groves;
from this, only your worth will rise to brave
its happy green in honour from your grave.

['Voy le jour cler . . .']


Gone languid now in my long-lingering hope
the spirit with the body fails, winds down,
and one is numb to every fleshly wound,
the other ignorant of its mortal foes.
    Thus I, deprived of hope, can scarcely say
whether I live to admiration or shame,
but this I know, that since I was shut out
from your dear grace, my happiness was lost:
you willed it; it is that shut hateful gate
my dark and sad archives perpetuate.

['Fait paresseux . . .']


Pierced as my spirit is by beauty, by that beauty
honour and wonder for this age to revere,
conniving at that pleasing cruelty
which in my pain, in joy appears to me,
I dream, and gaze: and gazing marvel at
her soft laughter, and grace of hand and heart.
    And then my wonder dies out in such sweetness
that deeper meditation lets me pass,
and meditating so, my soundless cries
climb and descend to both the centre and the stars.

['Tout en esprit ravy . . .']

173

Every length and breadth of every sea,
each tract of this revolving massive sphere,
all hills and peaks in gentle or dizzy air,
regions remote from night or turned from day,
all space, O my too rigorous friend, will be
filled with your sweet but changeless cruelty.
    In this way you outstrip the centuries
and climb above the courses of the stars
through power of your name, which leaps my sighs
to breast the ocean of the universe.

*['De toute Mer tout long . . .']*


Almost beside myself with sudden change:
the prick and tingle: reasonless sense: the mood:
already my body in unbridled surge
boiled with the working of my youth and blood.
Then would unthought-of pleasure course in me
perfectly free, and extremity of joy.
    Yet when my youth was urged so easily
to move itself in lust and liberty,
it was this self myself had to forget,
to keep another heart in memory yet.

*['Près que sorty . . .']*


At that happy centre, the impenetrable heart
where one child vainly brings his divine power,
my life arrived in such a wretched hour
that now forever self-exiled from my breast,
in the free sap and flourish of its spring
determined to possess that sacred centre,
all the pursuit of liberty forgotten,
feeding on meditation dark and cold:
it follows night alone, knows day no longer;
in the glooms of darkness all its glories are rolled.

*['Au centre heureux . . .']*

When (but O how seldom!) I see beside me
her who is goodness, her who is graciousness,
I turn from being fire and turbulence
to ice that hardens and constricts to deride me.
    Then I lift up my eyes to read that face
which has induced in me such desperate change:
but vision and intelligence are gloom;
I leave the labyrinth, and the fire revives:
so we find mountains steadily become
colder the more they soar to the solar fires.

['Quand (ô bien peu)...']


When death has stripped off from my sombre soul,
after the revolutions of time, this frame,
I would not want, to watch the ages go,
a pyramid or mausoleum fame.
    But rather, Lady, less cold and dry than stone
(if I am worthy) your breast should be my tomb;
    since in our lives between earth and heaven here
you unrelentingly have been my war,
so after death, in such suave grave entranced,
I might find love and peace in you at last.

['Quant Mort aura...']


Nothing, or little more, would serve to melt
all motion from this quickened image away,
a dissolution contemplated yet,
my spirit seeing its stricken flesh arrayed
in death's equivalent everlastingness,
raised up again from an impermanent sickness.
    If I should strive to end my strife with peace
am I to fear rebirth in vaster life?
When our day fades before the hosts of night
light breaks, not fails, at the Antipodes.

['Rien, ou bien peu...']

Perhaps you wonder why two elements
as contrary as these were laid together
within my tomb: this water, and this fire:
uneasiest of all companionships! –
ah, they are present as inevitables,
to show you by the most transparent symbols
that just as my living body once displayed
weeping and the fever of love in roughest fight,
so after death even in a grave's redoubt
I cry and burn for your ingratitude.

*['Si tu t'enquiers pourquoy . . .']*


Such blessed fire will burn on bright and clear,
and openly illuminate the world,
as long as earth subsists; such fire will hold
while love is still what living men revere.
  I do not see a massive difference
between that ardent fever of our hearts
and the life, the goodness which will follow us
beyond the broad and endless heaven of stars.
  Unblighted by the oblivion of men,
our juniper will grow for ever green.

*['Flamme si saincte . . .']*


## Garcilaso de la Vega

One moment my hope rises up on wings,
the next, grown weary of its high estate,
it turns and falls, and leaves me, like my fate,
wide open to the diffidence it brings.
  What man would bear such harsh revisitings
of evil to good? O wearied heart, be great!
Make strength in misery your surrogate;
wait for the calms that follow buffetings.
  And I myself will promise by main force

to break obstructions none have dared to break,
bristling with thousands of impediments.
  No death or stumbling-blocks or prison-doors
can keep you from my sight, though they should make
my naked ghost gaze through its fleshly rents.

*['Un rato se levanta . . .']*


  Your face is written in my soul, and when
I want to write about you, you alone
become the writer, I but read the line;
I watch you where you still watch me, within.
  This state I am and always will be in.
For though my soul imprints a half-design
of what I see in you, the good unknown
is taken on a trusting regimen.
  What was I born for if not to adore you?
My ills have shaped you to the bent they give.
I love you by a daily act of soul.
  All that I have I must confess I owe you.
For you I came to life, for you I live,
for you I'd die, and do die, after all.

*['Escrito 'stá en mi alma . . .']*


  Rough are the roads that led me to this place.
I stand here in such fear I cannot stir.
If I should move, or take one step, my hair
is seized to make all effort powerless.
  Yet I must strain, even in death's embrace,
to make my life my latest counsellor;
I see the best, but still the worst is dear,
through fate, or through a sin's deep-rootedness.
  This too: the meagre time our fates allow,
the years I swung perverse from their supports
at the beginning and in the midst of life,
  my inclination, unresisted now,
and death's sure end to such a world of hurts
make me a laggard in my godly strife.

*['Por ásperos caminos . . .']*

Sweet gifts, by me found something less than sweet,
though joyous gifts enough when God so willed!
You are knit into memory, I am killed
when you and memory conspire to meet.
   Who would have told me, when my whole heart beat
with joy for you, that those times would be stilled,
and that your image must one day be filled
with heavy grief such as these words repeat?
   Since one hour was enough for you to take
the very gift you gave me for my aim,
take too the misery you left to break.
   If not, I must suspect you made the same
reward of happiness as you were to make
of these sad memories I die to name.

['¡O dulces prendas...']


While there is still the colour of a rose
and of a lily in your countenance,
and you with such an ardent candid glance
can fire the heart, and check the flames it shows;
   and while that golden hair of yours that flows
into a knot can leap into a dance
as the wind blows with livelier dalliance
upon the fairest proud white neck it knows:
   gather together from your happy spring
fruits that are sweet, before time ravages
with angry snow the beauty of your head.
   The rose will wither as the cold wind rages,
and age come gently to change everything,
lest our desire should change old age instead.

['En tanto que de rosa...']


I came to a valley in the wilderness
where no one walked across the waste but me,
and there I saw a sudden misery,
a dog, distraught, wild with unhappiness.
   Its howl would mount into the emptiness,

178

and then it would go sniffing eagerly
for tracks, run on, turn back, and stop – to be
fretted again by a desperate distress.
    And it was this: the dog had missed the presence
of its master; could not find him; felt its loss.
See what straits they drive to, the ills of absence!
    The dog's bewilderment tore my heart across;
I said to it in pity: 'Cling to patience:
I am a man, yet absence is my cross.'

*['A la entrada de un valle . . .']*


## Torquato Tasso


To what joys could I aspire
when I am so far from you who are all my desire?
And yet by sleight of mind
I cross the hills and fields and streams and seas
to be near you again and find
my heart blaze up in the light of your eyes, and be pleased
by the very pain that is kind
for one who is infinitely happy to die in that fire.

*['Io non posso gioire . . .']*


So far from you, my dear!
I have no heart, no life; Tasso is not here.
No more, alas, no more
what I once was, but a piece of darkness, a shade,
a sound like the sound of pain,
a desolation, a voice: and this is nothing more
than what your absence has made;
I still have a mortal sickness – if death was near!

*['Lunge da voi, ben mio . . .']*


179

No flowers by these shores
bear such a lovely red
as the red that blooms along the lips of my love,
and no air that blows
in June by the lily-bed
or by river and rose has a song as sweet to sing of.
Ah may I only miss
the music of those dear lips in the pause of a kiss!

['Non sono in queste rive . . .']


Most perfect kiss –
this softest recompense
for serving you with my tireless faithfulness!
and O most happy hand
that trembles like a bird
and yet is bold to touch your gentle breast,
while sweetness has entranced
the soul that seals our lips to swoon to its rest!

['Soavissimo bacio . . .']


What were the dews I saw,
the lamentations or the tears
scattered abroad from under the cowl and shawl
of night, from the sweet white face of the stars?
And why did the snowy moon throw and strew
so pure a shower of sparkling drops across
the fresh and glistening grass?
Why were the winds that blew
through the dark air before daybreak so bleak,
wheeling and wailing as in grief?
Shall I say they are all witnesses, when you depart,
dear heart of my heart?

['Qual rugiada . . .']

Silent the forests, the streams,
waveless-sheeted the sea,
winds in their caves unblustering, at peace,
sombre the night, and white
its moon of deepest and marmoreal quiet:
let us too lie like secrets
locked in love and its sweetness –
love have no breath, no voice,
no sound a kiss, no voice or sound my sighs!

*['Tacciono i boschi...']*


Tarquinia, if your studious eyes
are set on the rolling heavens,
I could wish to be those skies:
if I could feel the fervours
of your sweet gaze
lighting my sight and face –
O then I should rise and surprise
your thousand graces with my thousand eyes.

*['Tarquinia, se rimiri...']*


## Giambattista Marino


My hidden treasure is love
and my heart is its treasurer;
may he lock up my longings there!
And O my sighs, mysterious witnesses
of the love I steal, voices
that my lips are parted to utter again and again –
keep your silence before men,
for this, alas, all schools of love can teach:
a sigh in itself is speech.

*['Ardi contento e taci...']*

That pair of gleaming snakes,
twisted into little orbs of enamel and gold,
which your lovely ear shakes,
Lilla, as pendants: they hold
some message, don't they? Yes, yes, I know:
these are the mysterious insignia of others'
pain, cruel, gratuitous;
like a biting snake you go
cruelly wounding others, your deaf ear takes
no prayers, tears, heartbreaks.

['*Quegli aspidi lucenti*...]

*from*
RITES OF PASSAGE
(1976)

## INTRODUCTORY NOTE

The first translations I made – from Verlaine, in 1937 – were naive
attempts to convey the enthusiasm I felt for the sudden discovery
of a foreign poet: Verlaine said something to me in his language
which no poet in my own language had quite said before, and I
wanted to show, if I could, what this quality was. This has been
my guiding principle throughout, and the selection of transla-
tions in the present book is a selection of the poets to whom I have
felt particularly attracted or for whom I have felt a special affinity.
As far as method is concerned, I have aimed at a conscientious
faithfulness, and have hoped that enthusiasm and affinity would
take care of the poetry. Despite the forceful exemplars of Ezra
Pound, Robert Lowell, and Christopher Logue, I have persis-
tently refused myself their freedom of approach, and have tried
to work within a sense of close and deep obligation to the other
poet. That it is possible to do this without losing the rhythms and
exhilarations necessary for the creation of even translated poetry,
is no doubt related to temperament, and the translator has to
gauge and use his temperament in deciding on his working
methods. I have not included in this volume any poems not done
directly from the original texts, because although versions done
with the help of native collaborators can be justified by the
results, especially if the translator knows something of the lan-
guage and is able to keep his eye on the text, it seemed fairer to
present the results of immediate poet-to-poet impact. 'We see,
we saw not what did move'.

\*

I would like to express my thanks to Haroldo de Campos for help
in translating his 'Servidão de Passagem'.

185

**Andrei Voznesensky**

AUTUMN IN SIGULDA

From the last carriage I watch the place go by,
goodbye,

goodbye my summer,
we must go,
axes stun the dacha now,
my house, nail up the timber,
goodbye,

my woods have lost their leaves,
they are empty and sad
like the case the music leaves
an accordion gone dead,

we are people,
we too are emptied out,
we issue,
                as it is written,
                                out

from walls,
                from mothers,
                                from women,
for ever, summer or winter,

goodbye dear mother,
at the windows
you grow translucent like a larva,
tired, tired with the days,
let us sit down together,

friends, enemies, live on,
adieu,
out from me now
whistling you run,
as I issue from you,

o my country, let us say our goodbyes,
I'll be a star, a willow tree,
no weeping, no beggarly cries,
only my thanks that life could be,

at the butts with my 10 shots
I thought I'd knock up 100, but –
my thanks that I could not,
and thanks and thanks redoubled that

in my transparent shoulder-blades they thrust
the gift of my vision, it fits
like the rubber
                        glove that trusts
a man's red fist,

'Andrei Voznesensky' – so it will be,
and perhaps briefly neither word nor pet dog, but me,
here against the burning of your cheek,
'Andryúshka',

my thanks that we met in the fall
in these woods, you asked me something,
dragging your dog by its collar,
the dog struggling,
my thanks,

I have come to life again, my thanks for this autumn
when you made me see myself clear and plain,
the woman wakened us at eight, my
thanks for the holiday record we played
that groaned out its slangy jangle,
my thanks,

but o you are going away, going away,
                        as a train goes, you are going away,
out from my empty pores you are going away,
each of us goes, we separate, we go on our way,
was this house wrong for us, who can say?

you are near me and somewhere far off,
Vladivostok is no farther off,

I know our lives come round again
in friends and lovers, grass and grain,
changed into that, and those, and this,
nature abhorring emptiness,

my thanks for the leaves that are scattered,
a million spring to their relief,
my thanks for what your laws tell me,

but a woman is fluttering along the embankment
after the train like a fiery leaf!..

Help me!

*[Osen' v Sigulde]*


PARABOLIC BALLAD

Our destinies fly like rockets, in parabolas,
occasionally along a rainbow but more often in the shadows.

Who was that fiery redhead painter – Gauguin?
You can't keep a bohemian in a business programme.
To land in the royal Louvre, starting from Montmartre,
he had to
                describe
                            an arc through Java and Sumatra –
just took off, leaving behind him the lunacy of money,
the clucking of matrons, the fetid academy,
took off and cancelled
                            terrestrial gravity.
Beery shamans sniggered over their glasses: 'The
plumb-line's shorter, the parabola's steeper,
copying the heavenly tabernacles'd be better!'
But he left them there, he roared up like a rocket
through a blast that snatched their ear-flaps and coat-pockets,
and he dropped into the Louvre – not the tourist-door Louvre
but an angry
                paraboloid
                            crash through the roof!

188

Well, truth-seeking's as unpredictable as diabolo.
Maggots make for cracks – man has his parabola.

I knew a girl once, she lived quite near,
we studied together, sat tests. But see
where I got to! –
                            was it on the wings of demons I
reached those reeling equivocal luminaries of Tbilisi?
Forgive me for such a jesterish parabola.
Dear shoulders, frozen, in a shadowy passageway...
Oh how you rang out in the gloom of the Universe
like an antenna-rod, so vibrant and tense!
I fly on still,
                    called to my terrestrial
touchdown by your clear-cold earthly signal.
How hard it is for us to take that parabola! –

But pronouncement and prognosis and paragraph are
swept aside by art, by love, by history

tracing their parabolic trajectory!
Galoshes flounder through a Siberian thaw...
Can the plumb-line be a short-cut after all!

*[Parabolicheskaya ballada]*


AUTODIGRESSION

*To J.-P. Sartre*

I am a family
as in the spectrum there are seven 'I's' in me

like beasts unbear-
able but the most blue's
                            an oboe-blower!

let spring come
and I dream
            I'm
            an eighth one

*[Avtootstuplenie]*

189

## THE FIRST ICE

In the telephone box the girl freezes,
her face is smeared with running tears
and lipstick, she huddles, peers
out from her chilly collar, aches –
blows upon her thin little paws –
icicle-fingers! Earrings flash.
Back – alone as she is, along
the long, lonely, icy lane.
The first ice. The first time, it was,
first ice crackling in phoned phrases –
the frozen track shines on her cheeks –
first ice on her insulted ears.

*[Pervy led]*


## FOGGY STREET

Fog scumbles the suburbs like tumbler pigeons.
Policemen bob like corks.
Fog stations!
Fog century is it? Pleistocene epoch?

Everything's in pieces, disconnected as delirium.
People have been screwed loose...
I drift along.
No I don't. I'm wrestling in a cottonwool noose.

Noses. Cap-bands. Tail-lights.
They loom double: what a hall of mirrors!
Galoshes all right?
Watch your loaf with your feet there!

Like a woman who's just left your kisses,
blurring out and yet returning to vividness –
a widow, no longer your lover –
yes she's yours – no she's a stranger...

Kerb? Excuse me. Passers-by? Oh.
Venus! Ice-cream? Sorry!...

People I know?
Nah! Iagos in homespun, what a story!

You?! Standing there squeezing your ears,
              by yourself, in a man-sized coat! –
with whiskers!
And that hairy ear – is that hoarfrost on it or not?

I stumble about, I struggle, I'm alive though;
              fog, fog, undissolving.
Whose cheek is this – brushed against in the mist? – Hullo!
Hoy there! O
fog, fog...voices...unavailing...

Great to unveil this fog and send it sailing!

*[Tumannaya ulitsa]*


GOYA

I am Goya!
The enemy flew like ravens over my appalling
              field: picked out my
                        eye sockets.

I am sorrow.

I am war's own
voice. I am cities fired in the storms of
nineteen-forty-
one.

I am hunger-horror.

I am also the throttled
neck of the old woman hanged in the naked square, her body
              like a bell rocking –

I am Goya!

O grapes of wrath! I
have driven on the West, have launched my volleys-
I am the ash of the uninvited guest!
And I have hammered in hard stars like coffin
nails on the memorial sky.

I,
Goya.

[Goya]

WINGS

The gods are dozing like slummocks –
Clouds for layabouts!
What hammocks!

The gods are for the birds.
The birds are for the birds.

What about wings,
all that paraphernalia?
It's too weird, I tell you.
What did the ancients see in these things?
Nearer
and nearer
to the fuselage
clouds press them in,
to a vestige-
ality of winginess on our things,
our marvel-machines, strange
to them. Men have unslung
something new, men don't hang
out wings, men are with it, bang.
Man, men are winged!

[Kryl'ya]

EARTH

We love walking
barefoot on the earth,
on the yielding, misty, homely earth.
But where? In Ethiopia?
Perhaps in Messina?
In the desert? In Havana?
In a village in Ryazan?
We are men.
We love walking about the earth.

Currents of the earth stream through us like a shudder.
Yet we are insulated from it, under
a shield of asphalt, cobblestones, cars...
We forget the smell of earth in our city affairs.
But suddenly we smile – at a green sapling
that bursts through city granite
                              like a geyser
                                        springing!...

An earth in dreams appeared to me, without trenches and chains,
without detonation of mines: a dream of telescopes,
of lime-trees, eucalyptus, peacock rain-
bows, lifts on crazy ropes
and showers of aluminium!
A world of seas, of trains, of women –
a world of puffing and
                        fructifying,
                              marvellous as man!...

Somewhere on Mars he goes, a visitor from Earth.
He walks. He smiles. He takes out a handful of earth –
a tiny handful of that burning,
half-bitter, homely,
far-whirling,
heart-catching earth!

                                        *[Zemlya]*

## NEW YEAR LETTER

Oh the guests, tight as hot-water bottles!
What a ravenous napkined row –
their hands laid out like lobsters
red on the plates. You go
restlessly among all this
tableware. You cool your cheek
on the ice-bucket, throw off your shawl. It's
hot! 'I'm nearly stifling' – you speak...
But my window opens full
on the towered city; there's a garden here;
and the snow has a pungent apple-smell,
and the flakes hang in the air.
They don't flutter, they don't fall,
they wait, they don't shake, light guests
watchful as ikon-lamps on a wall
or drifts from summer cigarettes.
They waver, and yet scarcely so,
touched now by your tiny foot
neat in its Polish boot...
Sweet smell of apples in the snow.

*[Novogodnee pis'mo]*


## ITALIAN GARAGE

The floor's a mosaic
like a carp's back.
The dark garage
                    sleeps in a palazzo.

Motorcycles are Saracen interlopers
or sleepfast grasshoppers.

Neither Paolos nor Juliets –
shuddering sweating Chevrolets.

Giotto frescoes, like mechanics,
are reflected in the car-hoods.

Wraiths of wars and raids loom.
Dark garage,
what's in your dream?

Halberds?
or tyrants?
or birds
from restaurants?...

A single motorcycle blinks –
the reddest of the tinks.

What's it anxious for? Tomorrow's
Christmas. Is it to be a Christmas omelette?

Oranges, ovations...
Those that crash
have resurrections!

We weren't born for survival kicks,
but to give the speedometer its licks!...

The blood-red, the doomed, the scorcher! Scorch on!
The hotrod girl has her swan-song.

*[Ital'yanskii garazh]*


SELLING WATERMELONS

Moscow is milling with watermelons.
Everything breathes a boundless freedom.
And it blows with unbridled fierceness
from the breathless melonvendors.

Stalls. Din. Girls' headscarves.
They laugh. Change bangs down. Knives –

and a choice sample slice.
– Take one, chief, for a long life!

Who's for a melon?
Freshly split! –

And just as tasty and just as juicy are
the capbands of policemen
and the ranks of motor-scooters.
The September air is fresh and keen
and resonant as a watermelon.

And just as joyfully on its own tack
as the city-limit melon-multitudes,
the earth swings
in its great string bag
of meridians and latitudes!

*[Torguyut arbuzami]*


RUBLYOV ROAD*

Motor-scooters roaring
past the sanatorium!

Behind the handlebars
like Rublyov† angels: loving riders.

As in the fresco of the Annunciation
with its strident white tone
see their women scattering a shine
behind them, like wings on their spine!

The splaying of their dress!
Tugged back from the handlebars!
Thrust into my shoulders
a wing's white fleece!

Shall I fly off?
              Drop down
like a falcon?
A stone! –

* In south-west Moscow.        † The great ikon painter (*c.*1370-1430).

Autumn.
The skies. The good
red woods.

[*Rublevskoe shosse*]


NEW YORK AIRPORT AT NIGHT

*The Façade*

My self-portrait, retort of neon, apostle of the heavenly portals –
the airport!

Ikons of duralumin shine and soar
like X-ray photos of the soul.

How fearful it is
                    when your sky is fixed
in the smouldering tracks of
unknown capitals!

Twenty-four hours a day
                        you are filled up like a sluice
with the starry fates
of freightmen and loose

women. Your alcoholics drain the bar, like angels!
You speak to them with tongues!

You lift them up,
                the beats and bums.

You say 'Advent' –
                roll on your drums!

*The Airfield*

Place of waiting . . . escorts, destinies, trunks, marvels . . .
Watch five Caravelles
                drift dazzlingly
                        down from the heavens!

197

Five night-birds let down their yawning undercarriages.
Is there a sixth of these voyagers?

It seems to have got lost –
                                    a maverick, a tiny stork, a star!...

Cities dance below it
                    on electric grids.
Where is it floating
                    droning, fooling –
and burning
          like a cigarette in the mist?...

It fails to understand the forecast.
The earth is closed to it.


*The Interior*

The forecasts are bad. And you, in the storm of anxiety,
linger in your entrance-halls, your guerrilla army.
Governments snore on
                              in oblivious pairs.
Quiet as a chemist, the control tower plots their flight.
A huge eye stares out to other spheres.
Window-cleaners
                    make you weep like midges,
stellar commando, prodigy of crystal,
how sweet, how terrible
                              to be a son of the future
where there are no more fools or
                                        wedding-cake stations –
only poets and airports!
The sky moans in the aquarium glass,
welded to the earth at last.


*Structures*

Airports – accredited legations
of sun and ozone!

A hundred generations –
                         could they touch this
mastery of immaterial structures?
Instead of a stony mass
like an idol
          a cool
glass of dark blue – without the glass.
With its hushed grilles and counters
it's like a vapour
                    of anti-matter.

Brooklyn's a blockhead, a devil in hard stone.
The monument for this age
is the airport alone.

                              *[Nochnoy aeroport v Nyu-Yorke]*


BELLA AKHMADULINA

This girl's been given a sparkle.
Not a Spangle, but a sparkle,
her asking spark, her risky spark,
audacious Olympic spark for the dark!
Can kindle a heart – and a stove as well.
can set
          the earth
                    on fire
                              like hell!
A blunt spark burns in the stub.
The hussy's twisty chuckle's stuck.

                              *[Bella Akhmadulina]*

## VIOLETS

Gods have hobbies, the bull
gave Europa a roll.
A couple of centuries later
the dove was Christ's maker.
Who's in the pipeline this fall?

Bobby Fischer breathes a prayer.
Vertinskys knit (both sisters).
Mona Lisa like a seamstress
smiles to keep the pins in.
A lover of pinks and phlox
sent a hemisphere up in smoke
at Majdanek. The beggar's thin
hands amass bank pass-
books! Worlds are sand-grains in Gobis!
No matter how you rack your brain,
you only see God's hobbies,
Unum Necessarium's not shown.

Gods have soft underbellies.
Umbrella-makers despise umbrellas.
The umbrellaless go tetchy, sobbing:
'Why can't we have such a hobby?'
Don't break a lance with dissenters,
save it for a lance-collector.
Gods want what is Caesar's,
Caesar needs what God has.
Spartacuses grace ministers' chairs,
Mothers Superior devour Nabokov.
And faith is peddled by rockers.

Gods have Mexican whiskers –
let them hang from these bonces
like handles from big cisterns
asking to be flushed. But mister,
don't. Don't knock the bonzes.

Is there no ontology lobby?
Why should the stork's hobby
be sent down from on high

in a shiver of gold to levy
a woman's heavy cry?
(Simpler the test-tube baby?
Feel free then to press your hobby,
phillumenist, on all and sundry!)

God is full of answers, but
mainly it is: 'Go to God!' . . .

. . . Gods have hobbies, like man –
if bowling worlds begins to bore,
you take your jeans and watering-can,
become a violet-grower!

Even violets have a hobby –
they grow grief in men.

People are ashamed of sorrow,
so I'll jest you to the end:

'Why'd they crucify you, Mac?'
'To let me play at hide-and-seek,
kid. I love to squint and
peer through these holes in my hand.'

*[Fialki]*

**Yevgeny Yevtushenko**


STALIN'S HEIRS

Voiceless that marble.
        Voicelessly the glass flashed.
Voiceless the sentry stood
        in the wind like a man of bronze.
But a ghost of smoke left the coffin.

A breath squeezed through the cracks
when they carried it out by the Mausoleum doors.
Slowly the coffin hovered,
    its edges grazed the bayonets.
It too was voiceless –
    it too! –
        but voicelessly loud with dread:
inside, a man was
    blackly clenching his embalmed fists,
pressing himself to the cracks,
    pretending to be dead.
He wanted to be able to remember them all,
    all his burial party:
young lads from Ryazan and Kursk,
    rustic recruits:
in order that some day, somehow
    he would gather strength for a sortie
and rise out of the earth
    and fall on them, the rustic dolts.
He's thought up something.
    He's only refreshing himself with a nap.
And I make this appeal now
    to our government, I make this prayer:
to double
    and treble
        the guard at Stalin's slab,
that Stalin may never rise,
    or the past rise with him there.
When I say 'past' do you think I mean
    what is most heroic or treasured,
Turksib,
    Magnitka,
        the flag over Berlin?
No, my meaning is
    of a different past, measured
by denunciations,
    by arrests of the innocent,
        by neglect of the good of men.
We sowed seed honestly.
We honestly made metal pour
and honestly marched and
    stood in ranks and were soldierly.

Yet he was afraid of us.
    He believed in a great end but ignored
that the means
        must be worthy
            of the majesty of the goal.
He was frightened.
    Schooled in the laws of the struggle,
he littered the globe with the heirs of his throne.
It looks to me
    as if the coffin has a telephone:
the Enver Hoxhas
    still receive Stalin's instructions.
How far does the cable from this coffin stretch even yet?
No: Stalin hasn't given in. There are ways
    of dealing with death, he reckons.
Out of the Mausoleum surely it was
    him
        we fetched?
But how are we to fetch
    the Stalin out of Stalin's successors?
Some of his heirs trim roses in retirement,
yet secretly trust
    such retirement is temporary.
Some too
    are first at the microphone abusing Stalin but
these are the ones
    who when night comes
        yearn after the old story.
You can see how today
    it's hardly by chance that the heirs
of Stalin go down with thromboses.
    To them, who were once his props,
the days when the labour camps
    are empty are disasters,
the times when halls overflow
    for the reading of poetry are a blot.
The Party has told me
    I shall not cease
        from mental fight.
If someone repeats, 'The fight
    is over!' – I have no skill
        to bury my disquiet.

So long as Stalin's heirs go
    walking in the light,
I'll feel him,
    Stalin, in the Mausoleum yet.

*[Nasledniki Stalina]*


## Boris Pasternak


'MY SHAME, MY SHAME . . .'

My shame, my shame, you are my burden! My conscience,
in so many early-shattered, still-living dreams!
To be a man! and not a vacant assemblage
of temples, lips, and eyes, cheeks, shoulders, palms!
Then by cry and whistle and symbol of stanzas,
by the strength of my longing and by its innocence
I'd yield to them all, I'd make them my attackers,
I'd storm your walls, my ignominiousness!

*['O styd . . .]*


THE APPROACH OF WINTER

The door was opened, and through the kitchen
the air from the yard rolled in like steam.
Time rolled back in that sharp instant,
as old as evenings in a child's dream.

Days are dry as glass, and quiet.
Out in the street, five steps away,
winter stands at the threshold, shyly;
hesitates to come in today.

It's winter, and everything older, and newer.
The willows waver out and glide

into the grey miles of November
like blind men without stick or guide.

Ice on the stream; the sallows tremble,
and transverse on that naked ice
like mirror on a dressing-table
the sky's black shell lies to entice.

And there in front, at the intersection
of paths half drifted over in snow,
a birch-tree watches its reflection,
a star in its hair, in the glass below.

It secretly suspects, however,
that winter's marvels filter through
to every cottage in the heather
as much as to the midnight blue.

*[Zazimki]*


'O HAD I KNOWN . . .'

O had I known that it ends like this,
the day I sprang to my debut,
that lines and blood together kill,
chokethroat, strike us through and through!

All joking with that cryptic thing
I should have bluntly set aside.
Far, far off was its origin,
doubtful, doubtful my first bite.

But old age – old age is Rome where
neither patter nor legerdemain
nor read-out speech redeems the player
cued for complete decease unfeigned.

Let feeling once dictate its line,
and drive its slave onto the stage –
then art is at an end, and life
stirs in the lungs of earth and fate.

*[O, znal by ya . . .]*

205

## VERSES ON PUSHKIN: THIRD VARIATION

Stars plunged. Promontories weltered in waters.
Salt blinded. There was a drying of tears.
Bedrooms went black. Brains plunged. Whispers
rose from Sahara to the Sphinx's ears.

Candles guttered. And blood in the colossus
seemed then to congeal. Lips melted, shed
the blue celestial smile of wildernesses.
At ebb-tide hour, the night went down and fled.

Breeze from Morocco came scratching the sea.
A simoom breathed. Archangel snored in snows.
Candles guttered. Pushkin's *Prophet* lay dry
in its first draft, as the Ganges sun arose.

*[Stikhi o Pushkine]*


## DAYBREAK

*from* Dr Zhivago

In my fate you were everything
till the war began, and chaos came,
and long, long was the time when nothing
was heard of you or of your name.

Now after many many years
your voice has stirred me once again.
All night I read your will, released
as from a faint to the world of men.

I want to be where people are,
the morning crowds, the lively faces.
I'll set them on their knees, and tear
all things in splinters from their places!

So I run madly down the stairs
as if in a first innocence
seeing the white snow this street wears
and the pavement's desertedness.

Rooms light up everywhere: snug homes!
Tea is gulped, and trams are chased!
In these few minutes the night forms
of the town unrecognizably effaced!

The blizzard's gusts throw on the gate
a thickly-tangled net of flakes.
All eat and drink not to be late –
half-plates, half-cups, as the clock shakes.

For them I feel, for all I feel,
as if I lay in their skin.
Snow melts. My melting is as real.
I knit my brows if dawn is grim.

People with no names live in me,
stay-at-homes, children, even trees.
When all have conquered me, I am free.
These are my only victories.

*[Rassvet]*


MARCH

*from* Dr Zhivago

The sun burns till we pant in its fire.
Surges sweep through the frenzied ravine.
Spring, like the milkmaid in the byre,
runs through its hands a seething sheen.

Snow thins, its lost vitality crawls
on twigs like bad blood in blue veins.
But new life smokes in the cows' stalls,
and pitchfork-teeth take growing-pains.

These nights, these days and nights! Patter
of drops at noon, icicle-nooks
emptying sapless on eaves, chatter
of all the loosened, sleepless brooks!

Framed in a half-open stable-door,
pigeons peck oats in the snow outside.
Can this rich, loaded season soar?
The dung of March reeks far and wide.

[Mart]

THE WEDDING PARTY
*from* Dr Zhivago

Crossing by the courtyard under their accordions,
guests at the bride's house, from evening till morning.

Felt-covered doors of their host must deafen
fragments of chatter from one until seven.

But at time of dawning, when beds are so belovèd,
strains rose once more as the guests departed.

Again the accordionist cast showers of hand-claps,
bead-glitter, gaiety and buzz of the party.

Voices of a folk-song, voices, voices,
called from their revels to the sleepers in their places.

Who is that white one, in the hum and the tumult,
gliding to the whistling, sinuous as a peacock –

shoulder, head, and right arm in a dancing movement,
a peacock on the pavement, a peacock, a peacock?

At once the buzz and fervour, and the folk-dance foot-beats,
dropped into the vanishing-pit, drowned was their music.

Busy was the yard now, wide-awake and working,
its voices came striking through the pealing laugh and talking.

Pigeons in a whirling flock of slate-grey smudges
rushed up from the dovecotes to the vast sky's edges.

Someone must have wakened with the thought of sending them,
winged with wishes of years of life, after all the wedding-guests.

Life is only a moment, life too is only a dissolving
of ourselves in all others as by an act of giving:

only a wedding's gladness thrilling up through a window,
only a song, only a sleep, only a slate-grey pigeon.

*[Svad'ba]*


## WINTER NIGHT
*from* Dr Zhivago

A snowstorm made the earth tremble
through its whole frame.
*A candle-flame upon a table,*
*only a candle-flame.*

Like midges swarming in the summer,
winging to a spark,
the flakes flew in a thick shimmer
to the window from the dark.

The blizzard blew. Its rime and stubble
clung to the pane.
*A candle-flame upon a table,*
*only a candle-flame.*

High up on the bright-lit ceiling
shadows were tossed:
hands cross-clasped, feet cross-leaning,
fate in a cross.

And two small shoes fell with a clatter
to the floor, useless,
and wax drops from the night-light spattered
weeping upon a dress.

And all things faded, misted, feeble,
a grey-white dream.
*A candle-flame upon a table,*
*only a candle-flame.*

The candle felt a hidden shaking
blow hot temptation:
wings raised, like an angel's, taking
a cross-like station.

All February, storm rocked the gable
and found there the same
*candle-flame upon a table,*
*only a candle-flame.*

*[Zimnyaya noch']*


*from* THE WAVES

Deep in the greatest poets' lives
such a naturalness is traced
that having known it man arrives
at the last in an utterly silent place.

Sure of his kinship with all that is,
acquainted with futurity,
he must end in the strangest of heresies,
an unimagined simplicity.

*[Volny]*


'IT'S AN ILL THING . . .'

It's an ill thing to be famous.
It isn't fame that scales the cliffs.
Don't build archives, save your labour.
Don't tremble for your manuscripts.

Creation aims at self-surrender,
not at rumour or success.
Some nobody becomes a legend,
and shames the thousand lips he threads.

Life must be lived without pretences,
lived so that at the end of all
you'll pluck love from immensity
and hear the future's welcome called.

Blanks should be left in destiny,
not in the midst of documents,
chapters and texts of life be vetted
by margin-strokes, though not of pens.

You must plunge into obscurity
and let your unknown tracks dissolve
into the invisibility
of lands dissolving in the fog.

Over your trail, footstep by footstep,
others will follow where life leads,
but you yourself should be incurious
to sift the gains from the defeats.

And you must never, for one byway,
step aside from what you are,
but be alive, only alive, be
only alive to your last hour.

*[Byt' znamenitym . . .]*

211

## Yevgeny Vinokurov

### THE NIGHTINGALE

The nightingale was working among the leaves...
Strike the anvil! Roll the blocks about!
Hoist your load under the stars! Rise, breathe!
Like a labourer, a docker soaked in sweat.
Strike the anvil! Strike! Smash granite slabs!
Night singer, knowing nothing of exhaustion.
Sing in the darkness! Love your terrible jobs,
doubling as hammerman and stonemason.
Cut down the oaks! Twist their branches to sheaves!
Dig up the clay and sling it on your back!
... The nightingale was working among the leaves.
He worked like a fiend until the day should break.

*[Solovey]*

## Salvatore Quasimodo

### MAN OF MY TIME

You are still the one with the stone and the sling,
man of my time. You were there in the cockpit
winged with hatred, dials set for death
– I saw you – in the armoured car, at the gallows,
at the torturer's wheel. I saw it! – it was you,
devoting your exact science to destruction,
without love, without Christ. You kill today
as always, as your fathers killed, as the beasts
that saw you for the first time also killed.
And this blood smells as rank as in the day
one brother said to another brother: 'Let us
go to the fields'. And that cold, stubborn echo
has penetrated now to you, to the bones of your life.

212

Blot from your memory, O sons, the clouds of blood
that mount and mount from the earth, forget your fathers:
their tombs are sinking into the ashes, the wind
and the dark birds cover over their hearts.

*[Uomo del mio tempo]*


## THE RAIN IS WITH US AGAIN

The rain is with us again,
the speechless air is shaken by it.
Swallows brush the waters squandered
beside the lochans of Lombardy,
they skim like seagulls over tiny fish;
hay smells sweet beyond the orchard-walls.

Another year consumed,
without an elegy and without a cry
raised to startle and conquer a single day.

*[Già la pioggia è con noi]*


## INSTEAD OF A MADRIGAL

The sunflower leans to the west
and already it watches the day
go foundering down and the summer air
grows thick and already it curls the leaves
and the dockyard smoke. Into the distance
with a dry scurry of clouds and a tearing
of thunderstorms it goes: the sky's last game.
Still, my dear, as for years past, we see here
the end of change in the thin trees bound
by the Naviglio canals. But it is always
our day and always that disappearing sun
held by the thread of its tender ray.

I leave off remembering, I have no more memories;
reminiscence mounts up again from death,

but life is without an ending. Every day
is ours. One of them will stop for ever,
and you with me, when we think it grows late.
Here on the bank of the canal, swinging
our feet like children, let us look
long at the water, at the first branches
caught within its darkening green.
See: the man who silently approaches
is hiding no knife in his hands, but a flower,
a geranium, not a fear.

*[Quasi un madrigale]*


## MY COUNTRY IS ITALY

More and more the days grow distant and scattered;
more and more they return to the hearts of poets.
There the camps of Poland, the plain of Kutno
with the piled hill of corpses set alight
in clouds of naphtha, there the barbed-wire fences
set up for Israel's quarantine, the blood
among the excrement, the burning exanthema,
the shuffling lines of wretches long since dead and
struck down on the graves their own hands opened,
there Buchenwald, the harmless wood of beech-trees
with its accursed furnaces; there Stalingrad,
and Minsk in the marshlands and the sickening snow.
The poets don't forget. O crowd of the degraded,
of the defeated, of those whom mercy has pardoned!
Everything overturns, but the dead are not sold.
My country is Italy – a stranger enemy –
and what I sing is its people, and it is also
the cry below the roaring of its seas,
the pure still mourning of mothers, my song is its life.

*[Il mio paese è l'Italia]*

## THANATOS ATHANATOS

And must we then deny you, God
of the tumour, God of the living flower,
and set a negative beside that stony
dark 'I am', and yield ourselves to death
and have each tombstone cut with our one
and only certainty: 'Thanatos athanatos'?
Let the name go – and then what memory
will remain of the dreams of man, the tears,
the angers of man, man who is confounded
by questionings nothing comes to assuage?
Our dialogue's transformed; for now
the absurd is what grows possible. There
past the haze of mist, within the grove
the leaf in essence waits with patience,
the river is true as it strikes its banks.
Life is no dream. Man is true,
true is his grief jealous of silence.
O God of silence, unlock solitude.

*[Thànatos Athànatos]*

## LETTER TO MY MOTHER

'*Mater dulcissima*, the mists are coming down now,
the Naviglio canal half-heartedly pounds its banks,
the trees swell up with water, burn with snow;
I am not sad, here in the north: I am not
at peace with myself, but I have no forgiveness
to await from anyone, there are many whose debt to me
is the tears owed from man to man. I know
you are ill, I know you live as poets' mothers
live, in poverty, sure in the measure of love
for distant sons. Today it is I
who send you a letter.' A line at last, you'll say,
a line from a boy who ran away at night
in a short coat, some verses in his pocket. Poor boy,
too guileless, he'll be killed some day – some place –
'Yes, I remember, it was from those dreary marshalling-yards

215

where slow trains left with oranges and almonds
for the mouth of the Imera, the magpie river,
the river of salt and eucalyptus. But now
I am thanking you – as I want to – for the irony
you set on my lips, lips as gentle as your own.
That smile has often protected me from pain.
And if I should now have tears for you –
for all who wait like you, not knowing what
they wait for: such tears must be. Ah good death,
forget to touch the clock that ticks on the kitchen wall,
every day of my childhood crossed the enamel
of its face, was lost upon its painted flowers:
forget to touch the hands, the heart of the old.
Oh but some answer, some voice –? Death of compassion,
death of quietness. Goodbye, my dear, goodbye, my

*dulcissima mater.'*

*[Lettera alla madre]*

ROAD IN AGRIGENTUM

A wind is alive there, I remember it
kindled in the manes of the horses that slanted
galloping across the plains, the wind
that chafes and darkens the sandstone and the hearts
of desolate caryatid and telamon, cast down
on the grass. Soul of the ancient world,
old grudge-grey soul, you return with that wind,
you sniff the subtle mosses that re-clothe
the giants heaven has overthrown! Alone,
how alone in the space that is left to you!
And worse: to break your heart to hear again
the sound that dies far out towards the sea
where streaks of day already follow Venus:
the sad vibrations of a jews'-harp, held
in the carter's mouth as he climbs up
a hill still sleek with moonlight, and slowly
rolls through the murmur of saracen olive-trees.

*[Strada di Agrigentum]*

216

NOW THAT THE DAY BREAKS

The night is ended, the moon
slowly dissolves in the stillness
and sinks in the canals.

And what a vivid September clings
to this flat open land: the fields
are green as southern valleys in spring.
I've left my friends behind
and hidden my heart within the ancient walls,
to be alone – to remember you.

How far off you are, farther than the moon,
now that the day breaks
and horses' hoofs are stamping on the stones!

*[Ora che sale il giorno]*


ON THE BOUGHS OF THE WILLOWS

And what had we to do with singing
when the foot of the stranger lay on our hearts,
and the dead were left unburied in the squares
on the brittle icy grass, and the children
cried like lambs, and black was the mother's
shriek as her steps came up to her son
crucified upon a telegraph-pole?
On the boughs of the willows, we too
(making our vow) hung up our harps.
They trembled a little in the grave wind.

*[Alle fronde dei salici]*

217

## SNOW

Evening comes down: and again you leave us,
O beloved images of earth,
trees, animals, poor folk encased
in soldiers' greatcoats, mothers
whose wombs are sterile with tears.
And the snow lights us from the fields
like moonlight. Oh but the dead – Strike
on the forehead, strike right to the heart.
If only someone would cry out in the silence,
in this white ring of buried things –

*[Neve]*

## FROM THE ROCK-FORTRESS AT UPPER BERGAMO

The cry of the cock pierced you, in the air
on the far side of the walls, beyond the towers
freezing in a light you never knew,
the riveting cry of life, and the rustle
of voices within the cells, and the call
of the bird like a sentry announcing daybreak.
And yet you had no words to utter for yourself:
the circle you were now in had no great radius:
and antelope and heron alike were silent,
lost in a puff of malevolent smoke,
amulets of an almost unborn world.
And so the February moon came over
the earth, blandly, but to you
a form in memory, lit at its own quiet.
Now you in turn are going noiselessly
among the castle cypresses; and here
anger's appeased by the green of the tender dead,
and a distant pity seems akin to joy.

*[Dalla rocca di Bergamo Alta]*

218

ELEGY

Icy messenger of the night,
you are back here, clear on the balconies
of shattered houses, to light up again
the unknown graves, the broken remains
smoking over the earth. Here lies
our dream. And you turn alone
towards the north, where everything runs
without light to death: and you resist.

[Elegia]


LAMENT FOR THE SOUTH

The red moon, and the wind, and your colouring,
a northern woman; and the stretch of snow...
You see my heart is on these meadowlands,
in these waters clouded by the mists.
I have forgotten the sea, the great
conch-shells blown by Sicily's shepherds,
old music of carts along the roads
where carob-trees shimmer in the stubble-haze,
I have forgotten the cranes and herons, passing
high over the green and airy uplands
through fields and waters of Lombardy. But
man's cry is raised in man's country: everywhere.
No one now can take me back to the South.

Sick, sick is the South of dragging the dead
to river-banks in its malarial marshes,
sick of its solitude, sick of its chains,
sick in its very mouth
of all the blasphemies its folk have spoken,
howling death to the echo of its wells,
drinking the blood that lies in its heart.
For this its boys return over the hills,
halt their horses under quilts of stars,
nibble acacia flowers by the tracks
grown newly red, still red, still red.
No one now can take me back to the South.

And in this twilight we are still here
charged with our winter, and with you I rehearse
my own unlikely counterpoint
of delicate and of raging things,
a love-lament where no love sings.

*[Lamento per il Sud]*

VISIBLE, INVISIBLE

Visible, invisible,
the man with the cart at the horizon,
held in the road's embrace, calls out,
his voice answers the voice of the islands.
I too am not one to go adrift,
around me the world rolls, I read over
my history as the night watchman does
in his rainy hours. The mystery's not
without lucky approaches, stratagems, hard attractions.
My life, mercilessly smiling people
of my landscapes and my streets,
has no handle to its doors.
Death's not what I'm preparing for,
I know things at their root and source,
the end is an arc of earth where a traveller
goes, the invader of my shade.
I have no acquaintance with shades.

*[Visibile, invisibile]*

THE SOLDIERS CRY AT NIGHT

Neither the Cross nor childhood nor
Golgotha's hammer nor the memory
of an angel is enough to tear out
war. The soldiers cry
at night before dying, they are strong,

they fall at the feet of words
learned under the arms of life.
Love numbers the soldiers,
the nameless bursts of crying.

[I soldati piangono di notte]

## TO THE NEW MOON*

In the beginning God created the sky
and the earth, and then placed lights in the sky
at the appointed time, and at last he lay
at rest, having reached the seventh day.

After a few thousand million years
man, made in his image and resemblance,
without taking rest, and with his secular
intelligence,
and without fear, placed in the quiet sky
of one October night
other lights the equal of those of old
that have rolled and rolled
from the beginning of the world. Amen.

[Alla nuova luna]

* On the launching of the first Russian sputnik, October 1957.

# Guillevic

## THE SKERRY

I
Whit says scaur to makar?
– I dinna heed ye.

Whit sall the scaur haud?
Eerie granderie,

and the bygane shoom o tides
and the bygane lowe o the sun.


II
Lauchs nane, the scaur.
The skerry isna drucken.

Nae leam o brunstane,
scaur's nicht is daurk.

Daith garsna
skerries trimmle.

In scaur's hoose
faur ben is fear.

In thir broo and mou
aa's fey, aa's clear.


III
Forby – the gledness:

nae frichtsome thing is
to thon craig fremit.

Fae craig and fae rig
the shairdit stane-shooer

faas, that wund and snaw
staw as the scaur was sleepin.


IV
Clinty-face needna
be a face forpynit.

Clinty-face needna
be an apen buik.


V
Dansars birl i the stane,
a lowe leams i the stane
gin the stane gies the word.

Reel and lowe arna
ayont, but intil the stane.

Reel's the fey thing
that cam faur ben.

Lowe's the hert o the
gleeds o the gledness.


VI
Nae clint or climpet's a
kirk-o-comthankfu.

Ootby the frichtsome
bides aye ootby.

Gledness i the clints
is a clinty gledness,

haary the haaf
or bausont wi bew.

VII
The faur-oot thing and the fremit thing,
skerry skances it, skerry kens it.

Mibbi it blesses it,
for 'fremit' maks 'hame'.

(No that partial to
alluttermichty pooer.)


VIII
Whiles, in nicht o the warld
ye'se hear thae blae sea-thruchstanes
granin and gowlin lang and lang.

Scaurie shallmillens droont
i the eerie sea-onding:

thruchstanes didna ken
that they culd girn and grane.


IX
Whiles, a gret sklinter o scaur
breks aff and draps to the sea,

draps and fooners dumfoonert
doon through the freath and swaw.

Scaur-sklinter
and nae mair –

steid for strathspey
that strathspey fortravails.


X
But the warst thing is aye
when yir ain sel's fremit –

when ye're wud and ye're fey
but nae Brahan seer –

when ye're naethin mair nor a stane's mindin,
a haun streetched ower the fremit tides.

[*Les Rocs*]

## Eugenio Montale

BLOW AND COUNTERBLOW

1

'Arsenio' (she writes me), 'here I am "taking the air"
with my gloomy cypresses all round and thinking
the hour has come to suspend the very-long-
by-you-for-me-desired suspension
of every earthly illusion: it's time
to hoist the sails and to suspend
suspended time.

I know the clouds are louring, I know the turtle-doves
have taken their nervous wings to the south.
Living on memories is beyond me now.
I'd rather have the bite of ice than the numbness
of your sleepwalking, O tardy wakener.'

2

Hardly out of adolescence
I was flung for half my life
into the Augean stables.

No two thousand oxen there for me, not
once did I see an animal;
yet it was difficult to penetrate
the passageways silting up with manure,

panting for breath; it was human bellowings
that grew louder there day by day.

He was never to be seen.
The ragtag-and-bobtail waited, though,
for the present-arms: choked funnels,
pitchforks, spits, a stinking pile
of meat balls. But
not once did He hold out
corner of robe or point of crown
above the ebony, the excremental battlements.

And then year after year – who could keep count
of seasons in such darkness? – some hand
probing invisible vents
pushed its memento through: a curl
of Gerti's, a cricket in a cage, last sign
of Liuba's exile, the microfilm
of a euphuistic sonnet dropped
from Clizia's drowsy fingers,
a clack of clogs (the lame
maid from Monghidoro)
                              until from the cracks
the spray of a submachinegun drove us back,
worn-out navvies caught in the act
by the constables of the mud.

And finally the thud: the incredible.

To free us, to drown the net
of tunnels in a lake, took no time at all
for Alpheus, askew. Who expected it
now? What was the meaning of that new
swamp? and the breathing in of other, equal
stenches? and the whirlpooling round on rafts
of dung? and was that sun, that sickening
worm from the sewers laid on the chimney-pots;
and were these men perhaps,
real living men,
the huge ants on the wharves?
................................................................
                                        (I think

226

it may be you no longer read me. But now
you know all about me,
about my prison and my afterwards;
now you know no mouse grows
eaglewards.)

*[Botta e risposta]*

## William Shakespeare

### THE HELL'S-HANDSEL O LEDDY MACBETH

*[Macbeth's Castle. Enter Leddy Macbeth, with a letter Macbeth
has scrievit her.]*

L.M.
Aye, ye are Glamis, ye are Cawdor, and ae thing mair
ye sall be, ae thing mair. But och, I traistna
sic herts as yours: sic fouth o mense and cherity:
ower-guid for that undeemous breenge! Ye'd hae
the gloir, the gree, the tap-rung, but ye want
the malefice the tap-rung taks. Ye'd hae
the pooer, gin pooer cam by prayin; ye carena
for fause pley, but ye'd win whit's no won fair.
Yon thing ye'd hae, gret Glamis, that caas 'Dae this
to hae me, or hae nane' – and then yon thing
that ye mair fear nor hate to dae. Come ye,
come ye, I maun unfauld, maun speak, maun whup
wi this tongue's dauntonin aa thing that hinners
your progress to thon perfit circumgowdie
aa thae wanearthly warnishments and weird
shaw as your croon to be.

*[Enter a castle carle.]*

Ye bring me news?

C.C.
This nicht ye hae a guest – the king.

L.M.
                              Are ye wud?
Your maister's wi the king. I'm shair he kens
we maun mak preparations for the king?


C.C.
My leddy, it is true. Ye'll see erelang
oor laird hissel. The message cam fae him:
wan o his men run on aheid, tellt me it
aa pechin and forfochten.


L.M.
                              Tak tent o'm,
his news is guid. *[Exit castle carle.]* – Pechin? The gorbie itsel
micht hauch and rauch to tell me Duncan's come
like a deid man in-through my castle-waas.
Cwa sichtless cailleachs o the warks o daith,
transtreind my sex, drive into ilka sinnow
carl-cruelty allutterly, mak thrang my bluid,
sneck up aa yetts whaur peety micht walk furth,
that nae saft chappin o wemen's nature shak
my fey and fiendly thocht, nor slaw my steps
fae thocht to fack! Cwa to thir breists o mine
you murder-fidgin spreits, and turn their milk
to venim and to verjuice, fae your sheddows
waukrife ower erd's evil! Cwa starnless nicht,
rowed i the smeek and reek o daurkest hell,
that my ain eident knife gang blinly in,
and heaven keekna through the skuggy thack
to cry 'Haud back!'

                                                    *[Macbeth I.5.16-55]*

## Giacomo Leopardi

THE BROOM

*And men loved darkness rather than light* – John 3.19

Here on the barren spine
of the stupendous mountain,
that destructor, Vesuvius,
which takes joy from no other tree or flower,
you scatter tufts of loneliness around,
sweet-smelling broom,
patient in the wastelands. As indeed I saw you
where your stems added beauty to the solitude
of the dead tracts that brood
round Rome: that she was queen of cities once,
set in an empire gone,
your stalks with their grave silent presence seemed
to witness to the traveller, out of oblivion.
Now I see you again upon this ground,
lover of sad unpeopled places, unfailing
comforter of fortunes overthrown.
These fields that are strewn
with unbreeding ashes, sealed down with lava
turned hard as stone
and echoing to each visiting foot:
where the snake hides and wriggles, snug in the sun,
and where the rabbit returns
to its well-trodden warren underground:
the plough, and villas, and laughter
were here once, and the yellowing grain, and music
of the deep lowing herds;
and gardens and great mansions,
retreats, establishments
for stately leisure; and those famous cities
which the insolent mountain from its mouth of fire
roared down on, struck like lightning, crushed
with all their people. Now one desolation
transfixes everything,
and in it you sit, gentle flower, as if
commiserating others' griefs, and send
upwards a breath so very dearly sweet

it must console the desert wastes. These slopes
should be seen by any man who loves to praise
and exalt our human state: let him see here
how much of human kind
stands in the care of loving nature. Here also
he can exactly find
the measure of man's living power, a force
in instant jeopardy to his hard nurse,
the earth that with the lightest tremor cancels
a part of it, and with
others hardly less light can suddenly always
annihilate it all.
These are excellent slopes
for viewing the human soul
with its 'grand destinies and progressive hopes'.

Here, here see your face,
century of empty pride,
abandoner of the path
renascence thought marked forward to our days,
turning your steps into the past again,
giving the retreat your praise,
calling your failure advance!
Your prattling voice has drawn the brilliant, born
under your bad star, to flatter you
as father, though they mock
you sometimes as they talk
behind your back. But I
shall not go down to the grave with shame like theirs;
I hope I can still release the scorn that flares
for you in my heart, and try
to make it felt – or some of it, although
I know how history
crowds out those who over-offend their age.
Well, that is an evil
I must share with you; I have laughed at it before.
Liberty is your great dream, yet you'd make thought
an era's slave again –
thought, which was our only
tentative step out of chaos, which alone
moves us to culture and manners, best, sole
guide of our general fate!

It seems that the lot of men
was harsh, the truth displeased you, the narrow place
which nature gave us. Therefore you miserably
turned your back upon the light that made
it clear: and you run from that light, calling
its followers cowards, and only
those who are foolish or clever
in mocking themselves or others and can extol
the human condition above the stars have 'soul'!

A man who lives poor and in poor health
yet is well-thinking and generous of spirit
will call and count himself
neither wealthy nor hardy,
nor does he put on a ridiculous show
of setting up as beau
or being a prince of men,
but rather lets his state appear, not shamed
by penury of strength or savings, speaks
openly of what he is, rates what he has
at its unflattered price.
And so the higher flights
of faith in the greatness of man I decline as witless:
a creature born to perish, schooled by hardships,
saying 'I was made for happiness',
filling volume on volume
with the stench of his boasting, his earthly promises
of new high destinies and pleasures known
neither on this globe nor in the whole of heaven –
and this to people whom
a wave of the disturbed sea,
a puff of malignant wind, a shift of the crust
destroys so thoroughly
that later ages wonder where they lie!
It is a noble nature
that ventures to look up
through mortal eyes upon
our common fate, and tell with a frank tongue
that hides no grain of truth
how frailties, evils, low estate are ours
by reason of being born:
one who reveals his strength

and greatness in suffering, refusing to add to
the angers and hates of his brothers
(worst harm of all within
our human miseries!) but rather transferring
the blame of grief from man and placing it
in the true seat of guilt, the mother of men
with the stepmother heart. She is the one
he calls his enemy! And since he believes
the brotherhood of men
to be, as indeed they are, united and set
against this enemy yet,
he takes all men to be confederates
among themselves, embraces
them all with a true love,
extends and expects a ready, meaningful help
as agonies and hazards strike and pass
in the common war of man. And to be armed
offensively against one's kind, to strew
a neighbour's path with spike
and block he sees as utter madness – like
a man hard pressed upon the battlefield
who at the crucial assault
forgets his enemies and begins a sharp
contest with his own friends,
spreading the panic of a whistling blade
that cuts its own troops down.
When thoughts like these are known
to ordinary folk, as once they were,
and when that terror which first
drew mortal men so close
in social links against unpitying nature
has been won back in part
by true recognition, then will justice, mercy,
fair and honourable dealing
in the dialogue of cities, find another root
than the presumptuous idle fables which
have had to prop the common probity
of men – if one can call
error a prop of what is bound to fall.

I often sit at night
upon these desolate slopes:

draped in the dark and solid fall of lava
they seem rippling still; and above the joyless
waste, in purest blue,
I watch the far-off flashing of the stars
whose fires are mirrored in
the sea, and the whole world is shimmering
with sparks that circle through the empty spaces.
And when I fix my eyes upon these lights,
mere points to human sight
yet truly so immense
that all this land and sea in fact is but
a point to them: to them
not only man but this globe
where man himself is nothing
is utterly unknown; and when I see
still farther off in boundless distances
what look like knots of stars
shining to us like mist, and think that to them
not only man, not only earth, but the whole
system of our stars infinite in number
and mass, together with our own gold sun,
is either unknown or must appear as they do
to the earth, a point, a node
of nebular light: how then do you appear
as I sit thinking there,
O seed of man? And recalling
your poor and worldly state which the mere soil
I press on testifies: and then again
your own belief that you crown
all things with mastery, finality,
and what a favourite tale you cherish still,
how the creators of the cosmic scene
came down onto this murky grain of sand
called earth, on your behalf, and often held
sweet talk with you: and when I see these myths
in their absurdity refurbished to insult
wise men even today, in an epoch
that seems ahead of all
in knowledge and in culture: what feeling then,
O luckless seed of man, what thought for you
knocks on my heart when all is said? Laughter?
Pity? Which comes first and which comes after?

A little apple drops down from its tree,
pulled to the natural earth
by simple ripeness in late autumn days,
and crushes at a single stroke, lays waste
and buries the trim colony
of ants whose homes were hollowed
out of that yielding clay
with such hard labour to them, their works and wealth
amassed with long exertions all that summer,
trials of diligence followed
by a provident folk: so also, plummeting down,
hurled from a thundering womb
up to the fathomless sky,
a night and ruin of rocks
and ash and pumice mingled
with boiling streams, or the vast
torrent of metals and molten
boulders and sizzling sand
falling along the hill-flank,
raging down unrepulsed
through the grass, smashed and convulsed
and covered over in a few moments of time
those cities which the sea
washed at the edge of the shore:
and now above the cities the goat browses,
and on the other slope
new cities rise, they stand upon the stool
of the entombed ones and the prostrate walls
the bitter mountain seems to tramp to dust.
Nature has no more care
or praise for human souls
than for the ants: and if she slaughters men
less terribly than them,
this is no great wonder,
for man's fecundity and ants' are worlds asunder.

Eighteen hundred years
and more have passed since those great populated
places vanished, crushed by the power of fire,
and still the peasant's fears,
as he watches his vines struggle in these fields
to nourish life on sterile cindery clods,

cause him to keep one eye
warily on the fatal peak
which never yet was moved to become gentle
but still sits awe-inspiring there, still threatens
destruction to him and his children and their
pitiful handful of possessions.
And often the wretched man
stretched on the rustic roof
of his home, lying there all night sleepless
in the wandering breeze, and time and again
jumping to his feet, gazes along the course
of the dreaded flux which waits to boil and pour
from unimpoverished cells
along that gritty crest and raise its glow
on Margellina and
the port of Naples, on Capri and its sand.
And if he sees it coming down, or if
he ever hears a gurgling ferment in
the depths of his garden well, he hurriedly
wakens his children, rouses his wife, and runs
with them, taking what things they can, far off
till looking back he sees
his nest and home, his field –
his tiny, only shield against starvation –
caught by the red-hot flood
which crackles as it comes and over these
victims settles, relentless, without appeal.
After long forgetfulness
extinct Pompeii returns to daylight like
a buried skeleton
brought out into the air
by worldly greed or pity; and the traveller,
paused in the empty forum,
looks through the stricken rows
of colonnades and gazes with intentness
up to the mass of the divided summit
with its smoking crater-ridge
still menacing the ruins scattered there.
And in the secrecy and horror of the dark
through vacant theatres,
through mutilated temples and through stark
shells of houses where bats hide their young,

235

the glow of the deadly lava
like terror wandering with a sinister
torch through empty palaces, runs on
and reddens in the shadows
of the distance and paints every place it meets.
So nature, unaware of man and eras
man calls ancient, unaware of links
from ancestors to sons,
stands always green, or rather sets her feet
on such a lengthy road
she seems to stand. Meanwhile kingdoms decay,
peoples and tongues die out: she does not see it:
and man presumes on his eternity.

And you, yielding broom,
decking these ravaged fields
with your sweet-smelling groves, you too
will soon go down before the cruel fires
of that great subterranean dominion:
they will return to their station
as before, their hungry hems will crawl
over your soft thickets. And you will bend
your innocent head with unreluctant nod
under that deadly load:
but not a head you bent till then in vain
with cowardly entreaty praying for
your future killer's grace: not lifted up
in frantic vanity towards the stars,
or over this wasteland where
your birth and growing-place
were yours not by your choice but that of fate:
but wiser and less weak,
so much less weak than man, since you could rate
your truly fragile race
with no self-won, no destined deathless state.

*[La Ginestra]*

TO HIMSELF

Now, and for ever, you may rest,
my worn-out heart. Dead is that last deception.
I had thought love would be enduring. It is dead.
I know that my hoping, and even
my wishing to be so dearly deceived, have fled.
Rest, and for ever. The strife
has throbbed through you, has throbbed. Nothing is worth
one tremor or one beat; the very earth
deserves no sigh. Life
has shrunk to dregs and rancour; the world is unclean.
Calm, calm. For this
is the last despair. What gift has fate brought man
but dying? Now, undo in your disdain
nature and the ugly force
that furtively shapes human ills, and the whole
infinite futility of the universe.

*[A se stesso]*


INFINITY

We are old friends, this lonely hill and I –
and this hedge too, shutting out from sight
so much of the horizon's farthest reach.
But here I sit and brood, and boundless are
the spaces spread beyond it, unearthlier
the silences, and deep, so deep the stillness:
I build these in my thought; build this brief truce
for the heart's fears. And when I hear the wind
moving and ruffling through these leaves, I set
its voice against that infinite thing, that silence:
and I look back over eternity,
and the dead seasons, and this season here
with its life, and the sound of life. And so my thought
drowns in the midst of this immensity;
I never foundered in a sea so sweet.

*[L'Infinito]*

## THE CALM AFTER THE STORM

I hear the end of the storm
as the birds strike up their song, and then the hen
ventures on the road again,
repeating its quiet note. See how the sky
breaks up, goes blue behind the western heights!
The countryside grows bright,
the stream shines clear across the valley floor.
Every heart rejoices, on every side
the day's work comes to life,
a hum is heard once more.
The workman looks out singing at his door,
and looks up, work in hand,
at the glistening sky; the women
come hurrying to be first to draw the water
left by the new sweet rain;
the fruit-seller passes by
as before, from lane to lane
crying his daily refrain.
See how the sun has come back, see how it smiles
on the roofs and the hills! Servants throw open
balconies and terraces and galleries; below,
bells are heard jingling on the far highway;
the carriage creaks as it resumes the miles
the traveller begins again to go.

It rejoices every heart.
And when is life so sweet
as now, or so complete?
When does man show such art
and love in the labour of his hands? –
picking up old threads, or searching for new strands?
When is he less conscious of his troubles?
Pleasure, born of suffering:
joy, empty: the fruit
of a terror that has passed, and passing, shaken
with fear of death the man
who once abhorred his life:
a long inquisition, frightening
people to shiver and sweat
speechless and cold and pale in impending strife

238

visibly gathered against us,
wind and cloud and lightning.

Charitable nature! These
are the gifts you have to give.
These are the happinesses
you offer mortal men. The end of pain
we take as happiness.
Pain you have scattered with both hands; sorrow
grows without effort; such pleasure as is born
at times by miracle, a prodigy cradled
in grief, becomes our greatest gain. O breed
of men eternally dear! happy indeed
if you have breathing-space
from pain: blessed all the more
if death should heal you of the pain you fear!

*[La quiete dopo la tempesta]*


VILLAGE SATURDAY

Now as the sun goes down the young girl comes
home from the fields, with grass
in a bundle and carrying in her hand
a rose and violet nosegay for her dress
and hair tomorrow, to face
tomorrow's holiday
with a festive beauty, as the custom is.
The worn old woman sits
with neighbours on the stair, sits spinning, glancing
out where the day's last light is disappearing,
recalling stories of the good old times
when she too would put on her holiday best
and would be dancing, dancing
the whole night through, in her supple days of youth,
in the midst of the lads who found her – then! – entrancing.
Already the air grows dark,
a clear deep blue the sky, and shadows slipping
already from hills and roofs
that whiten underneath a young moon's arc.

Now a sharp peal of bells,
and the festive day is signalled;
the sound comes over like
a reassurance of the heart.
The children with their cries
as they crowd the tiny square
jumping here, running there,
turn joy into a sound:
while the farm worker with his hoe returns,
whistling, to his meagre meal,
and thinks how his one day of rest comes round.

Then, when all the surrounding lights are out,
with silence round about,
you hear the tapping hammer, hear the saw
of the joiner still awake
behind the shutters of his shop, working
furiously by lanternlight
to finish his job before the brightening dawn.

Of all the seven, this day is most favoured –
filled with a happy hope:
tomorrow's hours will stop
on sadness, disenchantment, the return
of every mind to its familiar labours.
Lad's life of joy! Your
manhood buds full.
How like a day it is, swelled tight with gladness,
a pure day in its brightness
unfolding to your earthly festival!
Be happy, boy; such moments are like grace,
their state is sweet. From me
no further words; but may you never see
your long-sought festal day with different face.

*[Il sabato del villaggio]*

## HOLIDAY EVENING

The night is windless – windlessly soft and clear;
the moon pauses gently on the rooftops,
hovers by the orchards, lights each far-off mountain
in a picture of calm. Already, oh my dearest,
the walks have all gone silent, and the darkness
gathers about the winking balconies
where a few lamps appear: you are asleep,
folded in natural rest in your still rooms;
no cares assail you: and least of all the knowledge
or guess that you have pierced me to the heart.
You are asleep: I face this sky, which seems
a blessing to men's sight, and I salute it,
and salute nature, that old omnipotence
which shaped me for affliction. (Hope? said nature:
hope I deny you; as for a shining eye –
only the tears you shed will shine in yours.)
This day was a holiday: but all its amusements
you have ended with sleep, remembering perhaps
in your dreams how many took to you today,
how many you took to: it is not my name
(I dare not hope) that comes to your mind. So here
I ask what life I can look for, and on this ground
I throw myself; shudder; call out. Such days of horror
in years of youth! And oh, when my ear catches,
quite near, the workman's late and lonely song
along the road at night, as he goes home
from pleasures of the day to his poor retreat:
how desperately my heart is seized by thoughts
of everything earthly slipping through as if
it left no track to trace! Here is this day,
this holiday, that has fled, hungrily followed
by common and unfestive days; time comes
hurrying every human act into the wings.
Where today is the clamour of ancient throats?
Where today are our great forefathers crying,
and the vast power and arms and roar of Rome
that covered land and sea? There is nothing now
but peace and silence; the world rests its case,
our passions are not roused by them, they have gone.
When I was very young, and holidays

241

were ardently looked forward to, the great day
came and went, and left me wretched, wakeful,
pressing my pillow; and at the dead of night
a voice that rose up from the streets, singing
and dying little by little into the distance,
seized my heart fiercely, as it seizes still.

*[La sera del dì di festa]*


THE SOLITARY LIFE

The morning rain! – while the young cooped-up hen
hops about its prison, flapping its wings,
and the countryman comes to his balcony
and looks out, and the rising sun shoots
quivering rays among the shower-drops as they
fall: and softly pattering upon
my cabin roof, rain is the sound I wake to;
I get up, and I bless the light thin clouds
and the first twitter of birds and the breathing
air and the smiling face of the hills:
for I have seen and known you, oh too much,
black city walls where pain and hatred follow
hatred and pain; and in unhappiness
I live, and so will die, soon, soon! Nature
perhaps shows some faint pity still to me
in this place, but how different it was once,
how good, how long ago! For you too turn
your face from misery; you too, despising
our disasters, our anxieties, O nature,
kneel at the throne of happiness. No sky,
no earth yields luckless man a single friend
or leaves him an escape except cold steel.

I sit sometimes in a lonely place,
on rising ground, at the edge of a lake
ringed with majestic soundless trees. And there,
when midday rolls across the sky, the sun
mirrors its painted and unmoving image,
and no wind shakes a grass-blade or a leaf,

242

and no wave ripples, and no grasshopper
chirps, not a flutter on the branches
or even whir of butterfly – no sound,
no stir I hear or see in all this place.
These banks enclose a flawless stillness, and
to me as I sit motionless there the world
and I myself seem fading into oblivion,
already I see my limbs dissolved, no movement
or soul or feeling left, their ancient stillness
diffused in those pervasive silences.

Love, love, you have flown off so far
from my heart: it once was warm for you,
not warm but ardent. With its cold hand
misfortune seized it, it is turned to ice
in the flower of my years. My breast remembers
the day you entered it. It was that dear,
that unrecapturable time when youth
looks out at the unfolding scene of this
unlucky world and that world wears a smile
like paradise. The young lad's virgin heart,
his purest hope and longing beat and leap
within his breast; already the poor clay
girds itself to meet the work of living
as if life was a dance, a game – But I,
O love, had hardly known you when my life
was crushed by fate: even then; and then these eyes
were fitted only for a haunt of tears.
Yet there are times upon the bright hill-slopes,
at silent daybreak and when the sunlight
pours down the roofs and the low hills and the fields,
and I catch sight of a young girl's sweet face;
or there will come a summer night made still
with peace, when I have sauntered on, and paused
among the country houses, watching wide
over the lonely land, and hear a girl
weave her fine thread of song as she works on,
adding the night to day, in empty rooms;
and then I feel this stony heart of mine
begin to tremble: but oh, it soon returns
to its old iron sleep, for every pulse
of gentle hope is exiled from my breast.

Dear moon, dear spell of moonlight, the hares
dance in the spellbound woods; at dawn the hunter
curses what he finds, tracks crossed and tangled
to lead him astray, and he is led astray
and misses all their lairs: I welcome you,
night queen, good queen. Unwelcome to some:
when your beam lights up crags and thickets, or falls
through ruined buildings on the white-faced brigand's
knife-blade, where he cocks an ear for the telltale
rumble of wheels far off, or horses' hoofs
or tramp of footsteps on the silent road:
ready without warning and with startling clash
of steel and with his hideous voice
and grisly churchyard looks to freeze the blood
of the traveller and to leave him lying soon
stripped and half-dead on the rocks. Unwelcome too
in city streets: when your white gleam embraces
the lecherous adventurer as he drifts
sidling by the house-walls, clings to shadows,
stops in the darkness, goes in fear of every
streaming open balcony and the blazing
of the lamps. Unwelcome to black-minded souls –
but oh to me your face is always kind
and always will be, over those slopes you light
before my eyes, those happy hills and fields
you open and unfold. And yet I once attacked
your beams and beauty – innocent as I was –
when they brought light to thronged and busy places
uncovering my face to curious looks,
uncovering others' faces to my own.
But now I can only praise that light, whether
I watch you sailing the clouds, or looking down
in tranquil dominance from your starry plains
upon this home of man so fit for tears.
You will see me many times, silent, alone,
wandering by the woods and the green banks
or sitting on the grass, happy enough
if I have heart and spirit left to sigh.

*[La vita solitaria]*

244

## Anglo-Saxon Poems

THE RUIN

Wonder holds these walls. Under destiny destruction
splits castles apart. Gigantic battlements are crumbling,
roofs sunk in ruin, riven towers fallen,
gates and turrets lost, hoarfrost for mortar,
rain-bastions beaten, cleft, pierced, perished,
eaten away by time. Earth's fist and grasp
holds mason and man, all decayed, departed.
The soil grips hard. There a hundred generations
of the people have dwindled and gone. This wall bore well,
moss-grey and reddened, the revolutions of kingdoms,
stoutly withstood tempests. That great gate fell...
Magnificent rose the fortresses, the lavish swimming-halls,
the profuse and lofty glory of spires, the clangour of armies,
the drinking-halls crammed with every man's delight,
till that was overturned by steadfast fate.
The broad walls were sundered, the plague-days came,
the brave men were rapt away by the bereaver,
their war-ramparts razed to desolate foundations,
their city crumbled down. The restorers lie asleep,
armies of men in the earth. And so those halls are wastes,
the old purple stone and the tiles and wood are lying
scattered with the smashed roofs. Death crushed that place,
struck it flat to the hill, where once many a man
brilliant with gold and adazzle with costliest war-trappings,
happy, proud, and wine-flushed, glittered there in his battle-
    armour,
gazed over his treasures, on the silver and the curious stones,
on the rich goods and possessions, on the preciously cut jewels,
and on this splendid city of the far-spread kingdom.
The stone courts stood then, the hot stream broke
welling strongly through the stone, all was close and sweet
in the bright bosom of the walls, and where the baths lay
hot at the heart of the place, that was the best of all...

*[Wraetlic is thes wealstan...]*

245

## THE SEAFARER

This verse is my voice, it is no fable,
I tell of my travelling, how in hardship
I have often suffered laborious days,
endured in my breast the bitterest cares,
explored on shipboard sorrow's abodes,
the welter and terror of the waves. There
the grim night-vigil has often found me
at the prow of the boat when gripped by the cold
it cuts and noses along the cliffs.
There my feet were fettered by frost,
with chains of zero, and the cares were whistling
keen about my heart, and hunger within me
had torn my sea-dazed mind apart.
The theme is strange to the happy man
whose life on earth exults and flourishes,
how I lived out a winter of wretchedness
wandering exiled on the ice-cold sea,
bereft of my friends, harnessed in frost,
when the hail flew in showers down.
There I heard only the ocean roar,
the cold foam, or the song of the swan.
The gannet's call was all my pleasure,
curlew's music for laughter of men,
cries of a seagull for relish of mead.
There tempests struck the cliffs of rock,
and the frozen-feathered tern called back,
and often the eagle with glistening wings
screamed through the spindrift: ah what prince
could shield or comfort the heart in its need!
For he who possesses the pleasures of life
and knows scant sorrow behind town-walls
with his pride and his wine will hardly believe
how I have often had to endure
heartbreak over the paths of the sea.
Black squalls louring: snow from the north:
world-crust rime-sealed: hail descending,
coldest of harvests –
                              Yet now the thoughts
of my heart are beating to urge me on
to the salt wave-swell and tides of the deep.

Again and again the mind's desire
summons me outward far from here
to visit the shores of nations unknown.
There is no man on earth so noble of mind,
so generous in his giving or so bound to his lord
that he will cease to know the sorrow of sea-going,
the voyages which the Lord has laid upon him.
He has no heart for the harp, or the gift of rings,
or the delight of women, or the joy of the world,
or for any other thing than the rolling of the waves:
he who goes on the sea longs after it for ever.

When groves bloom and castles are bright,
when meadows are smiling and the earth dances,
all these are voices for the eager mind,
telling such hearts to set out again
voyaging far over the ocean-stream.
With its sad call too the cuckoo beckons,
the guardian of summer singing of sorrow
sharp in the breast. Of this the prosperous
man knows nothing, what some must endure
on tracks of exile, travellers, far-rangers.
And now my own mind is restless within me,
my thought I send out through all the world
to the floods of ocean and the whale's kingdom,
until it comes back yearning to me
unfed, unquenched; the lone flier cries,
urges my desire to the whale's way
forward irresistibly on the breast of the sea.

And keener therefore when they strike my heart
are the joys of the Lord than this mortality
and loan of life; it is not my faith
that the riches of the earth will be everlasting.
One of three things to every man
must always loom over his appointed day:
sickness, old age, or enemy's sword
shall drive out life from the doomed man departing.
And then it is best that those who come after
and speak of the dead should be able to praise him,
that he in this world before his end
should help the people with deeds of courage

against the malice of foes and the devil,
so that afterwards the children of men
will exalt his name, and his praise with angels
will remain for ever, everliving glory,
bliss among the hosts. Great days have gone,
pomp and magnificence from the world's dominions.
Now there are neither kings nor emperors
nor gold-givers such as once there were
when in their realms they dealt with the utmost
honour, and lived in the nobility of fame.
Fallen is all this chivalry, their joys have departed.
And the world is wielded by shadows of men
ruling under affliction. Oh glory brought low,
splendour of this earth grown withered and old
like man himself now through all the world!
See age come up to him, and his face go pale,
a grey head in grief recalling friends gone,
the children of men given back to the earth.
Nor can body of flesh when life has fled
taste for him any sweetness or be sensible of sorrow,
nor will hand have touch, nor the mind its thought.
And though he should strew the grave with gold
where his own brother lies, with numberless treasures
in a double burial, none will go with him
on that voyage, nor can gold avail
for the soul with its sin before God's wrath
who hoards it here while he still has breath.

Dreadful is the terror of the Creator, when the world has turned
  through time.
He established the great abyss, the leagues of the earth and the
  sky.
The fool has no fear of the Lord: death falls on him unwarned.
The blessed man lives in humility: on him heaven's mercies
  descend:
he trusts the power of his Maker in the battlements of his mind.

*[Maeg ic be me sylfum . . .]*

## THE WANDERER

The solitary man lives still in hope
of his Maker's mercy, though with anxious mind
over the ocean-roads he has long to go,
rowing in his boat on the rime-cold sea,
voyaging out his exile while fate is fulfilled.

The words of the wanderer recalling hardships,
savage encounters, falling of kinsmen:
'In the doom of loneliness dawn after dawn
I lament my cares; there is none now alive
to whom I might dare reveal in their clearness
the thoughts of my heart. It is true I know
that the custom shows most excellent in a man
to lock and bind up all his mind,
his thought his treasure, let him think what he will.
Nor can the wearied work against fate,
nor painful remembrance have present aid;
those after glory must often hide
a dark thought deep in their mind.
So I in my grief gone from my homeland
far from my kinsmen have often to fetter
the images of the heart in iron chains,
for now it is long since the night of the earth
lay over my lord and I then forlorn
wintered with sorrow on freezing seas,
seeking in sadness some gold-giver's dwelling,
if only I could find whether far or near
one to show favour to me in the mead-hall,
one to give solace to me friendless,
to treat me with kindness. He who has felt it
knows how care is a cruel companion
to the man deprived of his dear protectors:
wandering is his, not winding gold,
a breast of grieving, not world's glory.
He remembers the retainers at the giving of treasures,
and how he in his youth was feasted and pleasured
by his friend and lord; that joy quite gone!
This is his suffering who has so long missed
the counselling voice of his cherished prince,
when sorrow and daydream often together

seize the unhappy man in his solitude:
it all comes back, he embraces and kisses
the lord he is loyal to, lays on his knee
hands and head as he did long ago
when he knew the triumphs and treasures of the throne.
Then the unfriended man wakens again,
watches in front of him waves of grey,
sea-birds swimming and flashing their wings,
snow falling, hoarfrost thickened with hail.
Then the heart's wounds are the more harrowing,
graver is his longing for that loved man.
Grief is revived when the vision of kinsmen
gathers in his mind and he greets them with joy
and eagerly searches the dear faces;
but fighters and retainers float off and dissolve,
and the mind receives from these seafarers
scant song of speech; care comes again
to him who must send his ceaseless heart
in its weariness over the frozen waves.

There is no cause indeed in all the world
why my thoughts here should not grow dark,
when I ruminate the life of noble men,
how they suddenly left the halls in death,
warriors in their pride. And so this earth
from day to day declines and decays,
nor is any man wise before his due
of worldly years. Wisdom is patience:
to be neither too temperless nor too sharp of tongue,
nor too feeble in fight nor too heart-heedless,
nor too deep in fear, in pride or in greed,
nor ever too boastful of things unknown.
A man should be wary in uttering his vows
till he stands proud in sure knowledge
of where thought and mind are ready to bend.
The wise man perceives how terrible is the time
when all the wealth of the world lies waste,
as now scattered throughout this earth
walls are standing where winds howl round
and hoarfrost hangs, in crumbling courts.
Wine-halls are sinking, kings are at rest
bereft of joy, all the flower of men

has fallen by those walls. War took some,
bore them from the world; one the winged ship
drove over the deep; one the grey wolf
gave to death; and one sad-faced
a man buried in a cave of the earth.
So the Maker of men laid waste this globe,
till those old cities, the labour of titans,
stood in their desolation silent after revelry.

He then who ponders wisely in his mind
and goes over this life in its darkness and its origins
with insight of heart recalls the carnage
of far-off myriads and speaks these words:
"Where has the horse gone? the rider? the treasure-giver?
the halls of feasting? Where are man's joys?
The dazzling goblets! The dazzling warriors!
The splendour of the prince! Ah, how that time
has gone, has darkened under the shadow of night
as if it had never been! Now in the place
of that beloved chivalry a wall is standing
marvellous in height, sculptured with serpents.
The men have been seized by the strength of spears,
by death-hungry weapons, illustrious destiny,
while tempests beat on this steep stone,
the blizzard falling binds the ground,
the terror of winter roaring in darkness
when the night-storm blackens and sends from the north
fierce hail-showers in malice to men.
All the kingdom of the world is in labour,
earth under heaven revolves through its cycle.
Here riches will pass, here friends will pass,
here man will pass, here woman will pass,
and the whole foundation come to dissolution."'

So spoke the wise man in his mind, sitting in meditation by himself.
Good is the man who holds faith: he must never too readily tell
the grief he has in his heart, unless he has solace before him
in the daring a man may win. Blessed is he who implores
his grace and comfort from heaven, where the dooms of us all
    are shored.

*[Oft him anhaga . . .]*

SEVEN RIDDLES

1

A meal of words made by a moth
seemed to me when I heard the tale
curious and phenomenal:
that such a mite like a thief in the night
should swallow up the song of a poet,
the splendid discourse and its solid setting!
But the strange robber was none the wiser
for all those words and all that eating.

[*Moththe word fraet . . .*]


2

My garment sweeps the world in silence,
whether indoors or troubling the waters.
Watch me taken over human houses
by my armour-trappings and by soaring airs:
see how the power of the clouds carries me
far and wide above men. My adornments
loudly and melodiously sound and resound,
sing bright and clear, when I rise from my rest,
a spirit moving over field and flood.

[*Hraegl min swigath . . .*]


3

Here is my head beaten with a hammer,
cut with sharp tools, carved by a file.
Often I swallow what stands before me,
when I thrust hard, clashing in my rings
against a hard object; pierced from behind
I have to push forward the thing that keeps
the delight of my master's mind at midnight.
Sometimes again I retract my nose,
guardian of treasure, when my master's aim
is to take the spoils of those he has had killed
by avenging force with wishes of blood.

[*Min heafod is . . .*]

4

I am not loud; where I live's not silent.
The Lord laid down our course of life
inseparable. I am swifter than he is,
I am stronger sometimes, but he persists more steadily.
At times I rest; he runs on always.
I dwell in him every day I live.
Divide us and you doom me to death.

*[Nis min sele swige . . .]*


5

Sometimes my master miserably binds me,
sends me under the vast swell
of the flourishing fields and forces me to be still,
drives down my strength supine into darkness,
furiously into a den where the earth presses
crouching on my back. From that monstrous place
no way of turning I know but to trouble
and stir the home of man: Heorots
rock, dwelling-houses, walls tremble
terrible above hall-counsellors. Tranquil they seem,
sky over landscape, sea in its silence
till I drive upward, rise from my prison,
in the hand of him who guides me, who gave me
in the beginning my bonds and fetters, bound me
never to bend but the way he beckons!

Sometimes from above I shake the waves,
wreathe the ocean-stream, throw to the shore
the flint-grey flood: foam's in the fight
of wave against sea-wall: mountainous above the main
it looms in darkness, and black on its track
its neighbour travels in the water-tumult
till they clash breaking at the brink of land,
at the soaring bluffs. There the ship seethes
through the sailors' clamour, the steep rock-falls
quietly stand for the sea's assailing,
for the crash in the stone-split when crested mass
crowds to crush cliffs. There over the boat
a hard strife hangs if the sea should seize it

253

with its freight of souls in fearful hour,
torn if it should be from course and command
riding foam-white with its life outfought
on the back of the waves. Unblest, awesome,
manifest to men, each terror I unwrap
adamant in my wayfaring, and for whom will it be still?

Sometimes I career through what clings to my back,
the black wave-pourers, press far apart
the sea-feeding cloud-brims and suddenly let them
slap again together: it is the king of sounds
bursting above cities, boldest of crashes
when cloud on cloud edge to edge
cracks dark and sharp. Creatures of blackness
scurrying in the sky shower down fire,
fire-pallor, fire-flare, with tremors roll on
dull, din-resonant above the distraught,
all battle forward, letting fall
rustling from their breast wet mist and gloom,
rain from their womb. The dreaded army
advances in its feud, fear arises,
a great anxiousness among mankind,
all places are appalled, when the quicksilver phantom
shoots in flashes with his sharpest weapons.
The fool fears nothing of those mortal spears,
but the fool lies dead if the living God
lets an arrow fly to him from the far whirlwind
right to his heart, through the falling rain
a falling bolt. Few remain
whom lightning pins at weapon's point.

I establish that strife in its origins
when I go out among the cloud-congress
forcing through its press with my vast host
on the bosom of the stream – the lofty war-throng
breaks into great sound. Then again I bow
low down to land in the hollow of the air
and load on my back what I have to bear,
admonished in the majesty of my own master.
So I act and battle, a servant but glorious,
now beneath the earth, now beneath the waves
sunk in humility, now over the main

rousing the ocean-streams, now risen up
flinging the sky-wrack far and wide
in my vigour and race. Say what is my name,
or who shall raise me when I cannot rest,
or who shall support me when I must be still.

*[Hwilum mec min frea . . . ]*


6

I caught sight of a wonderful creature,
an air-vessel, luminous, elegantly adorned,
bringing booty held in her horns,
bringing booty home from the foray.
She wanted a bower to be built in the fortress,
a snug retreat, if so it might be.
A wonderful creature topped the crag then,
a creature known to every country,
seized the booty and sent the wanderer
unwilling home – she slid back west
vowing vengeance, and soon vanished.
Dust rose skyward, dew fell on earth,
night took its way. No man afterwards
could guess the course of the creature's journey.

*[Ic wiht geseah . . . ]*


7

A strange being slipped along the waves,
lovely on shipboard, shouted to land,
loud and resounding. Hair-crawling laughter
made earth shiver. Edges were sharp.
A cruel creature, grudging engagement
but grim in encounter, it savaged, ravaged
the stove-in ship, bound bad spells round it,
spoke with cunning on its own creation:
'My mother is of dearest maiden kin,
she is my daughter fully developed
and brought to greatness as all men believe,
all living folk, she will walk in delight
through fields of every earthly land.'

*[Wiht cwom aefter wege . . . ]*

# Friedrich Hölderlin

THE RHINE

In the shadowy ivy I sat, at the entrance
to the forest, just as the golden noon
came down to visit the source
from rocky steps of the Alps
which to me are a heavenly fortress
raised into place by gods, as old
opinion has it, but where still
there's many a secret resolution born
that touches man; and there
I sensed, without expecting it,
a destiny, for in those warm shadows
I had only set my soul
roving through many matters
of thought and on to Italy
and Morea's far distant coasts.

But now I heard, from the mountains,
far down from the silver peaks,
down under the glad green
where woods shudder over him
and the tops of overlapping rocks
look down at him, there,
day after day, in the coldest abyss,
the youth's lament and cry
to be released, and others heard,
his parents who gave him life, Earth-Mother and
Thunderer, they pitied him
even as he blustered and blamed them, but
the place was shunned by mortal men,
for it was terrible to hear
the demigod raging there
as he rolled in the dark of his chains.

This was the voice of the noblest of rivers,
of the free-born Rhine,
he had hoped for other things, up there with his brothers
Ticino and Rhône, when he left them

for a wandering life and his imperious
impatient spirit drove him towards Asia.
But when did destiny
bow to a wish?
Yet none so blind
as the sons of gods. For man and the beasts
know where they must build
their homes, but to those raw souls
the flaw has been given of never
knowing where they must go.

Immaculate births are riddles. Even
song can scarcely illuminate them. For
as you began so you will be,
whatever the exigencies, the training
accomplish, it is birth
that counts for most,
and the ray of light
reaching the newly born.
But where is there anyone
left so free
his whole life long to carry out
his very heart's desire, so
happily born from benevolent heights
as the Rhine, from such
a holy womb as his?

And so his word's a shout of joy.
He won't, as other children will,
whimper in his swaddling-bands;
for where the banks begin
to creep to his side and snake about him,
thirsting to wind him around
in his careless boyhood, eager
to train him and to defend him well
with their own teeth, he laughs,
tears through the snakes, shoots off
with what he has won, and if a greater force
fails soon to tame him, and
he grows and grows, he'll come like lightning
to split earth open, and the woods fly after him
like things bewitched, and the mountains sinking in shoals.

But a god wants to keep for his sons
this rushing life, and smiles when rivers,
chafing wildly at the curbs
of the holy Alps, angrily
miscall him from the depths.
For it is on such forges
every pure thing is hammered out,
and it is beautiful
how coming down from these mountains
and turning quietly through German earth
he seems at peace and his yearnings are ended
in good works, the rich land is his –
Father Rhine, nourishing well-loved children
in cities he has founded.

Still, he never forgets it; never.
For the house shall vanish
and the statues crack and the day
of men be warped awry
before his kind will forget its beginnings
and the pure voice of its youth.
Who was the first to distort
the bonds of love
and knot them into snares?
Then obdurate men, assured
of the fire of heaven, deriding
their own right, despising thus
their mortal paths, and choosing
presumption as their end,
strained to exalt themselves to the height of the gods.

But the gods have their own
undying life; and Heaven, if it needs anything,
needs heroes, needs
humanity, needs
all things mortal. For
spirits of Heaven can in themselves feel nothing,
and therefore someone else (if I may say this)
must surely feel, show sympathy
for the sake of the gods
who need him; and yet their decree
is that a man shall smash his house and

bury his own father and child under the ruins
if he should aim to be like them
and kick like a fanatic
against the pricks of inequality.

He therefore is the luckiest man
who has found a fitting destiny
where recollections of wanderings
and of sorrows recalled not in sorrow
still roars up on a solid shore,
and he can gladly gaze,
there and far off, at the bounds
which God has marked out for him
in his stay, from the day of his birth
He then is at peace, blessed by
a modest spirit, for all he desired –
which is Heaven – has now come of itself
to embrace him for his boldness,
smiling without compulsion upon his calm.

Demigods besiege my thoughts now
and I must seek them out, dear as they are,
for their lives so often stir
my heart in its longing.
But what can I call him, the stranger
like you, Rousseau, who with a soul
unconquerable, strong to
endure, a firm understanding,
a sweet talent for listening,
and for talking in such a way
that he gave out the speech of the purest
like the wine-god, from a divine abundance,
mad, heavenly, lawless, and
intelligible to the good, but rightly
struck the irreverent, the wretched blasphemers, blind?

The sons of the earth, like their mother, are
all-loving, and therefore these happy ones
receive, without labour, everything.
And this is what startles man in his mortality,
shocks him when he thinks of the heaven
and the weight of joy which his own

welcoming hands have amassed
on his shoulders; often then
what seems best to him is to be
all but all-forgotten, there where the ray
cannot burn, in forest shade,
beside the lake of Bienne and its fresh green,
and out of a reckless poverty of song
to learn like beginners from nightingales.

And wonderful it is then to rise
from holy sleep, to stir
in forest coolness, now at dusk
to wander towards the softer light
when he who built up the mountains
and mapped out the path of the rivers
after he had also guided,
smiling, the striving life
of men, those poor few breaths,
like sails with his winds,
is himself at rest,
and day the imagemaker
seeing more good than evil
bows to his pupil, the earth.

– Then gods and men celebrate their union,
it is a celebration for all the living,
and at that moment
fate moves on even terms.
And the fugitives look for shelter
and the heroes for sweet sleep
but the lovers
are what they were; they are
at home, where the flower rejoices
in its innocent fervour and the spirit
sighs round the dark trees; but
the unreconciled are utterly changed, contending
to be first in holding out a hand,
before the friendly light
goes under and the night comes on.

Yet to one all this
will pass in a flash, to another

remain longer.
The eternal gods are
filled, always, with life; but still
a man can guard the best
in his memory, even till death,
and then he is a witness of the supreme.
Only, each has his limits.
For it is tough to bear
bad times, but good times – tougher.
But one wise man in Plato
was able from midday to midnight
and right to the glimmer of dawn
to keep a clear head at the banquet.

Sinclair my friend! God may appear to you
on the sultry path under fir-trees or
in a dark oak-wood sheathed with steel or
in clouds, you know him, since you know in your youth
the strength of his goodness, and his glorious smile
is never locked from you
either by day when
the living world seems fevered in its fetters or
by night when everything
swims in formlessness and primordial
chaos has come again.

*[Der Rhein]*

**Federico García Lorca**

MURDER

*(Two Voices at Dawn in Riverside Drive, New York)*

– How did it –?
– Scratch on the cheek,
that's all. Claw
pouncing on a green
shoot. Pin plunging
to meet the roots of the scream.
And the sea stops moving.
– But how – how?
– Like this.
– Get away from me! That way?
– Sure. The heart
went out alone.
– Oh no, oh god –

*[Asesinato]*

SLEEPLESS CITY

*(Brooklyn Bridge Nocturne)*

No one sleeps in the sky. No one, no one.
No one sleeps.
The moon's creatures prowl and sniff round their cabins.
Living iguanas arrive to gnaw the insomniacs
and the heartbroken man on the run will meet at streetcorners
the quiet incredible crocodile beneath the soft protest of the stars.

No one sleeps in the world. No one, no one.
No one sleeps.
There is a dead man in the farthest-off graveyard
who for three querulous years
has grumbled at the shrivelled landscape fixed to his knees;

and the boy they buried this morning cried so much
they had to call out dogs to give him his quietus.

Life is no dream. Watch out! Watch out! Watch out!
We fall downstairs to eat damp earth
or climb to the snowline with a dead dahlia chorus.
But there is no oblivion, no dream, only
living flesh. Kisses bind mouths
in a maze of fresh veins
and the one whose pain vexes him will be vexed without rest
and the one whom death terrifies will be bowed under it.

One day
horses will neigh in taverns
and rabid ants
will attack the yellow skies lurking in cows' eyes.

Another day
we shall see a resurrection of dissected butterflies
and then as we stroll through a sponge-grey boat-still scene
we shall see our rings flash and our tongues spill roses.

Watch out! Watch out! Watch out!
For those who still guard the claw-tracks and the cloudburst,
that boy weeping because the invention of the bridge is beyond him
or that dead man left with a head and a shoe,
they are all to be taken to the wall where iguanas and snakes are
        waiting,
where the bear's teeth are waiting,
where the mummied hand of the child is waiting
and the camel-skin bristles and shivers in raw blue fever.

No one sleeps in the sky. No one, no one.
No one sleeps.
But if any eye should shut –
lash him awake, boys, lash him!
Imagine a panorama of staring eyes
and bitter sores kept flaming.
No one sleeps in the world. No one, no one.
No one sleeps.
I say it here.

No one sleeps.
But if anyone should find a glut of night moss on his temples –
open the trapdoors and let the moon look down on
the sham wineglasses, the poison, and the skull of the theatres.

*[Ciudad sin sueño]*

## CASIDA OF WEEPING

My balcony I've drawn, I've shut it –
who could bear to hear this weeping?
And yet the grey walls cannot hide it –
there's no sound but the sound of weeping.

Singing angels are few, are few –
barking dogs are few, are few –
hundreds of violins in the shadow of a hand –

and yet the weeping is a vast dog,
and the weeping is angel and violin,
vast the angel and vast the violin,
the wind is choked with the crying, leaving
no sound but the sound of weeping.

*[Casida del llanto]*

## CASIDA OF THE ROSE

The rose's gaze
was not on the sunrise:
it lay on a timeless tree,
it gazed on another place.

The rose's gaze
was not on sign or on sense:
outpost of flesh and dream,
it gazed on another place.

The rose's gaze
was not upon the rose.
Still with all sky to seek
it gazed on another place.

*[Casida de la rosa]*

## CASIDA OF THE DARK DOVES

It was through the laurel boughs
I saw the two dark doves.
One dove was the sun
and the other was the moon.
'Where, little neighbours, where
is my tomb, is it there or here?'
'Tomb in my tail' (said the sun).
'Tomb in my throat' (said the moon).
And I, as I still travelled
with the living earth at my belt
saw the two eagles of snow
and a girl naked as day.
One eagle was the other
and the naked girl was neither.
'Where, little eagles, where
is my tomb, is it there or here?'
'Tomb in my tail' (said the sun).
'Tomb in my throat' (said the moon).
It was through the laurel boughs
I saw two naked doves.
One dove was the other
and the two doves were neither.

*[Casida de las palomas oscuras]*

## GACELA OF THE FLIGHT

Often and often I have lost myself in the sea.
My ears have been rich with fresh-cut flower-spray,
my tongue has been rich with love and agony.

265

Often and often I have lost myself in the sea
as easily as into the heart of a boy.

No one who gives a kiss can fail to feel
the smile that fills the race without a face;
no one who touches the newly born can fail
to recall the horse's dull and motionless skull.

The reason? The roses probe the forehead for
its under-contour of unyielding bone;
and man's hands find their labour and limit in
imitating those roots below the loam.

As easily as into the heart of a boy
often and often I have lost myself in the sea.
I am blind to the water, I go still on my way
in search of a doom of light that can only destroy.

*[Gacela de la huida]*


## GACELA OF THE BITTER ROOT

One root is bitter,
one world of a myriad windows.

Not even the littlest fist
shivers the door of the water.

Where – where – where are you gone?
One sky, myriads of terraces.
Myriads of bees, angry battles.
And one root, and that bitter:

bitter.

A pain for the sole of the foot,
a pain for the heart of the face.
And pain for the throbbing trunk
of night raw from the blade.

O Love, my enemy:
your root in my teeth is bitter!

*[Gacela de la raíz amarga]*


SONG OF THE LITTLE DEATH

Lawns of the leprous moons
and blood at the heart of the world.
Lawns of inveterate blood.

Light of days gone and to come.
Skies of the leprous grass.
Light and darkness of sand.

I found myself with death.
Lawns of the leprous earth.
A little thing was death.

The dog above in the eaves.
My left and lonely hand
crossed a great tableland
of flowers dry as leaves.

Cathedral made of ashes.
Light and darkness of sand.
A little death for man.

A death and I a man.
A man alone, and it
a little death, so little –

Lawns of the leprous moons.
The snow shudders and moans
on the far side of the door.

A man: what more? As before –
it, and that lonely man.
Lawns, love, light, and sand.

*[Canción de la muerte pequeña]*

267

**Luis Cernuda**


A GLASGOW CEMETERY

Walls with gaping railings, and behind them
black earth holding no grass and no trees,
only wooden benches where the old folk
sit in silence in the long afternoons.
All round are houses, shops are near,
children play through the streets. The trains pass
close by the side of the graves. The people are poor.

Rain has soaked the rags that hang in windows:
patches on the grey tenement face.
Blotted already are the In Memoriams
cut on these tombs two centuries ago
over the dead who have now no friends to forget them.
Huddled the dead are, hidden. Yet when the sun shines and June
    comes
even old buried bones must feel some June-day touch.

No leaf here, no bird. Stone only, and earth.
Hell is like this? – Pain without forgetfulness,
clamour and wretchedness, huge cold without hope.
No place for death to sleep in silence. It is always
life that among the very graves roves like a whore
plying her trade under the unstirring stars.

Dusk comes down out of a cloudy sky;
smoke from the factories floats off, lost
soon in grey dust; voices are heard from the pub;
then one passing train
shudders and echoes loud like a black trumpet-blast.

Not the last judgement yet: sleep, if you can,
sleep on, anonymous dead, in your long calm.
God too perhaps forgets you, not just man.

*[Cementerio de la ciudad]*

## Leonid Martynov

YOU MUST LIVE!

The threads break,
the joints give,
they lose their heart for work.
But the flower brazens it out in its vase:
'You must live!'
And the inches chirp in their yards:
'You must live!'
And the steam sighs in the machine:
'You must live!'
And the petrol coughs in the limousine:
'You must live!'
And the waves seethe in the sea:
'You must live!'

You must live!
And live, maybe,
a very long time...

And everything relentlessly
repeats the unbroken chime:
'You must live!'

*[Nado zhit'!]*


THE ETERNAL WAY

Tonight
the Milky Way is hanging
over the crater of an extinct volcano.
as if, high in its heaven, it was trying
to peer at the dumb mouth of this volcano.
But maybe the galaxy has been puffed out too
up from the crater of an extinct volcano,
its starry tail waving through the blue
up from the crater of an extinct volcano?
All things are possible. With your thoughts on fire

you're on the summit of an old volcano.
Maybe tomorrow it's a meteorite
I'll find on the steep sides of this volcano,
and maybe on some shoulder I'll unearth
no more than a volcanic bomb. I'd say
it's clear to no one anywhere on earth
what gulf his feet are stumbling round all day,
not knowing top or bottom of that drop,
and everything unsteady and uncanny...
It seems to me
that I myself am propped
over the crater of a silted-up volcano.

*[Vechny put']*


## THE SHEEPSKIN COAT

Perfumes –
coxcombs in striped hats –
saunter insolently through the village,
but in the lumber-room, what's that
in the dark corner, on its hind legs?

Not the sheepskin coat. Only its smell begs
there in the lumber-room, hiding in the dark,
still standing there on its hind legs
like a stuffed bear where the shadows are.

*[Tulup]*


## 'ALONG THE BEACH...'

Along the beach after the tempest
I hear the grinding of your stones.
Sea, sea, you are the greatest
abstract artist ever known.
I renegue from the controversy,
the debate has been scoured bare –
whatever you've depicted, sea,
on pebbles here or pebbles there.

*['Na poberezh'e...']*

FACT

Bulldozer,
selfloader,
snocat...

You'd think I put them all in paint
and sketched in every detail pat,
as if I'd a whole world to create,
and snatch the veils off when I want,
and cart off I say where and what

But what then did I not force out?

Ah yes, old ploughs the feather-grass beat,
the steppes the black tornado caught,
the desert acres, the hayloft
newly erected, empty and lost.

Visibly, the automobile rolled out,
bulldozer, selfloader, snocat,
and muffled everything in such dust,
weighed things down with a great weight.

That's how they fall into memory's net.

But you know, this too's reality and fact,
to make you less able to forget
bulldozer, selfloader, snocat!

*[Byl']*

'OUTSIDE...'

Outside,
like thunder clearing its throat,
the black sheepdog began barking.

It was stifling.
Somewhere on the second floor
they suddenly, heatedly started arguing.

271

Someone there set a side-question afloat.
Well, it all finished on a friendly note,
and lightning was indifferently scratching
the night, when thunder grumbling in its throat
slunk off, like the black sheepdog that was barking.

['Na dvore ...']

THE GREEN RAY

The clouds at last drifted away.
The whole sky was starry, rosy, till
I caught sight of the green ray.
You too – look hard. It's early still!

[Zeleny luch]

## Jacques Prévert

PROCESSION

A gold old codger with a watch in mourning
A working queen with a man of England
And toilers of peace with guardians of the sea
A hussar of the company with a black butt
A coffee-snake with a spectacle-mill
A rope-hunter with a head-dancer
A meerschaum field-marshal with a pipe in retreat
A babe in black with a gentleman in arms
A gallows-composer with a music-bird
A spiritual collector with a stub-director
A grinder of Coligny with an admiral of scissors
A Bengal sister with a St-Vincent-de-Paul tiger
A professor of porcelain with a patcher of philosophy

A superintendent of the Round Table with knights of the Paris
    Gas Company
A St Helena duck with Napoleon and oranges
A Samothrace keeper with a cemetery victory
A tug of a large family with a deep-sea father
A member of the prostate gland with a hypertrophy of the French
    Academy
A big horse *in partibus* with a great circus bishop
A conductor of the wooden cross with a little bus chorister
A *terrible* surgeon with a dental *enfant*
And the general of the oysters with a Jesuit-opener

*[Cortège]*

## Henri Michaux

YOU THOUGH

You though, when will you come?
One day, stretching out your hand
over my lease of living ground,
at the hour of harvest when despair is my truth;
in a thundering second of time,
plucking me with imperiousness and dread
from my own body and from the flaking body
of my thought-pictures and their ridiculous world;
sounding me with your unspeakable lead,
milling my metal with your daunting presence,
erecting in a flash above my incontinence
your straight and all-outsoaring cathedral;
shooting me not as a man
but as a shell in vertical flight,
YOU WILL COME,

You will come, if you exist,
taken by bait of my bungling;
by my hateful self-hegemony;

273

coming from space, from there or nowhere, from under my
    unhinged ego maybe;
flicking me as a match into your immensity,
and goodbye, Michaux.

If not, what then?
Never? No?
Well then, Jackpot, in whose lap would you fall?

*[Mais toi, quand viendras-tu?]*


HUGE VOICE

Huge voice
slorps and swallows

Huge voices slorp
and swallow and
slorp and swallow

I laugh, I laugh by myself up another
up another
up another sleeve

I laugh, I have the laughing shotgun
my gunshot body
I, I have, I am flung

somewhere else!
where else!
else!

What is a hole in the wall?
what is a rat after all?
a spider-fall?

I was a bad farmer and my father vanished from sight
No, don't bring me light
He vanished just like that

The word of command faded
No more voice. More choking at least
Renewed after twenty years.
But what is it I hear?

Huge voice that destroys our voice
Huge father regalvanized giant
from wretched or blind events

Huge house that covers our boughs
our joys
that covers cats and rats

Huge cross that damns our rafts
that undoes our souls
that scrapes our graves

Huge nothing voice
shroud voice
voice to crack our columns

Huge 'oughts' 'laws'
oughts oughts oughts
Huge hieratic starchpots.

Huge business
majestic in sham
chilling us

Were we born for grubbing the rocks?
Were we born with broken fingers to devote
a good life to a bad riddle?

to I don't know what for I don't know who
to an unknown who for an unknown what.
Always towards more cold

All right! here there is no singing
You won't get my voice, huge voice
You won't get my voice, huge voice.

You will do without it, huge voice
You too will move out and go,
– You will move out and go, huge voice.

[Immense voix]

## VOICES

I heard a voice in these black times and I heard: 'I shall break them, these men, I shall break them and already they are broken although they still fail to see it. I shall break them down into something so small it will no longer be possible to tell man from woman, and already they are hardly what they once were, but they think because their organs still know how to pierce each other that they remain different, the one this, the other that. But the suffering I shall give them will be so fierce that it will not matter any more what organs they have. I shall leave them only the skeleton, a trace of their skeleton to attach their misery to. Enough running! What good are legs to them anyhow? Small, their movements from place to place, small! And it will be so much better. A park statue has only one gesture whatever happens: I shall turn them into stone like that; but smaller, smaller.'

I heard that voice and I shivered, but not so much, for I admired its sombre dedication and its enormous though seemingly crazy programme. That voice was only one among a hundred voices which rang through the heights and depths of the atmosphere both East and West, and they were all aggressive, bad, malignant, promising man a future of graves and tears.

But man who is driven here to distraction and held there in coolest steadiness had reflexes and reckonings in hand for such a dire time, and he was ready, although in general he must have appeared on the contrary to be hunted and pithless.

A pebble trips him but he had been walking for two hundred thousand years when I heard the voices that in their menaces and hatred thought they could terrify him.

[Voix]

276

LANDSCAPES

Landscapes at peace or devastated.
Landscapes of the road of life rather than of the surface of the
    Earth.
Landscapes of Time trickling slowly, almost motionless and
    occasionally as if backwards.
Landscapes of rags, jagged nerves, *saudades*.
Landscapes to cover wounds, cold steel, gunbursts, evil, eras,
    hangmen, mobilization.
Landscapes to abolish cries.
Landscapes like pulling a sheet over your head.

*[Paysages]*


LABYRINTH

Labyrinth, life, labyrinth, death
Labyrinth without end (says the Master of Ho).

Everything harries, nothing frees.
Hara-kiri reborn, new pain.

Prison opens on prison
Passage opens another passage:

Thinking he rolls reels of life, man
Rolling only nothing.

Nothing issues anywhere
Centuries also subterranean (says the Master of Ho).

*[Labyrinthe]*


CARRY ME OFF

Carry me off in a caravel,
in a sweet and antique caravel,
in prow or foam as you may prefer,
but far off lose me, far off lose me.

277

In the carriage and pair of a past year.
In the false velvet of the snow.
In the breath of a little knot of dogs.
In the nerveless ranks of dead leaves.

Carry me off whole, carry me in kisses,
in rising hearts, in breathing breasts,
on the carpet and smile of hands' palms,
in the long galleries of joint and bone.

Carry me off, or bury would be better.

*[Emportez-moi]*


## REST IN MISERY

Old Misery now, leave your plough,
oh Misery of mine, sit you down,
rest you,
rest let us both a while, us two,
rest,
you detect me, you test me, you attest it to me.
I am your destruction.

Old playhouse and haven and hearthstone of mine,
my vault of gold,
my future, my very mother, my farthest border.
Into your splendour, into your soar, into your shudder
I give myself, wrecked, up.

*[Repos dans le malheur]*


## THE FUTURE

When the mah,
When the mah,
The marshes,
The maledictions,
When the mahahahas,

The mahahaborrances,
The mahahamaladyhahas,
The matrimatraitrimahahas,
The hungorduregardenings,
The hunkockroachmen,
The hundropopolies of festero pro festero,
The gloss of cephalophilth,
The plagues and pounds of flesh, the putrefactions,
The mortifications, the slaughters, the founderings,
The sticky, the noisome, the finished,
When the honey gone gritty,
The ice-floes losing blood,
The frantic Jews rushing to ransom Christ,
The Acropolis and the barracks changed into cabbages,
Looks into bats, or else gone bearded, like a box of nails,
New hands into Severn bores,
Other vertebrae made of windmills,
The sap of joy beginning to scald,
Caresses turned to sharp attacks, and the body's most sweetly
      knit organs to sabre-clashes,
The rosy caressing sand become lead on the limbs of all beach-
      lovers,
The gentle tongues, impassioned wanderers, changing into
      knives or hard pebbles,
The delicious sound of the running streams changing into forests
      of parrots and steam-hammers,
When the Appalling-and-Unappeasable, bursting out at last,
Claps his myriad germy rumps on this closed, centred, hook-
      dangled globe
That turns and turns about itself and never wins free,
When suffering, the farthest branch of being, survives alone at
      one fine growing terrible point,
Sharper and more intolerable at every second...and the obstinate
      surrounding extinction shrinking like panic...
Oh wretchedness, wretchedness!
Oh last recollection, each man's little life, each animal's little life,
      little lives like dots:
And then no more.
Oh emptiness!
Oh Space! Space without stratosphere...Oh Space, Space!

                                                      [L'avenir]


279

**Robert Rozhdestvensky**

HISTORY

History!
As a boy it seems
                    I was naive
I believed too long,
                    believed too deeply
that you
were more precise than any mathematics,
less questionable
than the commonest platitude.
But what then –
                    boys
                        become men.
Your winds
                tug
at their faces.
The seconds demand
from the centuries an
account!
I'm speaking now
                    in the name of the seconds...
History is
            beautiful as a red sky.
History is
            hateful as poverty.
Making people new –
and then scuttling off
in the face of some degradation.
History right,
                history senseless!
How often you've been called
– remember! –
bad
    (when you were
                    magnificent!),
good
(although you were
                    shocking and disreputable!)!

How you've depended
                    on empty caprice,
on egocentricity,
on a soul's stupidity!
How afraid you were of dictators
                    who measured
you by their own
personal yardsticks!
Swearing by you
          they stupefied the people!
Cloaking themselves in you
they plundered
the world!
They put a puff of powder on you!
                         And rubbed a bit of
                                   rouge on you!

And dipped you in the dye again!
And clapped you in new clothes again!
You were crammed full
                    of raucous cries
and you specialized in transformation-scenes:
wretches
into titans...
History!
Prostitute
          history!
What is it for,
all that dust?
You call it archives?
NO
     MORE
             LIES!
Press the dry fingers.
To the people
             open up a living heart.
Look
at your deathless creatures
sleeping it off –
what managers they are
                    and family men!
Gulping down
          a modest breakfast –

hurry, hurry –
kiss their wives –
exeunt.
A waft of
        stirring greenery
wraps them about.
The sun beats in their eyes.
The hooters halloo.
The imperturbable smoke
            floats from the chimneys.
You will be yet
the most exact
science!
You will be yet!
You must be!
We
want it
that way.

                          *[Istoriya]*

## Bertolt Brecht

'WHEN THE TIMES DARKEN'

When the times darken
will there be singing even then?
There will be singing even then.
Of how the times darken.

            *['In den finsteren Zeiten']*

THE RETURN

My native town, how am I to find it?
Following swarms of bombers
I come home.
Where then does it lie? Where those monstrous
mountains of smoke are piled.
In the flames yonder:
that's it.

My native town, how will it receive me?
The bombers come first. Deadly swarms
tell you I'm in their wake. Firebursts
announce the native son.

*[Rückkehr]*


**Hans Magnus Enzensberger**


ECONOMIC MIRACLE

you believe you are eating
but it is no meat
they feed you it is
bait, its taste is sweet
(you think the anglers will forget
the line, or perhaps
they have taken an oath
to fast from now on?)

the taste of the hook is no biscuit
it tastes of blood
it tears you out of the lukewarm gravy:
how cold the wind blows on the beresina!
and you must squirm
on a foreign beach

on a foreign icefield:
greenland, nevada, clutch-
ing your limbs tight
on the nubian desert's hide.

don't worry! the anglers are blessed with
ancient expertise, their memory is good.
they wrap you in the love
of a butcher for his sow.
they sit patiently on the rhine,
the potomac, the beresina,
on the rivers of the world.
they take you to the grazing, they wait.

your teeth maul each other's throats.
shivering at the ghost of hunger
you mill round the deadly bait.

*[konjunctur]*


## DROWSING

let me sleep in the guitar tonight
in the night's confused guitar
let me rest
        in the shattered wood
let my hands sleep
           on its strings
my confused hands
          let them sleep
the sweet wood
       let my strings
            let the night
rest on the forgotten notes
my shattered hands
         let them sleep
on the sweet strings
in the confused wood

*[schläferung]*

284

read the timetables, my son, not the odes:
timetables are more precise. unroll the sea-charts
while you can. keep awake, don't sing. the day
is near when they will again stick lists
on the gate and brand the chests of rebels
with an iron pen. learn your incognito, learn
more than I did: change house, papers, face.
study the small betrayal, the squalid
escape from day to day. the function
of encyclicals is to kindle fires,
of manifestos to wrap salt and butter in
for the defenceless. rage and patience are needed
to blow down into the lungs of power
the subtle deadly dust that's ground
by those who have learnt many things,
who are precise – like you.

*[ins lesebuch für die oberstufe]*


CICADA

cicada short? cicada surplus?
who'll count the voices
                              beneath the basalt
in the scree in the marshes
in the savannas the voices
the songs where to
                              torrent and triumph
interchange and answer
                              who for?
looked after by what hands
beneath the wings of envy
beneath the snow of usury

singing to defy gods and jonahs
cicada short
                    cicada surplus

*[zikade]*

## ADVICE TO SISYPHUS

out of your control, what you do. good:
having seized the point, keep it.
but never be reconciled to it,
man with the stone. no one
is grateful to you; chalk marks,
the bored rain licks them up,
measure out death. not to rejoice
too soon is best, there is no career
in what's beyond your control. changelings,
scarecrows, cassandras are thick as thieves
with their own tragedy. say nothing,
speak one word only to the sun,
as the stone still rolls, but
never hug your powerlessness,
only feed the anger of the world
with your hundredweight, with your grain.
there is a lack of men doing
in silence what is out of their control,
uprooting hope like grass, trundling
their laughter, trundling the future and
their anger up the mountain-sides.

*[anweisung an sisyphos]*


## Haroldo de Campos


### TRANSIENT SERVITUDE

PROEM

fly of gold?
fly gone dry.

fly of silver?
fly of cinders.

fly of rainbows?
fly of rags.

fly of indigo?
fly of indigence.

fly of blue?
fly of flies.

fly of white?
poetry no-poetry.

\*

blue's pure?
blue's pus

to empty belly

green's vivid?
green's virus

to empty belly

yellow's vaunted?
yellow's vomit

to empty belly

red's fuchsia?
red's frenzy

to empty belly

poetry's pure?
poetry's purpose

to empty belly

\*

poetry in time of hunger
hunger in time of poetry

poetry in place of humanity
pronoun in place of noun

humanity in place of poetry
noun in place of pronoun

poetry of giving the name

naming is giving the noun

i name the noun
i name humanity
in mid-naming is hunger

i name it hunger

*


POEM

from sun to solar
solder
from salt to salty
saline
from stick to stone
stunned
from sap to sugar
sucked
from sleep to slip
slumped

sanguined
from seep to spurt

*


where does this grinding grind
where does this gear engage

grindstone man's grinding
grinding man's grindstone

gearchanged
gangrengaged

*

from profit to profit
pinched
from pinch to pinch
profited
from pole to pole
parted
from puddle to puddle
poleaxed

*

sun to salt
salt to stun
stun to sap
sap to sleeping
sleeping to bleeding

*

with man
            this bonegrind
with flesh
            this bloodgut
with bone
            this baregear

*

bland man
branded man

pillage man
peeled man

cudgel man
cudgelled man

sieve man
steel-safe man

*

sir man
serving man

super man
sub man

stacked man
sacked man

served man
swallowed man

*

trencher man
empty man

yakkity man
rabbity man

socko man
sick man

graft man
chaff man

*

who's lord
who's lout

who's the horse
who's on horseback

who's the exploiter
who's the spoil

*

who's hangman
who's hanged man

who's usury
who's used

who's plundered
who's plundering

*

who's whisky
who's piss
who's feast-day
who's fatigue-duty
who's lust
who's lice

*

flesh   filth   fury

bloodbath   bleeding   blood

*

grindstonemangrindingman

*

sugar
in these husks?

musk
in this armpit?

petunia
in these molasses?

*

indigo in this snakepit?

*

ochre
acrid
lizard
lazar

*

halter harness hot-seat
heaviness head-hot halter
hangdog half-tot anger

*

from dearth to dearth
from drouth to drouth
from deadhouse to deadhouse
from death to death

*

lonely grindinghood
bone-grindinghood

no mirage to brood
through savage wood

*

transient servitude

*[Servidão de passagem]*

**Eugen Gomringer**

UNTRACKED

untracked
being trackless

being trackless
lightfoot

lightfoot
being powerless

being powerless
dangerous

dangerous
being untracked

being untracked
trackless

trackless
being lightfoot

being lightfoot
powerless

powerless
being dangerous

being dangerous
untracked

*[beweglich]*

MAYBE

maybe tree
tree maybe

293

maybe bird
bird maybe

maybe spring
spring maybe

maybe words
words maybe

*[vielleicht]*


## FROM DEEP TO DEEP

from deep
to deep
from near
to near
from grey
to grey
from deep
to near
from near
to grey
from grey
to deep

from two
to four
from three
to one
from one
to four

from deep
to two
from four
to near
from grey
to one

*[von tiefe zu tiefe]*

## WORDS ARE SHADOWS

words are shadows
shadows become words

words are games
games become words

are shadows words
do words become games

are games words
do words become shadows

are words shadows
do games become words

are words games
do shadows become words

*[worte sind schatten]*


## FROM OCCASION

from occasion
        invasion

from invasion
        destruction

from destruction
        desolation

from desolation
        dereliction

from dereliction
        secession

from occasion
        secession

*[aus zufall]*

295

# THE BOOK OF HOURS (II)

your soul
my word

your soul
my question

your soul
my answer

your soul
my song

your soul
my poem

*

your word
my soul

your word
my question

your word
my answer

your word
my song

your word
my poem

*

your question
my soul

your question
my word

your question
my answer

your question
my song

your question
my poem

*

your answer
my soul

your answer
my word

your answer
my question

your answer
my song

your answer
my poem

*

your song
my soul

your song
my word

your song
my question

your song
my answer

your song
my poem

*

your poem
my soul

your poem
my word

your poem
my question

your poem
my answer

your poem
my song

*

your body
my look

your body
my strength

your body
my joy

your body
my grief

your body
my silence

*

your look
my body

your look
my strength

your look
my joy

your look
my grief

your look
my silence

*

your strength
my body

your strength
my look

your strength
my joy

your strength
my grief

your strength
my silence

*

your joy
my body

your joy
my look

your joy
my strength

your joy
my grief

your joy
my silence

\*

your grief
my body

your grief
my look

your grief
my strength

your grief
my joy

your grief
my silence

\*

your silence
my body

your silence
my look

your silence
my strength

your silence
my joy

your silence
my grief

\*

your coming
my beginning

your coming
my way

your coming
my goal

your coming
my death

your coming
my dream

\*

your beginning
my coming

your beginning
my way

your beginning
my goal

your beginning
my death

your beginning
my dream

\*

your way
my coming

your way
my beginning

your way
my goal

your way
my death

your way
my dream

*

your goal
my coming

your goal
my beginning

your goal
my way

your goal
my death

your goal
my dream

*

your death
my coming

your death
my beginning

your death
my way

your death
my goal

your death
my dream

*

your dream
my coming

your dream
my beginning

your dream
my way

your dream
my goal

your dream
my death

*

your tree
my blossom

your tree
my gift

your tree
my house

your tree
my year

your tree
my hour

*

your blossom
my tree

your blossom
my gift

your blossom
my house

your blossom
my year

your blossom
my hour

*

your gift
my tree

your gift
my blossom

your gift
my house

your gift
my year

your gift
my hour

*

your house
my tree

your house
my blossom

your house
my gift

your house
my year

your house
my hour

*

your year
my tree

your year
my blossom

your year
my gift

your year
my house

your year
my hour

*

your hour
my tree

your hour
my blossom

your hour
my gift

your hour
my house

your hour
my year

*[das stundenbuch (II)]*

300

**Yury Pankratov**

SLOW SONG

the   ship   goes   out   to   sea
the   ship   goes   out   to   sea
the   ship   goes   out   to   sea
far   out   far   away...

and   the   sea   goes   out   to   the   sky
and   the   sea   goes   out   to   the   sky
and   the   sea   goes   out   to   the   sky
high   up   high   above...

and   the   sky   goes   out   to   the   stars
and   the   sky   goes   out   to   the   stars
and   the   sky   goes   out   to   the   stars
the   green   ones   and   the   blue

and   the   stars   go   out   to   eternity
and   the   stars   go   out   to   eternity
and   the   stars   go   out   to   eternity
calmly   and   endlessly

and   eternity   goes   down   to   men
and   eternity   goes   through   to   men
and   eternity   goes   out   to   men
both   great   and   small

and   men   go   out   to   sea
and   men   go   out   to   sea
and   men   go   out   to   sea
and   men   go   out...

*[Medlennaya pesnya]*

## Edgard Braga

```
        one
fly       fire fly
fire      one fly
fire      fly  one
fire      fire fire
one       fly  fire
one       fire fly
        one
```

*[um lume vaga]*


```
white horses    rough waters

deep waters     smooth waters
rough waters    white horses
                        waters
                        waters

mares           white horses
rough           mares waters
white           rough mares

        mares   waters rough

        brief   white rough
                        waters
                            deep
                                rough
                                    brief
                                        smooth
                                            waters
```

*[água branca]*

302

in my glove of gold　　　　in my glove of silver
i hid men and nations　　　i hid my shame

　　in my glove of stone
　　i hid my death

　　in my glove of iron
　　i hid my silence

knight-at-arms knight-at-arms　　knight-at-arms knight-at-arms
throw your glove to the winds　　throw your glove to the winds

　　knight-at-arms knight-at-arms
　　throw your glove to the winds

　　knight-at-arms knight-at-arms
　　keep your glove
　　　　　　keep
　　　　　　the winds

*[na minha luva de ouro]*


living　　　　deadman　　living
deadman　　living　　　deadman
　　　　　alive
　　　　　living
　　　　　deadman
　　　　　living
　　　　　deadman
　　　　　alive
long live the　　　　　dead man

*[vive morto vive]*

303

ballad
ballad

    brooded
    brooded
    brooded
        beloved
        beloved
            bird
            bird
            bird
                ballad
                brooded
                beloved
                    bird

*[balada]*

        isle
        smile

        tranquil

*[ilha]*

one
    poor    plays
            one
ploy        poor
plays   one   ploy
one   poor   plays
plays   plays    plays
one     poor    plays
    ploy   poor
    one
    plays

*[um pobre joga]*

304

| white | swallow |
|---|---|
| yellow | swallow |
| black | |
| black | coat |
| yellow | swallow |
| white | |
| yellow | |
| black | coat |
| yellow | swallow |
| white | . |
| | black |
| | silver |
| | yellow |
| white | swallow |

*[andorinha branca]*

| | | | |
|---|---|---|---|
| yes | yes | no | no |
| no | no | yes | yes |
| one | yes | no | |
| one | yes | yes | |
| no | no | yes | |
| yes | no | no | |
| | one | no | yes |
| | | | |
| | one | yes | yes |
| | | one | no |
| | | yes | |

*[sim sim]*

305

*PLATEN: SELECTED POEMS*

(1978)

## NOTE

After army service at the tail-end of the Napoleonic Wars, Platen studied law and languages at Würzburg and Erlangen, but for the last decade of his relatively short life he lived in Italy. His career was punctuated by more or less unhappy homosexual affairs, which are often dealt with in his poetry in a surprisingly lightly coded way. He was a master of many poetic forms, including adaptations of classical and oriental metres, and his work has the permanent interest of that kind of writing where tight technical control fails to conceal a depth of romantic feeling.

[1996]

## THE PILGRIM* AT ST YUSTE

Night falls, the wild winds whistle more and more.
Spanish monks, unbar me your closed door!

Here let me rest, and waken to the chime
That hurries you to church at praying time.

What your house offers, that I must assume;
Show me a monk's habit and a monk's tomb.

Accept me, set me in a little cell.
Before me more than half the world once fell.

The head that now seeks tonsure and bows down
Was diademed with more than one proud crown.

The shoulder that a cowl has humbled here
Knew ermine and imperial tiring gear.

Not dead, but as the dead, I fall and crack
Like the old Empire crumbling at my back.

[Der Pilgrim vor St. Just]


## VESUVIUS IN DECEMBER 1830

Beautiful and dazzling is the clash of sea-waves
When choppy water races, seethes, and rages;
But fire is itself, it has no twin element
    For supreme power

Or hypnotic grace. Simply let anyone
Out of curiosity climb up to the crater
While darkness cumbers the world, marvelling
    At the rim of the sheer drop –

* The pilgrim is Emperor Charles V.

309

Till a thundering drum-roll quick-marches its forces
From the clifflike cone threatening crescendo
And red-hot boulders in golden hordes are bounding
    Out continually:

Their drive impelled through the fierce heat and vapour
Scatters them now across the ashy summits
Like massed rubies, now rolls them hard down the
    Craggy crater-walls:

While the lava flows calmly along the sombre
Earth. – A thick black smoke-cloud shadows
Your face, dear moon, smudges your silver,
    Your rest and your peace.

                              *[Der Vesuv im Dezember 1830]*


'LOVE IS MY BETRAYER'

Love is my betrayer.
Grief comes, grief hits hard.
Cheated everywhere!
Cheated, cast off, barred!

Tears – I cannot stop them –
Burning down my cheek,
Stop heart, heart who drop them,
Stop heart, stop here, break!

                              *['Die Liebe hat gelogen . . .']*


A SIGH IN WINTER

Look at that sky – so blue, so clear!
Why can't the earth be green!
The wind is keen, and so severe!
Such shining snow, and no thaw near!
Why can't the earth be green!

                              *[Winterseufzer]*

## 'AND I STARTED UP SHARP IN THE NIGHT'

And I started up sharp in the night, in the night,
Felt myself drawn on the pathway,
Let the lanes and their watchmen sink out of sight,
Made my step light
In the night, in the night,
To the gate with its Gothic archway.

The millstream poured through its rocky divide,
I leaned from the bridge, I stood gazing
At the waves far below me, they'd roll and they'd ride
So late and so light
In the night, in the night,
Running forward, but never reversing.

The stars wheeling high in melodious flight
Burned in their numberless places,
And beside them the moon, superb, calm, bright;
They glittered so light
In the night, in the night,
Through the blank receding spaces.

I looked at that sky in the night, in the night,
I looked down again at the mill-race.
How quickly your days have been ravaged by blight!
Now let it lie light
In the night, in the night,
Let your loud heart's remorse lie in stillness.

*['Wie rafft ich mich auf in der Nacht']*


## 'FAIN WOULD I LIVE IN SAFEST FREEDOM'

Fain would I live in safest freedom,
Free from the world, safe from its crowds.
Fain would I walk by quiet rivers,
Roofed by a shady tent of clouds.

Flurrying wings and summer feathers
Would brush my sullen days away.
Guilt-ridden men would shun the cleanness
Of air, the embrace of purity.

A boat upon a stream, for ever,
Grazing the bank but rarely, drawn
To reach a young rose, and returning
To the mid-current running on.

Watching the herds far off, at pasture,
Fresh-hearted flowers every spring,
Vinemen lopping the grape harvest,
Reapers at the heady haymaking.

For food I'd have the light of heaven,
Bright, unstained, it cannot change!
And I would drink the living wellspring,
That blood might rest, not race and range.

*['Ich möchte gern mich frei bewahren']*


TRISTAN

The man who has once fixed his eyes on beauty
Moves by that very act into death's keeping,
Grows dull to the minutest earthly duty,
Yet shivers still that death might take him sleeping,
The man who has once fixed his eyes on beauty.

The ache of love with him is everlasting,
Only a fool can hope through all this planet
For food that would not leave such passion fasting;
Beauty's arrow lodges, burns him, plans it:
The ache of love with him is everlasting.

God! he must sicken like the failing wellspring,
Wants to suck poison from each breeze, putrid
Decay from every flower he loves smelling:
The man who has once fixed his eyes on beauty,
God! he must sicken like the failing wellspring.

## 'WHITELY THE LILY WAVERS'

Whitely the lily wavers in the waters, to and fro;
Yet you can never say, my friend, 'It falters, to and fro.'
Its foot is rooted there so fast in the deep sea bed
Its head just cradles love, rocks love thoughts to and fro.

*['Im Wasser wogt die Lilie . . .']*


## TO A WOODBINE TENDRIL

Strange to find you here among the spruce-trees
In the waste land, it is late, dear blossom, late!
Raw and rude the breath of the breeze,
Already winter looms and cannot wait.

Scrawls of mist lay thick over the mountains,
And behind them the sun had long gone down,
When yearnings of the heart found me
And made me rove again through combe and down.

There your scent betrayed you to the wanderer,
Your whiteness that you wear so blindingly:
But I was lucky that no other
Wanderer saw you first and stole you away.

Was it your dream to wait here with your perfume
Till I could join you in this silent place?
Blooming far from plot or garden,
Here in the forest, under winter's face?

How estimably right the late-found flower
Should vein and swell the song the young man sings,
An image of renown or honour
That grows amidst so many dying things.

*[An eine Geissblattranke]*

313

## 'THE NEW SHOOTS SCATTER THEIR
SCENT FAR AWAY'

The new shoots scatter their scent far away,
The sun's bright shoots are sent far away;
The sea shines glass-clear – see the flashing
Fish fins all ocean-bent far away;
See the rose grow red as the nightingale
Its love companion sings faint, far away;
See the boy there on the hill, seeking
The castle of dreams, marble-veined, far away;
Let us hurry, either on foot like the pilgrims
Or riding off proud as the wind – far away!

*['Düfte sprüht die junge Sprosse fernehin']*


## 'TRUEST OF SAGES ARE YOU TO ME'

Truest of sages are you to me,
Your eye speaks softly true to me;
A friend of friends without a mask
You walk this long march through with me;
Not life alone but living love
Is what your life has proved to me;
The fragrant musk of love you bring,
The food of truth, as due to me;
Deep in your sphere I lay, my dear,
So warm, so bright it grew to me:
I saw you as the pearl of price
Above all other good to me.

*['Du bist der wahre Weise mir']*


## 'FORFAIRN'S MY HERT'

Forfairn's my hert, ye loe me nane!
Ye mak it apert, ye loe me nane!
I staun afore ye still to implore ye
Fae the lowe o my smert, and ye loe me nane!

314

Your word is sayed and never gainsayed
And ye made it assert ye loe me nane!
How sall the starns, how sall the sun
To thir een revert? Ye loe me nane!
The lily blaws, the jesmie and the rose,
But nocht for this hert: ye loe me nane.

['*Mein Herz ist zerrissen...*']


'TIME AND SPACE, TORMENT'

Time and space, torment; torment, the scope and span!
He who has proved this truth speaks to my state.
He who has watched the fought-for gladnesses of fate
Die in the very flash of wishing: he is the man;

He whose tracks in the labyrinth are gone
From unreturning, unescaping feet,
Whose heart is set and held at love's heartbeat
Only for despair to hammer cadence on;

He who has called on the lightning to destroy him
And on every tide and flood to wash him away
With all the pain that laboured to undo him,

Who envies the dead their stony panoply
Where love with fury and folly can no more sear them –
He hears my heart, and his way is my way.

['*Wem Leben Leiden ist...*']


'WHO HAS EVER HELD LIFE IN HIS HAND'

Who has ever held life in his hand,
Who has not lost trace of half his days
In senseless talk, in dreams, caught in some craze,
Suffering love, and sifting time like sand?

315

Yes, and the very man who's relaxed and bland,
Born conscious of a duty and a place,
Quick chooser of his way of life – his face
Must blench at life's unkind, unplanned command.

Good fortune all men hope for – just ahead.
And yet to bear good fortune here indeed
Is more for gods than men when all is said.

Who said it ever comes? We wish, we bleed,
But dreamers only dream it in their bed;
Runners hunt it with unavailing speed.

['Wer wusste je das Leben recht zu fassen']

'AT LEAST TO BE AT PEACE'

At least to be at peace, that is one of our cravings,
One of our oldest cravings, yet to reach tranquillity
We find ourselves mingling with the disturbingly fiery
    Company of youth and of wine.

Love's flames are checked by a delicate diffidence,
Among many carnations a discreet rose shows modesty,
A smile betrays the degree of heart-tenderness,
    Kisses lingering like honeydew.

But ceaselessly burning sighs? Why these? And glances
Burning, but why burning? Can they be envoys of happiness?
You are silent? Come then, bewilder the bold moonlight,
    Close the shutter fast, dear heart!

['Lange begehrten wir . . .']

VENETIAN SONNETS

I

At last I left the open sea behind
To watch Palladio's churches looming near
Out of the water; the waves that roll us here
And hug these steps are guileless now and kind.

We walk off on dry land with grateful mind,
The whole lagoon seems to rush back, and there
The doge's old, huge colonnades appear,
And what we seek, the Bridge of Sighs, we find.

Venice's lion, Venice's joy, how high
The kingly brazen wings are towering
From that gigantic stone they glorify!

I disembark with the awe and dread I bring.
St Mark's Square sparkles in the sun. Shall I
Be bold enough to be there, wandering?

*['Mein Auge liess das hohe Meer zurücke']*

II

This labyrinth of bridges and cramped streets
Which twist and cross and mix a myriad ways,
How shall I ever master it? This maze,
How can I penetrate its far retreats?

Let me climb St Mark's tower; the eye greets
Light and space, gazing from these terraces;
And all the great surrounding riches raise
One picture where a double grace competes.

There I salute the ocean, blue at noon;
And here the Alps, the wave that never broke,
Looming above the islanded lagoon.

See how this place drew an audacious folk:
They came, and palaces and temples soon
Rose from the very waves on props of oak.

*['Dies Labyrinth von Brücken und von Gassen']*

317

III

What joy it is when the hot day grows cool
To gaze on the gliding ships and gondolas
Lagoonward – in such quiet, still as glass,
All Venice vibrant, lapped in its soft pool!

And then again the eye is held in thrall
By the city's heart: church spire and palace face
Searching the clouds, the motley crossing place
Of the Rialto where the loud throngs crawl.

Gay all around is the dear swarm of souls
Moving in idleness, as if freed from care;
A queer soul can feel free here as he strolls.

Then that full chorus in the evening air –
The Riva where the storyteller calls,
The singer singing in St Mark's great square!

['Wie lieblich ist's, wenn sich der Tag verkühlet']


V

Venice lies in a dream landscape today.
Its very shadows lean from times long gone.
How close to the Lion Republic death has drawn!
How desolately the old jail doors sway!

Bronze horses brought here by the salt white way
Through heavy seas, from that church looking down,
Look alien now; under a Corsican frown
They took the bit that took their pride away!

What can have happened to that race of kings
Whose daring raised these marble roofs and walls
Now turned to sinking, slowly crumbling things?

The grandson's brow not fitfully recalls
The deep tracks of his forebears' venturings,
Hewn in the stone where a doge's graver falls.

['Venedig liegt . . .']

VIII

I seem to hear a long, undying 'alas'
Sighed from this air that scarcely stirs at all.
It drifts toward me from an empty hall
Once rich with joys and zest none could surpass.

Venice came down, though it thought ages would pass,
And the wheel of life turn back, before its fall.
The harbour's derelict, few boatmen call
Along that Riva where beauty brimmed its glass.

Venezia! How proud you once appeared,
A woman glittering in golden folds,
Painted as Veronese saw you, revered!

Today a poet stands in awe and holds
The doge's giant balustrades; stands seared
By the true tears no visitor withholds.

*['Es scheint ein langes . . .']*


X

Here, I admit, there are no green fields to see,
Nor can you float in fragrance from a rose.
What flowery banks you've known! Their memory goes.
Here, you scarcely feel that they should be.

Gently the starry night pours down its plea
For all to gather in the square. Long rows
Of distinguished beauties sit and interpose
Their grace in that arcaded dignity.

Crowd brushes crowd, milling through the heart
Of the square. Music blows off in shreds.
This is the life of Canaletto's art.

And here, three kingly flags above our heads
Stream from bronze pedestals in the wind. They chart
The glory Venice shed, and lost, and sheds.

*['Hier seht ihr freilich keine grünen Auen']*

XII

I love you, as the sum of all those forms
Which Venice in its paintings shows to us.
The very heart may yearn, 'Come close to us!'
But they stand silent, we pass by their charms.

I see you as the breathing stone whose arms
Hold beauty carved for ever motionless.
Pygmalion's rage is still. Victorious
I cannot be, but yours, yours through all storms.

You are a child of Venice, you live here
And stay here; this place is your paradise,
With all Bellini's angels flocking near.

But I – as I glide on, I recognize
I am cheated of a world so great and so dear;
Like the dreams of darkness it dissolves and flies.

*['Ich liebe dich, wie jener Formen eine']*


XIII

What is it life lets us win in the end?
What becomes truly ours, from its strongbox?
Gold of good luck, sweetness of pleasure – the locks
Spring back, they escape, and only pain has remained.

As for me, before my last hours have waned
I'll hazard one more tossing in the flux –
Gazing where marble courts and sea that plucks
My startled heart with 'Venice! Venice!' blend.

The eye roves anxious, searching as a knife,
Wishing its mirror was a resting place
For all that wavers in the visual strife.

But oh, at the last, leaving the last hot race,
In one last moment of this hurrying life
One lightning glance of love falls on that face.

*['Was lässt . . .']*

XIV

When I am deeply burdened, desolate,
My soul is drawn to the Rialto, to haunt
The stalls in dying daylight – not a jaunt
For trifles, but for the mind's ease I await.

A shadow on the bridge, I've often gazed
Down where the dull waves quiver sluggish and cold,
Where old half-crumbled walls are overscrawled
With branches of laurel, from bushes wild and crazed.

And there, where time has turned the posts to stone,
I stand and stare till all things disappear
In the dark doge-widowed sea that sleeps alone;

And in that silent space my listening ear
Catches at times a faint cry that is blown
Here from the far canals. Ah, gondolier!

*['Wenn tiefe Schwermut meine Seele wieget']*

*from*

*SWEEPING OUT THE DARK*

(1994)

# Claudian

## ON THE OLD MAN OF VERONA:
## A DECONSTRUCTION

Auld Fergus is richt bien an croose, ye ken,
Crawin on his ain dunghill seeventy years.
His stick hirples him ower the grun he crowled on
Langsyne. Gode, he wis feart tae lea the hoose!
His teeth ay chittert at the notion o chynge.
Aw furrin lochs were pysin! That export trock –
Nae thanks! The ermy? – na, thon's danger-money.
Boather the ombudsman? Naw, keep the heid doon.
He's sic a sumph he's niver been tae toon,
He gawks up at the lift – weel, it's free, man!
He coonts the months by kail and coarn and claver,
But disna ken his M.P. frae his elbuck.
Same auld fields, same sun an muin – aw's wan
Tae him, he plowters through, it's breid an bu'er.
He kent that aik as an aikorn wance? – big deal!
The scrunty foggage is as grey as him.
And Bennachie's as faur aff as Benares,
And as for Udny, oh man, yon's like Omsk.
Warst thing is, he's still quite hale and stuffie,
His sons and oys are hodden doon, pair loons.
Their backpacks are stashed fidgin for Albania:
He's gote his wee warld, but they wahnt the Wey.

[*'De sene Veronensi'*]

---

*Bien* comfortable; *croose* self-satisfied; *hirples* limps; *grun* ground; *lea* leave;
*trock* business; *sumph* fool; *lift* sky; *kail* cabbage; *claver* clover; *elbuck* elbow;
*wan* one; *plowters* works sloppily; *foggage* grass, grazing; *stuffie* sturdy;
*oys* grandsons; *hodden doon* held back; *pair loons* poor fellows; *fidgin* itching

## Michelangelo Buonarroti

### 'IN ME IS DAITH . . .'

In me is daith, I leeve in you alane.
Ye twin time aff and mark it, gie oot time
tae gar me loup or shauchle as ye will.

Leeze me on your mense! For I can sain
the saul that's no run through by bornheid time:
ye mak it staun and luk at Gode, stock-still.

*['In me la morte . . .']*


## Giacomo Leopardi

### THE AESOME BLACKIE

Therr ye sit, at the tap o the auld tour,
aesome blackie, giein the kintraside your sang
afore the cowslem taks wir licht awaw;
the haill glen swaws wi thae sweet rins o soun.
Aw roon, spring's bricht and braw
in ilka airt, and fields expreme their joy;
whase hert sees this, melts richt aipen and nesh.
Herk tae the baain sheep, the rowtin o the kye!
The ither happy burdies wheel thegither
in rival bauns, the braid lift taks their flisks
and flirts in thoosans, it's their hoaliday!
But you sit aye apairt, thochtfu; nae whisks

*Leeve* live; *twin* split; *gar* make; *loup* leap; *shauchle* shamble; *leeze me on* I am happy with; *mense* grace; *sain* bless; *bornheid* headlong; *staun* stand

*Aesome* solitary; *blackie* blackbird; *cowslem* evening; *wir* our; *swaws* ripples; *rins o soun* streams of sound; *in ilka airt* everywhere; *aipen* open; *nesh* tender; *rowtin* lowing; *kye* cattle; *bauns* bands; *lift* sky

alang the airs for you,
nae croods o friens; nae licht-hertit gemms;
yit your sang shemms
the best flooer o your life and o this May.

Wae's me tae see hoo near
your weys tae mine! Pleesure and lauchtir that gar
the halflin mind pit oan its pleyin-gear,
love that is youdith's furst confiderat
and the sherpest-taen sich o aulder years –
I've nae likin for thae, I kenna why;
seem tae flee them, faur aff,
like a gangrel body, a nyaff
tae his ain fowk, a traiveller
through his ain unhanty livin spring.
This day, which noo dwines doon tae the gloamin,
is taen here as a people's hoaliday.

Herk hoo the bells jow oot through the lown air,
and hoo the shoatguns aften crack their thunner
fae faur-aff villa tae villa reverbin awwhere.
Aw in their hoaliday claes,
the boays and lassies skail
fae their hooses and stravaig fae street tae street;
the gled hert and the wandrin ee are theirs!
Burdalane, I gaze
alang thae unthrang fields, gang my ain gate,
pit aff tae ither times aw gemms and ploys;
my een threid the douce air
and stap at the sun abune his faur hill-taps
steekin this lang lown day:
he draps and's gane, and whit he says by this
is, even gleddest youthheid canna stay.

You, solitar burdie, wance ye come
tae the eenin o the span your weird decreets,
I'm shair ye'll no decry
the life ye've leeved; the things ye thocht maist fain

---

*gemms* games; *gar* make; *halflin* young; *sich* sigh; *thae* those; *gangrel body*
wanderer; *nyaff* despised person; *unhanty* clumsy; *jow* toll; *lown* calm;
*skail* scatter; *burdalane* quite alone; *steekin* closing

were nature's alane.
But me, gin the years hain
me intae hatit auldness,
and thir een canna speak tae ithers' herts,
and aw the warld be tim, and my days tae come
mair seik and bleck nor aw the days that's gane,
my wiss tae be alane,
hoo will it seem? and hoo thae years? and me?
A cutty-stool I see,
and mony backwart luik and unappeasit grane.

[*Il passero solitario*]


FLINDER

ALICK

I tell ye, Malc, thon wes an eerie widdrim
I hud yestreen, it aw comes back tae mind
noo I see the muin again. I wes staunin
at the winnock that luiks richt ower the fields;
I kest my een up tae the lift, and wow
but the muin cam loose, in a gliff: I thocht
it tumml't doon, the muckle thing, cam near
and near, till it hud whumml't wi a scult
amang the stooks, breenged therr aboot the size
o a creel, and scowdert oot a michty boak,
a clood o flichters that soon hisht and pisht
like coaly gleeds a haun hes smoort ablow
the watter-troch. I sweer there wes nae differ:
richt in the middle o the field it wes,
the muin, and oot it gaed, gaed slawly bleck;
the gress aw roon began tae sneyster and smeek.
I luikit up again intae the lift:

*gin* if; *hain* protect; *thir* these; *tim* empty; *cutty-stool* stool of repentance;
*grane* groan

*Flinder* fragment; *widdrim* nightmare; *yestreen* last night; *winnock* window;
*lift* sky; *gliff* moment; *whumml't* tumbled; *scult* slap; *breenged* barged; *scowdert*
scorched; *boak* vomit; *flichters* particles; *gleeds* embers; *smoort* smothered;
*ablow* below; *sneyster* burn; *smeek* smoke

naethin wes left bar a skimmer, a smick, a neuk
it hud been claucht fae, and yon wes a sicht
that gart my bluid rin cauld: I'm shakkin yit.


MALC

As weel ye micht. It's aiblins on the cairds
the muin could traipse doon someday tae yir rigs.


ALICK

Wha kens? Is it no true hoo simmer gies us
shuitin-starns?


MALC

        Ay, but there's starns eneuch:
it's little skaith gif yin or twa sud faw –
there's thoosans mair. But we've allanerly
the aesome muin i the lift, and naebody
hes watched it faw, binna in dwam or widdrim...

                          *[Frammento: 'Odi, Melisso...']*



TAE HIS SEL

Noo and for aye, ye's be quate,
my forfochen hert. Gane is the graun swick
I thocht wad be ayebydin. Gane. I'm shair
yon swick, though sweet, is ower:
I hope for't and I streetch for't noo nae mair.
Quate, for aye. Eneuch
o that yaiseless pit-pat. Naethin is wurth
your eident flutherins, ye can sich and sab
tae a yirth that's deif. Whit's life


*skimmer* gleam; *smick spot; claucht* clutched; *gart* made; *skaith* damage;
*allanerly* only; *aesome* solitary; *binna* useless; *dwam* daydream

*Quate* at peace; *forfochen* worn-out; *swick* deception; *eident* eager; *sab* sob

but a wide wersh wanrufe; the warld's but a clart.
Quate, quate. It is
the last wanhope. For there is nae weird gien
tae livin men bar daith. Wha'd no miscaw
you, nature, grim
in your slee and ugsome pooer tae ding us doon,
and aathing circumjackless, howe, and tim.

*[A se stesso]*


# Aleksandr Pushkin


### AUTUMN (A FRAGMENT)

Then, what is not the target for my drowsy mind?
                                                Derzhavin


1

October has come – already now the wood
Casts its last leaves, its branches are all bare;
Autumn has breathed its cold to freeze the road,
Beyond the mill the stream still murmurs there,
But the pond's already ice; my neighbour's load
Of hunting-hounds is shot off with wild blare
To ravage winter crops in distant fields;
They bay until the sleeping forest yields.


2

Now is my time: I hold no brief for spring;
Tiresome thaw with its slush and stench – I'm ill
In spring, blood fevered, mind and heart panting
With longing. Rough-hewn winter meets the bill

---

*wersh* tasteless, insipid; *wanrufe* disquiet, restlessness; *clart* lump of filth;
*wanhope* despair; *weird* fate; *slee* sly; *ding* throw; *circumjackless* uncircumscribed;
*howe* hollow; *tim* empty

Far better; I love its snows; our sledge stealing
Through moonlight, swift, at its own airy will,
While a warm hand stirs from beneath her sable
To press my hand, and make her flush and tremble!


3

What a delight to glide on sharp-shod iron
Across the smooth unruffled river-glass!
Winter festivals all shimmer and fire! . . .
But snow for six months? No, I think I'll pass:
Even for bears in dens it might be fine
At first, but not at last. You can't amass
Pleasure for ever from Juliet in a sledge,
Or vegetate by stove and window-ledge.


4

Summer, you beauty! I would be truly yours
But for the heat and dust, the midges and the flies.
You drain our mental strength, and what tortures
You give us! Like the field, the body cries
For rain; to be where drink and freshness pours;  ·
Only to see old mother winter rise
Once more: pancakes and wine for her farewell,
Ice and ice-cream for her memorial.


5

Late autumn days are no one's favourite,
And yet, you know, I find this season dear.
Its still beauty, its shining placid spirit
Attract me like a Cinderella's tear.
I tell you frankly I can see no merit
In any other season of the year.
Such good, in autumn? Yes, I can discover
Its beckoning essence, and I am no boastful lover.

6

How to persuade you? Were you ever taken
By some unrobust girl wasting away –
Strange, but it's like that. She is stricken,
Death-bent, poor creature, unrepining prey
Of unseen jaws whose grip will never slacken;
She smiles still, with red lips that fade to grey;
Her face has twilight in its blood, not dawn;
Alive today, tomorrow she is gone.


7

Melancholy time, yet magic to the sight!
Leavetaking kinds of beauty please me best:
All nature withering in a sumptuous light,
The groves and forests gold-and-purple-dressed,
The wind-loud tree-crests, the airy delight,
The mists that roll to trouble the sky's rest,
The rare sun-ray and the first test of frost,
The distant menace of winter's grizzled ghost.


8

And with each autumn I bud and bloom once more;
The Russian cold is good and therapeutic;
The everyday routines no longer bore:
Hunger and sleep come sweetly automatic;
Joy dances lightly where my heart's tides pour,
Desire swirls up – I'm young again, an addict
Of life and happiness – that's my organism
(And please forgive this forced prosaicism).


9

My horse is brought; it shakes its mane and takes
Its rider out into the wilderness,
The frostbound glen where every hoofbeat strikes
Flashes, rings loud, while ice cracks in the stress.
But the short day goes grey, and the fire-flakes
Play up in the forgotten grate, now less,
Now more, now smouldering and now flaring:
I read there, or I feed my long thoughts, staring.

10

And I forget the world – and in dear silence
Am dearly lulled by my imagination,
And poetry wakens into consciousness:
My soul is rocked in lyric agitation,
It cries and trembles, and like a dreamer frets
To free itself in full manifestation –
And now a swarm of unseen guests draws near,
Both old friends and imagined shapes are here.


11

And brave thoughts break like waves along my brain,
And rhymes race forward to the rendezvous,
And pen beckons to finger, paper to pen.
One minute, and verse surges freely through.
So a stilled ship drowses on the stilled main,
Till look: a sudden leaping of the crew,
Masts are shinned up and down, sails belly free,
The huge mass moves and slices through the sea.


12

Great to sail off with it! But where to go?
What lands shall we now see: vast Caucasus,
Or some sun-blistered Moldavian meadow,
Or Normandy's snow-gleaming policies,
Or Switzers' pyramid array on show,
Or wild and sad Scottish rock-fortresses . . . ?

*[Osen']*


Corbie tae corbie flees and steirs,
Corbie tae corbie skreiks and speirs:
Corbie! whaur sall we tak meat?
And hoo kin we fin oot aboo't?

*Corbie* raven; *steirs* stirs, sets out; *speirs* asks

Corbie tae corbie gies repone:
Ah ken the brod oor denner's oan;
In aipen muir, unner a sauch,
A knicht liggs thonner, deid eneuch.

What kill't thoan boay, and forwhy,
His faucon kens that anerly,
And his mear sae corbie-bleck,
And his ying wife, tae this effeck:

The faucon's flittit tae the shaw,
The reiver's rid the mear awaw,
But the wife's aye waukin fur
Nae deid man but her leevin dear.

*['Voron k voronu letit . . .' Pushkin's untitled Russian version*
*of the old Scottish ballad 'The Twa Corbies'.]*

## Vladimir Solovyov

### THE WINTRY LOCH O SAIMAA

Happit in a flaffie mantie fae heid tae feet
Ye ligg like a stookie in a dwam, white, quaet.
The leamin skimmerin snawy air micht hint,
But disnae by the sleeest souch, o daith.

Naw naw, I hivnae socht ye yaiselesslie
In aw thon boddomless lown doverin.
Faur ben, my sicht is on nae blawflum o ye
Nikniven! – queen o pine and craig and whin!

*repone* reply; *brod* table; *aipen* open; *sauch* willow; *anerly* alone; *mear* mare;
*reiver* raider; *waukin* wakeful, watching

*Happit* wrapped; *mantie* gown; *stookie* statue; *dwam* daydream; *quaet* quiet;
*leamin* gleaming; *souch* breath; *lown* calm, hushed; *doverin* dozing; *ben* within;
*blawflum* deluding image; *Nikniven* medieval witch queen

Mackless as the snaw ayont the braes,
Thocht-hoatchin like the daurkest yuletide nicht,
Ye blinter wi the Merry-Dancers' bleeze,
Dochter o sooty Chaos, eerie-bricht!

*[Na Saime zimoi]*


## Aleksandr Blok

Nicht, causey, leerie, pothicar,
Aw'where a dreich and donnert licht.
Leeve for twinty-five year mair –
Naethin will chynge. Nane taks flicht.

Ay, ye can dee – re-stert it aw,
Aw'thing turns roon like a peerie:
Nicht, and the canaul's cauld swaw,
Causey, pothicar, and leerie.

*['Noch', ulitsa . . .']*


## Velimir Khlebnikov

GAFFIN-CANTRIP

Och, unsneck, snicherers!
Och, unsnib, snicherers!
Gar thaim smicker wi smirlin, gar thaim smirkle skirlinlie,
Och, snicher smirtlinlie!

*mackless* immaculate; *thocht-hoatchin* rich with many thoughts; *blinter* shimmer

*Causey* street; *leerie* lamp; *dreich* bleak; *donnert* dull; *peerie* top

*Gaffin-cantrip* incantation by laughter; *gar* make;
The original is a sound-poem built up on imaginative extensions of the word
*smekh* (laughter). Scots equivalents are similarly deployed here.

Och, the snorkstock o the besnorkit – the smue o the besmuit
    snicherers!
Och, snocher snowkilie, smirl o the snirkit snirters!
Snowkio, snorkio,
Smirl and snitter, sneeterers and sneisterers,
Snicherikins and snocherikins.
Och, unsneck, snicherers!
Och, unsnib, snicherers!

*[Zaklyatie smekhom]*

HA-OO!

Ha-oo! ha-oo! ha-oo!
Many of the black ones
Ha-oo! ha-oo! ha-oo!
Dogs of the rebellion
Ha-oo! ha-oo! ha-oo!
Scampered through the snow
Ha-oo! ha-oo! ha-oo!
To the nearby villages
Ha-oo! ha-oo! ha-oo!
To root up all the corpses
Ha-oo! ha-oo! ha-oo!
To drag off someone's arm
Ha-oo! ha-oo! ha-oo!
To bloody up their muzzles
In belly and in snow.

*['Gau! gau! gau!']*

COARSE TALK

COARSE TALK
Here's a kick in the teeth –
My kiss.
More red,
More scarlet,
A coarse rowan,

336

A fragged-out fragging,
A red cart-shaft,
Cherry-blossoms,
Crushed-up lips.
And the air screaming.

*[Gruby yazyk]*

## Vladimir Mayakovsky

FOR ALL THAT

The street's caved in like a syphilitic's nose.
The river's a libidinous ripple of spittle.
The park, in tiniest wisp of underclothes,
lies sprawled with its midsummer titill-

ation. I walked into the square,
pulled a burnt-out neighbourhood
over my head like a ginger hairpiece.
People are scared – foot by foot
a half-chewed shout crawls from my face.

But they won't bark at me, they won't condemn me,
they'll strew my prophet's path with flowers.
None of the caved-in noses will blame me:
I am your poet, I am yours.

Your terrible judgement is as terrifying as a teashop!
Prostitutes will hoist me alone like a monstrance
through the burning tenements, their gestures teaching
God to absolve and not to admonish.

And God will start crying over my slim volume! –
not words but spasms, lumps clamped together;
and he'll run through heaven with my poems under his arm
and read them out, panting, to those in his favour.

*[A vse-taki]*

**Eugenio Montale**

BOATS ON THE MARNE

Elegant delight of the cork-float
caught in the current that
wavers through inverted bridges
and the full moon pale in the sun:
boats on the river, frisky, summer-borne,
and a dull murmur from the city.
Row by the meadow, if the butterfly-hunter
should reach you with his net,
the tree-maze on the wall where dragon's
blood is re-done in red ochre.

Voices on the river, bursts of sound from the banks,
or rhythmic dip and rise of canoes
in the evening that ripples
through the manes of the walnut-trees, but where is
the steady procession of the seasons
that was a dawn without streets and without end,
where is the long wait and what is the emptiness
that leaves us nothing to defend?

This is the dream: an enormous
unending day flooding and reflooding
its almost unwinking glare between the dykes,
and the good work of man at every turn,
a veiled tomorrow carrying no terror.
And the dream was other things, but its reflection,
strong on the racing water, under the hanging
tit's nest, airy and inaccessible,
was supreme silence in the concerted
cry of midday and the evening
was a longer morning, the great ferment
a great rest.
                    Here . . . the enduring colour
is that of the mouse jack-in-the-box
among the reeds or the starling with its spurt
of poisonous metal swallowed up
by the misty bank.

Here is the dusk. We now
can go down till the Great Bear shows its face.

(Sunday boats on the Marne, a race
on the day of your anniversary.)

*[Barche sulla Marna]*


## WIND IN THE CRESCENT (EDINBURGH)

The muckle brig didna gang your wey.
Gid ye'd've gien the word, I'd have won through
to ye by navigatin stanks and syvers. But
aa my virr, wi thon sun on the winnocks
o the verandas, wis seepin slawly awa.

A birkie that wis preachin on the Crescent
speirit at me: 'D'ye ken whaur Gode is?' I kent
and tellt him. He shook his heid. I saw nae mair
o him in the wud wind that skelpit hooses and fowk
and gart them flee abune the taurry daurk.

*[Vento sulla mezzaluna]*


## XENIA II (5)

Giving you my arm, I have gone down at least a million stairs
and now in your absence every step is a void.
Even so our long journey was soon over.
Mine lasts yet, but without the accompaniment
of bookings and connections, of the snares
and the shames of one who believes
the world is what he perceives.


*Gin* if; *stanks* gutters; *syvers* drain-traps; *virr* vitality; *winnocks* windows;
*birkie* chap; *speirit* asked; *wud* mad; *gart* made

I have gone down a million stairs, giving you my arm
not, surely, to prove four eyes might beat two.
I went down them with you because I knew
that of our pupils, yours, dimmed as they were,
only yours were true.

['*Ho sceso . . .*']


## Attila József


ATTILA JÓZSEF

*Attila József*, believe me, I am very fond of you, this has come
 down to me from my mother, she was goodness itself, she
 brought me into the world
It is no use comparing life to a shoe or a dry-cleaner's, there are
 other reasons why we love it
Redeem the world three times a day and cannot strike a match?
 if that is all they can do I am finished with them
How good it would be to buy a ticket and travel to Oneself, it is
 there all right, alive, inside us
Every morning I wash my thoughts in cold water, then they
 become brisk and bold
Diamonds, planted beneath our heart, can nurture good warm
 songs
Some people are pedestrian even on horseback, in cars, in planes,
 I can loll at dawn and listen to larks, yet I have crossed the
 chasm
We must look after our real souls as carefully as our best clothes,
 and keep them clean to celebrate the feast-days in.

[*József Attila*]

HEART-INNOCENT

Without father, without mother, alone
without cradle, without shroud I go
without God, without land and home,
without kiss, without girl to know.

Three days and nothing to eat,
bite or banquet, fat or lean!
My twenty years, my strength and speed –
who'll buy this twenty-year machine?

And if no buyer comes – well then
I'll sell these years to the devil of hell!
become pure thief, heart-innocent,
yes, and be a killer as well!

They'll catch me, hang me like a lout,
lay me out in holy ground.
From then on my heart'll be proud –
death fattens the grass growing round.

*[Tiszta szívvel]*


MOTHER

All this last week I have been thinking
of my mother, thinking of her taking
up in her arms the creaking basket
of clothes, without pausing, up to the attic.

Oh I was full of myself in those days –
shouting and stamping, crying to her to leave
her washing to others, to take me in place
of the basket, play with me under the eaves –

But calmly she went on, lifting out the clothes,
hanging them to dry, she had no time to scold
or even to glance at me, and soon the line
was flying in the wind, white and clean.

341

I cannot shout now – how could she hear?
I see her, great, vast, yet somehow she is near.
The wet sky shines washed with her blue,
her grey hair streams where the clouds scud through.

*[Mama]*

MEDITATIVE

*Storm*

If you've seen a child seizing a cockroach,
that's how I nipped it, two fingers closed
under its arm, muttering: So the storm's here!
And its tiny lightnings scrabbled at the air.

*Mulberry-tree*

An ancient mulberry stands at the roadside,
thick-set, stocky, like a country wet-nurse.
Driver, sir, watch out! it has an iron hide!
But oh, beggarman, its fruits are soft to crush.

*Christian*

Fat sheaves all round me, I waste in hunger,
    stroked and stroked by sorrow.
Bright are the sky's stars I stand under,
    like a crown of thorns.
Does this make me a Christian, however grudging?
    Only if there are no wars.

*Punctuation-mark*

All this is a game you know. I'm writing here
in pencil. Gentry's money paid the paper.
These letters have no machine-gun rat-tat-tat
yet. Like poverty they gouge, like lice they bite.

*[Tünödö]*

UNEMPLOYED

Eighteen months now
the bird can't rise from the ground.

In submarine market-caves
I've stumbled under slippery crates.

Been with the Danube shipping,
a strangler's grip on the cold rigging.

Had a hawker's, not a reader's view
of Móricz, Barbusse, Zola, Cocteau, Shaw...

Sold golden bread, then
watched it eaten, but still kept thin.

No bacon, no stove. Night on the benches
and grassy places – with the angels.

*[Állás nélkül]*


KEEP GOING!

Mandarins hanged in Peking,
the dead man liked his cocaine.
– Go to sleep, you're rustling the straw.
The dead man liked his cocaine.

What does the poor man watch
through the window? Till and cash.
– Go to sleep, you're rustling the straw.
Through the window? Till and cash.

Buy yourself sausage and bread,
keep hardy, keep your head.
– Go to sleep, you're rustling the straw.
Keep hardy, keep your head.

343

You'll find the woman of gold,
she'll cook and never scold.
– Go to sleep, you're rustling the straw.
She'll cook and never scold.

*[Biztató (Kínában . . .)]*

## MY MOTHER

She would hold the mug in both hands,
one Sunday as evening approached
she smiled in her own peaceful way
and sat a moment in the half dark –

A small saucepan held the supper
she brought home from the fine folks' house,
we went to bed, and I lay thinking
how they had a whole pot to devour –

This was my mother, tiny, early dead,
a washerwoman's lot is to die early,
her legs shake from the loads she carries,
her head throbs as she bends ironing –

And her mountains are the dirty washing!
She has a tranquillizing cloudscape
of steam, and as for pastures new
the washerwoman has the attic –

She pauses with the iron: I see her.
Her brittle body was broken by
capital, grew thin, grew thinner –
think about it, proletarians –

She was bent, you know, bent from washing,
I never knew how young she was,
she wore a clean apron in her dreams,
and the postman greeted her then –

*[Anyám]*

344

It isn't me you hear crying, it's a growl from the earth.
Look out – the devil has lost his head – look out!
Crouch in the belly of the well –
squeeze against the window-pane –
hide behind the flash of diamonds –
beneath stones – in a swarm of flies –
oh, hide in the bread just drawn from the oven –
you, Poorman:
soak into the earth with a thunder-shower!
To plunge your face into yourself – wasted labour,
you are only washed in the waters of others.
Slip into a grass-blade: on its vein
you will stretch farther than the axis of this world.

O birds and foliage, machines and stars,
our sterile mother implores and reclaims her children.
So, Poorman, so –
and is this dreadful, or is it wonderful? –
it isn't me you hear crying, it's a growl from the earth.

*['Nem én kiáltok . . .']*


ODE

1

Here I sit on a shining wall.
The light young summer wind
rises like the warm welcome of supper.
I accustom my heart to the silence:
not hard.
Here
I regain what I lost,
I bend my head,
my head hangs down.

My eyes are on the mane of the mountains –
your splendid brow,
every leaf on fire!
On the street no one, no one;

345

I see your skirt lifted by the wind.
Your hair strays under fine leaves,
I see your soft breasts
trembling –
as Szinva brook runs down –
Oh what I see:
a magic laugh
shining on your teeth,
on the round white stones.


2

Oh how I love you!
You have been able to force
speech from the universe –
and from solitude, weaving its fitful deceits
in the heart's deepest place.
Now, as the booming leaves the waterfall,
you leave, you run subdued, until
I cry from among the peaks of life, singing
in those distances hung between earth and heaven,
that I love you, that it is you,
sweet would-be mother, that I love.


3

I love you as the child loves its mother,
as the silent cave loves its depths.
I love you as rooms love sunlight,
as the soul loves warmth and the body rest.
I love you as mortal men love living
and strive in its arms till death.

I am the keeper of your words, your smiles,
your moments – everything, as the earth keeeps
everything that falls.
My instincts, like acid on metal, have
engraved you on my mind; my existence
takes form at last, dear love, from your sweet essence.

Loudly the moments pass by;
dumb you remain, dumb, and I
have ears for you alone.
Glittering stars – already they are setting,
but you are always steady in my sight.
Breath of silence in the cave: your flavour
stings cold in the mouth; at times your hand
with its delicate veining will bend
mistily round the glass of water.


4

Oh but what substance am I made of,
moulded and carved by your simplest glance?
What mind, what light and miracle
that can make me reach the gentle
dales of your fertile
body, through the mist of absence?

As the word is released by reason,
I can delve into your enigmas!...

Your veins quiver like bushes,
ceaselessly, bushes of roses.
They move in the undying stream,
for love to flourish in your face
and your belly to bear its fruit.

The sensitive soil of your flesh
is sown with finest roots,
thin threads it knots, unknots, –
for the juices of the tiny cells
to crowd to a growing mass,
and the leafy bush of the lungs
to murmur up its praise!

And the deep undying matter advances
singing in its galleries, and rich life emerges
from tireless wells, from the very scourings
of buried pits, of burning kidneys!

In you, the swelling hills
rise, constellations wink,
lakes move, and workshops work:
a million beings, quick
insects,
bladderwrack,
cruelty and goodness;
suns shine, auroras go dark –
here, in your huge essence,
the eternal unconscious wanders.

5

Like clotted blood, in shreds,
these words
are dropped in your path.
Existence stammers:
only law has a clear voice.
My active senses, reborn day after day,
are ready even now
for silence.

But up to now everything cries aloud –
chosen out of two thousand millions,
you alone, you the living bed,
you the gentle cradle, you the fierce tomb:
into yourself: into yourself I
beseech you, receive me.

(How deep the sky at daybreak!
Armies shine in light of steel.
The glitter hurts my sight.
I am lost, in this air.
Surely my heart must break,
beating in the light.)

6  *After-song*

(The train takes me, I follow after you,
perhaps today I'll find you again,
perhaps my burning face will be cool,
perhaps you'll say, in your undertone:

The water's lukewarm, go and try it!
A towel for your body, dry it!
The meat is baked, end your hunger!
In my bed for ever linger.)

'ON THE PAVEMENT . . .'

On the pavement a small puddle gave a wink,
the shadows settled down upon the city
and all the cheeping swarming sparrows fixed
their claws in branches silently but firmly,
for anyone who sleeps must clutch more tightly
than people moving off in the waking world,
men and women, tramcars, revving taxis
milled around like the instincts and the mind.

Under a gateway I kissed a girl's mouth
and was soon lost melting into the crowd,
only to leave them, to make this poem flout
my cares and leave them, turn and turn about.
I brooded slowly to give it its shape,
my animal grief has all that human sense
of sadness which can recognize its face
in garish streets, in worse advertisments.

[A kövezeten]

I OPEN THE DOOR

I open the door. The congealed smell
of vegetables drifts slowly from
the kitchen which is filled, swept
through by the clawed stove's grin. The room

is empty, nobody. Sixteen years
ago, what I can never forget.
I sat on an oilskin-covered chair
in the kitchen, tried to whimper, could not.

349

I know very well my mother is gone,
but this absence gives me no rest,
and I know nothing. Am I a grown man?
(The washing-up bowl shows no rust.)

It doesn't hurt, but I was even unable
to touch her, I never saw her dead,
never cried. And it's incomprehensible
that this is what I see, for ever, ahead.

*['Ajtót nyitok']*


## EVERYTHING'S OLD

Everything's old here, the hoary storm
leans on a twisted stick of lightning,
trails through the thorn-bearded roses, piping,
with twig legs like theirs, tottering along.

Everything's old. Revolution
coughs as it crouches on sharp-edged stones
ready for pelting, and with hands all bones
holds a bright penny: my best creation.

Can I not have an old see-through hand,
so that I could trace my wrinkled brow,
lay my hand in my lap, and seem to show
that tears of mine were dropping to the ground?

My days of youth! that holy age!
Oho, I'm a frisky chilly fish
flung by flame into the twilight's dish,
my dying ash becoming weed and sedge.

*['Öreg minden']*

## THEY'D LOVE ME

I don't meditate on good and evil.
I work, and I suffer: that's all.

I make screw-propeller boats, crockery,
badly in bad times, well in ordinary.

Numberless my works! Only my love,
being aware of them, takes stock of them, my love

takes stock of them all, my love has faith
but is silent before creed or oath.

Make me a tree, and the crow, I believe,
would only nest if there was no tree near.

Make me a field, and the old farmer's hoe
will turn up nothing but the weeds I've grown.

You'd have to water potatoes with sweat
to see them thrive on my thankless earth.

I'm water? A marsh begins to form.
Fire? I'm ash. But if I was transformed

to a god, in place of the god they know,
men would love me in truth, with all their soul.

*[Szeretnének]*


## MY MOTHER WASHING CLOTHES A WREATH

My mother's dead now I don't know what to do with her
she held the mug in both hands
one Sunday at dusk she smiled gently
flowers came the name unregistered the porter never saw him
if it was China she lived in they would dispatch her to the dragons
but she stands up
far from me is the dragon now I'll hurry home for a handful of rice
and I will plait my wreath instead of you

351

she patched my coat saw how good I looked naked
nobody ever yet saw me naked
her laundering had stooped her permanently
I never realized what a young woman she was
in her dreams she had a white apron the postman touched his cap
    to her then.

*[Anyám a mosásban gyászkoszorú]*


## DEAD LANDSCAPE

The water smokes, the bulrushes
sag and wilt into the wilderness.
The sky cowers deep in its quilt.
Thick silence cracks in the snow-filled
    field.

Gross and greasy the silent sundown;
flat the plain, featureless and round.
Only a single barge, heard
slapping self-absorbed on the furred
    lake.

Newborn time rattles in the cold
branches of the icy wood.
Chittering frost finds some moss here,
ties up its skeletal horse here
    to rest.

Then the vines. And among them plums.
Damp straw on the stocks and stumps.
And a procession of thin stakes,
good for old peasants' walking-sticks
    in the end.

A croft – this countryside revolves
all round it. Winter with its claws
keeps cracking plaster till it falls
in pieces from the homestead walls:
    cat's-play.

The pigsty door gapes wide open.
It sags and creaks, the wind's playpen.
What if a sucking-pig trots in
and a field of corn should sport and spin
    on the cob!

The room small, the peasants small.
Dried leaves in the smoker's bowl.
For these ones, no prayer will work.
They sit there, deep in the dark,
    thinking.

The vines are freezing for the landlord.
His is the crackling of the wood.
His is the pond and under its ice
it is for him the good fish hides
    in the mud.

*[Holt vidék]*


## THE WOODCUTTER

I wade through the fresh timber-piles.
Sap-wood shines in the sun and cries.
My winged hair is powdered with cold.
Winter draws its nail on my neck.
Time passes with a velvet step.

Everything sparkles: the freeze-up like an axe,
the land, our brows, the sky, our eyes.
And from the jet of shavings where the day
breaks out, another woodcutter growls:
Bite the trunk deep, we don't want frills!

Break down the oaks without a word!
Why be a laggard if the tree should bleed?
Strike the trunk, strike the doomed wood,
the feudal puszta groans and howls!
– says the axe, the broad axe, as it smiles.

*[Favágó]*

## BLIGHTY NUMBERS

Farmworker-feet first
Amputated from the spade...Nothing now
Of the warm colour-drizzle to soak
The dryness of their eyes.

Clamour of bell-metal
Moulted into satanic tanks
Smashed their fine spine-steel
Into grenades.

Infiltrated lungs are
Marched through by gasping froth-fiends
And whole Siberias were interned
In their gentle brains.

These are the ones
Whose mothers received just something back
At the customs-post of more human pits
Where now all kinds of

Stammering Christs are
Calcifying into one, till the bacchanalia
Of death-rattles mounts up into a
Terror-sermon on the mount.

On their missing arms
The breadwinning palm is fixed as a fist,
It sears their heart, it rings out
The advent of Peace.

*[Rokkantak]*

## MARCH 1937

Soft rain is drifting like a smoke
across the tender fuzz of wheat.
As soon as the first stork appears
winter shrivels in retreat.
Spring comes, tunnelling a path
mined with exploding spikes of green.
The hut, wide open to the sun,
breathes hope and wood-dust sharp and clean.

The papers say that mercenaries
are ravaging the face of Spain.
A brainless general in China
chases peasants from hill to plain.
The cloth we use to wipe our boots
comes laundered back in blood again.
All round, big words bemuse and smooth
the voiceless miseries in men.

My heart is happy as a child's.
Flora loves me. But oh what arms
the beauty of love? For us, for all,
war stirs its withering alarms.
The bayonet contends in zeal
with the assaulting tank. Alone
I draw to us the force I need
against the fear I can't disown.

Men – women – all have sold themselves.
A heart? They keep it close as sin.
Hearts torn by hate – I pity you,
I shudder to see hatred win.
A little life on earth I have,
yet here I watch all life unfold –
O Flora, in this blaze of love
nothing surrenders to the cold!

May our daughter be beautiful
and good, our son be fearless, keen.
May they transmit some sparks beyond
star-clusters you and I have seen.

355

When this sun loses its great fire,
the children of our illumination
will launch towards infinity
their own galactic exploration.

*[Marcius]*


## EPITAPH FOR A SPANISH FARM-HAND

General Franco made me one of his crack troops,
  fear of the firing-squad ensured I was no deserter.
It was fear that kept me fighting justice and freedom
  at the walls of Irun. Death found me all the same.

*[Egy spanyol földmíves sírverse]*


## ELEGY

Smoke, under a low leaden sky, swirls hooded
in thick banks over the sad land:
and so my soul, back and forward,
sways like the smoke.
Sways, yet stays.

Iron soul you are – yet tender in images!
Going behind the heavy tread of the real,
look deep into yourself, see
where you were born!

– Here, under a sky once supple and flowing
across the loneliness of thin dividing
walls, where the menacing, impassively imploring silence
of misery slowly loosens the melancholy
so solidly
packed in the thinker's heart
and mingles it with the heart
of millions.

The whole dominion of men
begins here. Here everything is a ruin.
A tough euphorbia has spread
its umbrella over the abandoned factory yard.
Into a damp darkness
the days go down by stained steps
from shatter of paltry windows.
Tell me:
is it here you are from?
Here, where you are tied to your gloomy wish
to be like other wretched souls
in whom this age, the great age, is
straitjacketed: the others whose faces
are marked by every line that's made?

Here you rest, here where the rickety creak
of a fence still guards the greed
of the moral order,
and watches it all.
Can you recognize yourself? Here the souls
wait in a void for the towering beauty-filled
future, as the dark and desolate shacks
have dreams of houses, lifting high
a nimble web of murmurs. Set
in the dried mud, fragments of glass
stare with fixed eyes, cut off from the light,
over the tortured meadow-grass.

From the low hills a thimble
of sand rolls down at random... and there's a flash,
a buzz of some fly – black, green, or blue –
attracted here from richer neighbourhoods
by the rags,
by the leavings of man.
Good is mother earth, tormented in her care,
also in her way
preparing a table.
A yellow weed springs in a saucepan there!

What have you to say
to this dry heart's-leap of recognition which draws me –
to a landscape that is bone of my bone?

357

What of my rich torment – coming back, back here?
So a mother's son,
after the cudgels of strangers, will return.
Here, and only here, you may smile and cry, and
here, here only, can your sinew endure,
my soul! This is my native land.

*[Elégia]*

PROFIT

Pound your dough by the gas-flame,
or bake your red bricks with their cavities;
get the hoe to shatter your palm;
sell yourself as your skirt twists;
floor a mine-shaft, crawl the pits;
shoulder a sack through the markets;
learn a trade or don't learn it –
here you stand, there profit sits.

Rinse your silks in a petrol-stream;
pick onions, squatting in the grit;
kill the goat that bleats your name;
cut trouser-cloth to tailor's fit;
stick with it! Why should you stop it?
You'll get the sack, for what good that is!
Then beg? Or burgle? But laws hit –
here you stand, there profit sits.

Wring out verse in a lovelorn dream;
cure Prague ham for festivities;
cull herbs; sweat at the coal-seam;
keep ledgers, cover up their secrets;
wear caps with gold braid on the skip;
live in Paris or in Claypitts –
even with wages in your pocket
here you stand, there profit sits.

Attila, I could go on and bore you;
you know you don't live on salmon cuts –
you can hang about or they can employ you
but here you stand, there profit sits.

[Haszon]


'FREIGHT TRAINS SHUNT . . .'

Freight trains shunt on the tracks,
the dreamlike clanking
fits light shackles
on the silent landscape.

The broken stones
crouch in their own shadow,
glitter in
secret, show
they are in place
as never before.

Unknown the enormous night
this heavy night is but a shaving of,
as it drops down on us
like an iron splinter on dust.

Sun-born desire!
If the bed holds a shadow, would you tire
of lying awake
through the weight
of that whole night?

The freight shed
has a dusty lamp burning nearby
which shows itself but nothing else.
The mind in its longing is like this.
It flickers bravely, against
the great dead
light of the sky.

['Tehervonatok tolatnak . . .']

359

NIGHT IN THE SUBURBS

The light smoothly withdraws
its net from the yard, and as water
gathers in the hollow of the ditch,
darkness has filled our kitchen.

Silence. – The scrubbing-brush sluggishly
rises and drags itself about;
above it, a small piece of wall is in
two minds to fall or not.

The greasy rags of the sky
have caught the night; it sighs;
it settles down on the outskirts;
it sets off through the square, going where?
It kindles a dim moon for a fire.

The workshops stand
like a ruin;
within
the thickest gloom
a plinth for silence to assume.

On the windows of the textile factory
the bright moon now climbs
in a cluster of light,
the moon's soft light
is a thread at the boards of the looms,
and all through the idle night
the darkened machines weave the dreams
of the weaver-girls – the unravelled dreams.

Farther on, iron-works, nut-and-bolt-works
and cement-works, bounded by a graveyard.
Family vaults alive with echoes.
The factories sleep with their arms over
the sombre secret of their resurrection.
A cat comes poking a paw through the railings.

The superstitious watchman catches
a will-o-the-wisp – a flash of

brilliance – the cold
glitter of beetle-backed dynamos.

A train-whistle.

The damp explores the greyness,
probes the leaves of splintered trees,
lays the dust more heavily
along the streets.

On the street a policeman, a muttering workman.
A comrade rushes down
with leaflets in his hand:
sniffs ahead like a dog,
looks over his shoulder like a cat,
the lamp-posts watch him pass.

The tavern mouth ejects a sour glare;
puddles vomit from the window-sill;
the lamp inside shakes, gasping for air.
A solitary labourer stares.
The host is asleep, he snores.
The other one grinds his teeth by the wall,
his wretchedness gushes and weeps down the stair.
He hymns the revolution still.

The water cracks, goes stiff
like chilled metal, the wind
wanders about like a dog,
its huge tongue dangles
as it slobbers up the water.
Swimming like rafts on the stream
of the voiceless night, paillasses –

The warehouse is a grounded boat,
the foundry an iron barge,
while the foundryman sees a pink baby
taking shape in the iron mould.

Everything wet, everything heavy.
A musty hand maps the countries
of misery. There, on the barren fields,

on ragged grass – paper, and rags.
If only the paper could fly up! It stirs
slightly, weakly. See it try
to get on its way . . .

Filthy sheets are fluttering around
in your slapping wind, your wetting wind,
O night!
You cling to the sky as unthreaded
cambric clings to the rope, as sadness
clings to life, O night!
Night of the poor! Be my coal,
and the smoke at my heart's core,
cast me in your ore,
make me a seamless forge,
and make me a hammer that labours and rings,
and make my blade strike till it sings,
O night!

Grave night, heavy night.
My brothers, I too must turn out the light.
May misery be a brief lodger in our soul.
May the lice leave our body whole.

*[Külvárosi éj]*


'WELL, IN THE END I HAVE FOUND MY HOME . . .'

Well, in the end I have found my home,
the land where flawless chiselled letters
guard my name above the grave
where I'm buried, if I have buriers.

It will take me like a collecting-box,
this earth. For no one (sadly) wants
wartime leftovers of base metal,
wretched devalued iron coins.

Or an iron ring engraved
with noble words: new world, rights, land.

362

Our laws are still the fruit of war;
gold rings shine finer on the hand.

For many years I was alone.
Then all about me was a crowd.
It's up to you, they said, although
I'd have loved to follow them round.

It was like that, empty, the way I lived:
no one has to tell me it was.
I was compelled to play the fool
and now I die without a cause.

In that whole whirlwind of my life
I have tried to stand my ground.
More sinned against than sinning, I
leave that thought and laugh aloud.

Spring is beautiful, summer too,
autumn better, winter the best
when you leave your hopes for family
and hearth to other men at last.

['Ime, hát megleltem hazámat . . .']


## IN LIGHT, WHITE CLOTHES

*To Paul Ignotus*

I have chewed it all and spat it out,
everything that is not my food.
Up there, I neither care nor doubt:
soap-bubble or empyrean vault?
I know what is and is not good.

And like a little child, I know
only playing brings happiness.
I have so many games to show;
reality always turns to go,
appearance lives in steadiness.

The rich can have no love for me
as long as I am poor like this.
And the poor, I leave them equally
cold, how could I be consolatory
where love comes shameful and amiss?

I am the creator of my own love . . .
Star and planet feel my tread:
I set out for the gods above,
in opposition – heart calm enough –
in light, white clothes striding ahead.

*[Könnyü, fehér ruhában]*

# Gennady Aigi

## MOZART: CASSATION 1

*To S. Gubaidulina*

mozart divine mozart straw compasses
divine blade wind paper infarct mother-of-god
wind jasmine operation wind divine mozart
cassation twig jasmine operation angel
divine rose straw heart cassation mozart

*[Motsart: Kassatsiya 1]*

A NOTE: APOPHATIC

*K.B.*

but the night of this world should have been
enormous terrifying like the Lord-not-Revealed
such a thing could be endured
but murder-people
have seeped into the darkness of this white night:
terrifyingly-simple
terrifying Moscow night

*[Zapis': apophatic]*

LAKE AND BIRD

   The lake – so ravishingly-irregularly-round, so
distantly-translucent, that our appearance before this
is virtually a reverence.

   But in the very middle of it – on an unseen rock? –
is a bird: it trembles, flutters its wings, trembles –
and does not fly away, – and it is like: this place
was always so and always will be so.

   Suddenly – nothing but Sun. Happiness of Immensity.
And – with a single sigh-of-existence:

   'Amen'

*[Ozero i ptitsa]*

365

FIELD: HEIGHT OF WINTER

*To René Char*

god's-pyre! – this bright field
pushing everything right through (mile-posts and wind and distant
                                      dots of mills: more and more –
                                        as if out of this world – as if
                                        not in reality – withdrawn: o all
                                        this – unlacerating sparks
                                        flame of non-universal pyre)
I am – without tracks of whatever there may be
not universally shining
god's-pyre

                                      *[Pole: v razgare zimy]*


KRCH – 80

*(For the 80th anniversary of A.E. Kruchonykh)*

o I am
your surface
burning invisibly
from the interface *I-am-not* –

to the poet a name
crunching creative:

krch

krch

krch

## SENDING ROSES

to nephritic space
this greeting
of white! –

and let it ring out
there – as in an opal room
every roused velvetiness
with an eulenspiegelling of the stalk:

'till-till'

*[Pri posylke roz]*


## SUBURBAN HOUSE

*To my son Konstantin*

but from Homeland-Life
strange
secretive –

t h e    s o u l
g r o w s    g o l d
in the window-frame:

the willow
flowers –

– the child
stammers! –

secret meeting (flowering and chatter) –

in your – unstained – Homeland

*[Dom za gorodom]*

## THE BIRCHES RUSTLE

*To V. Korsunsky*

and I myself – murmuring:
'but maybe God...' –

birch-whisper:
'is dead...' –

and we
are the fallout – keeping it going? –

but why should it
not be like that? –

the dust howls up lonely and empty... –

(whisper of birches...
all living flesh murmurs...) –

and he will Resurrect
again?... –

...even without pain:

as for ever... –

the rustle – as from this!... –

...................................................... –
(as if forsaken – rustle of autumn)

*[Shumyat berezy]*

368

## ONCE MORE: PLACES IN THE FOREST

again t h e y a r e b e i n g s u n g ! they are! again t h e y
are resounding – everywhere – in unison! –

again about that time
wakening-time:

brightly
– by-the-meadow-of-suffering! –
motionlessly
and clearly – endlessly! –
and as if the morning was unwavering
in me: as in the world: absolutely:

and there they placed that place
in the midst of others related
to them:

place I once knew! –

it shone
like an hour of happiness:

with a high
clear centre:

hawthorn – keeping silent beside the singing
like god keeping silent – behind the resounding Word:

keeping silent – with a personality untouched:

one touch – and that is: n o m o r e G o d

*[Snova: mesta v lesu]*

369

**Ezra Pound**


LAMENT OF THE FRONTIER GUARD: A RESTRUCTION

*Murnin o the Merches-Gaird*

By the Nor'Yett, the wund blaws fu o saun,
Lanelie fae time's jizzen tae thir days!
The wid crines, the gress yallas at hairst.
I sclim tours an tours
　　　　tae vizzy the barbour straths:
Oorie barmekin, the lift, the braid desart.
Nae waw stauns noo i this clachan.
Banes blanchit wi a thoosan forsts,
Hie-humphit deid-knoks, owrheildit wi trees an gress;
Wha brung uz thir effeirs?
Wha brung the levin o the cankert coorts?
Wha brung the airmy wi its touk an tarantara?
Barbour keengs.
A douce spring, cheengit tae bluid-gowpin hairst.
A stramash o fechters, spreed owr this haill kintra,
Three hunner an saxty thoosan,
An dool, dool lik dash an dag.
Dool awaw, an dool, dool at retour.
Toom, toom faulds,
Wi nae a chiel o the fecht upo them,
　　　　Nae langer birkies tae gaird or tae breenge.
Och, hoo sall ye ken the doolie wae at the Nor'Yett,
Wi oor ledar Li Mu's name negleckit,
An uz, the gairdsmen, fother for teegers.

*[Pound's poem is a translation from the Chinese of Li Po (701-762)]*


370

*UNCOLLECTED POEMS*
(1937-1996)

# Endre Ady

## I AM BREAKING NEW WATERS

Courage, my boat! Tomorrow's hero boards you,
Let them guffaw their fill at the drunken oarsman,
Fly, my boat,
Courage, my boat: Tomorrow's hero boards you.

Scudding, scudding, scudding always onwards,
To new, new Waters, great and virgin Waters,
Fly, my boat,
Scudding, scudding, scudding always onwards.

New horizons shimmer in the distance,
Life is new and awesome every minute,
Fly, my boat,
New horizons shimmer in the distance.

I have no use for dreams of other dreamers,
I break waters of new wants, wounds, and secrets,
Fly, my boat,
I have no use for dreams of other dreamers.

Let dolts and dullards find some other minstrel,
I rise on pub-fumes or the Holy Spirit,
Fly, my boat,
Let dolts and dullards find some other minstrel.

*[Új vizeken járok]*

## LONG LIVE THE VICTOR

Don't tramp on it too heavily,
Don't stamp on it too heavily,
Our beautiful poor blood-slowed heart
Which – look! – still tries to race.

Sad black-starred folk the Hungarians.
Knew revolution and they brought us
The remedy, War, that Vampire,
Blackguards damned even in their graves.

A dull rumbling fills our barracks,
Oh how much blood they have to remember,
Oh crypts of mourning, crypts of horror,
Catafalque, catafalque at your door.

We were the idiots of the earth,
Poor drained-out Hungarians,
And now let the conquerors come:
Long live the victor.

*[Üdvözlet a gyözönek]*


## GIVE ME THOSE EYES OF YOURS

Give me those eyes of yours,
Let me plant them in my fading forehead,
Let me see myself as splendid.

Give me those eyes of yours,
Your blue sight always building fitly,
Adding beauty, adding pity.

Give me those eyes of yours,
That can find me beautiful
And can yearn and burn and kill.

Give me those eyes of yours,
Loving you I love myself too,
And it's your eyes I envy you.

*[Add nekem a szemeidet]*

## A STROLL IN THE COUNTRY

Silence all round, and I stroll in silence
across this small old Guignol-country
rinsed out by grubby autumn floods
and weeping eaves of each thatched cottage.
And perched on the crest of this great quiet,
strutting and swaggering, the peacock's envy,
a vulgar, all-usurping, gun-clutching
blackguardly rout of hunting gentry.

Here and there the gloomy thrust
of factory chimneys and urban towers:
how many crippled, begging, slaving
in Sin, live silent there in tears.
And heroes from old savage wakes
dress up to gnaw man's-heart today,
and serfs that once rebelled are nowhere,
they live serfs still if not swept away.

They are living still, but their soul is Silence,
there is silence, yes, but never such silence:
from half-a-country's choking breasts
revenges rattle, black and scarlet.
Town greets village with silence-sign,
a terrible word lurks dumb in these emblems:
soundless pit-shafts with damped-down curses
hoard their hellish unheard-of engines.

Silence will redeem everything here,
explosions dream in its deaf lap,
and this little thousandfold-strangled
land will explode. Let the usurpers clap
the grateful levy of this cold and silent
soil to their hearts, winter-secure:
at a flash, like an avalanche, unasked
the fury of buried guns will roar.

*[Séta az országban]*

## A GRACEFUL MESSAGE OF DISMISSAL

Let the spell break a hundred-and-first time
that has broken a hundred: I dismiss you yet again
for ever, if you believed I still held you dear,
and believed one more dismissal stood in line.
A hundred-times-wounded, here, I throw at you
the sumptuous king's-robe of my forgetting you.
Wear it, for the weather will come colder,
wear it, for I am sorry for us both,
for the huge shame of such unequal fight,
for your humiliation, for I don't know what,
and for you I am sorry, for you alone here.

How long, how silently it has been like this:
how often, to reassure you in your fate
by dazzling favours, you were given a golden
Leda-psalm, sent white-hot to the fairest
of the fair. I received nothing, withdrew nothing:
it was my grace to give you false belief
in kisses 'wont to wanton otherwhere'
and loves I was 'wont to love otherly':
and I am grateful for all these embraces,
and despite everything I thank such wisps
of Leda-gone as any man can thank
on leaving behind him an old listless kiss.

And for how long I have not sought you out
in gritty past, in muddy present, how long
since I took leave of you, on that slave-track
where your sex steps into its circumscribed fate.
For how long now I have looked for nothing
but what you might keep of my splendid self,
of the magical attributes my verse drew youwards,
so that you can find consolation, lonely, loving,
in having existed too, as well as the man
who left a world unclaimed at last to hang
adornments from his store upon a woman.

From this proud breast 'wont to be gaping great',
I had to see your stylish, majestic fall –
oh not the bitch-revenge of a jilted piece

who sets a raging ambush for her venging-mate:
not anything to mock your poor scant self
since you go branded by my Croesushood
and your once-been-mine was a belief for you,
to pass so deftly none can sense or tell,
the one in whom I planted my embrace
so that she too might take delight in it,
she who had been the merest question-mark
and needed me alone to find fulfilment.

Now will you frou-frou down, well-wilted flower
fallen from its dust-smothered prayer-book,
or will you rush about and rub threadbare
your borrowed halo, your sad bridle's power,
and what at last trembles to its blessing in a girl,
my own self-idolizing act of prayer?
I ask Fate now to ask your fate to leave
thinking it can twist round the fate in my stars,
and I am easy whether flood or fire devours
you, for through me you live, I saw you first
and you are long dead long out of my eyes.

*[Elbocsátó szép üzenet]*


## IN THE BOAT OF MEDITATION

Meditation, sad-straked boat,
I slip you off from my death-port:
We go
And I let my blue flag float.

My old, fast craft still beckons me,
But I leave the all of life behind me,
We go,
And may our wake efface memory.

This is marvellousness, the finest,
Our soul is being laid in state,
We go,
Our life and all: godspeed at last.

377

Between life and death is our ocean;
Drawn by a divine far-off confusion
We go,
Set on the waters of meditation.

Meditation, sad-straked boat,
I slip you off from my death-port:
We go,
Till sun-death cuts tomorrow short.

*[A tünödés csolnakjan]*


## Pierre Albert-Birot

THE POET SALUTES THE DIVINE
EJACULATOR MAGNIFICENT IN M
OVEMENT SCEPTRE STEADY IN H
AND HOW HANDSOME YOU ARE ER
ECT SUPERB IMPERIOUS SUN ZE
NITH LOVER HOW HANDSOME YOU
ARE WITH YOUR FORM TENSED A
ND AIMED AT THE FUTURE HOW
HANDSOME YOU ARE WITH YOUR
HARD POLISHED SUBSTANCE YOU
ARE MORE HANDSOME THAN ALL
HANDSOME THINGS A VISIBLE G
OD DIVINELY GIVEN TO EVERY
MAN THE POET WANTS TO REBUI
LD YOU A LUMINOUS TEMPLE AL
L HUNG WITH GARLANDS OF POE
TRY TO BE THE RESORT OF ALL
MEN COMING TO SEE YOUR GOLD
EN IMAGE HIGH AS THE TEMPLE
AND CELEBRATE YOU YOU WHOM
WE HAVE DENIED THESE TWO TH
OUSAND YEARS YOU THE CENTRE
YOU WHO ARE THE AFFIRMATION

O   COME   LET   US   ADORE   HIM

*[from Poèmes à la Chair]*

EVERYTHING GOES AT THE COMING OF THE BL
ACK TRIANGLE THE LYRICAL TRIANGLE THE
CENTRAL TRIANGLE SINGS DISTRACTEDLY
THE RISING OF THE MASTER & THE BL
ACK TRIANGLE BLINDS THE DESIRE G
AZING AT IT THE CENTRIPETAL D
ESIRE WITH GENTLE HANDS BUT
THE BLACK TRIANGLE IS A D
ESIRE WITHOUT HANDS & T
HE MALE IS SUBDUED BY
THIS CURLY GOD & TH
E BLACK TRIANGLE
IS IN MAN'S HAN
D & AT EVERY
MOMENT A W
ORLD END
S    EXPL
O D I N
G IN
S P
AC
E

[from *Poèmes à la Chair*]

## Guillaume Apollinaire

THE MIRABEAU BRIDGE

Under the Mirabeau bridge runs the Seine
        And our loves
    Must I remember them
Joy always came to remain after pain

        Come night again strike time again
        The days are running I remain

379

With hand in hand be calm and face to face
    While beneath
  Our bridge of arms shall pass
Waves that bear our insatiable gaze

    Come night again strike time again
    The days are running I remain

Love like that rilling water runs away
    Love rills away
  How slowly runs life's day
And how impatient is expectancy

    Come night again strike time again
    The days are running I remain

Pass day to silence and pass week again
    Not time gone
  Not our loves shall return
Under the Mirabeau bridge runs the Seine

    Come night again strike time again
    The days are running I remain.

*[Le Pont Mirabeau]*


## TIME TO COME

Let us take up the straw
Let us look at the snow
Let us write letters
Waiting for orders

Let us smoke our pipes
As we dream of love
Look at the trenches
Let us look at the rose

380

The fountain has not dried
Not more than the straw's gold has dulled
Let us look at the bee
And not be dreaming of what is to come

Let us look at our hands
Which are indeed the snow
The rose and the bee
As they are what is to come

*[L'Avenir]*


THE PARTING

And on their faces, pallor
And if they sobbed, broken

Like the pure snow petals or
Your hands my kisses taken
Leaves from the woods were shaken.

*[Le Départ]*


THE PRETTY REDHEAD

Here then I stand before all a man of some judgement
Knowing life and what the living can know of death
Having had experience of the griefs and joys of love
Having sometimes been able to make capital of my thoughts
Knowing several languages
Being well travelled
Having seen war with the Artillery and the Infantry
Wounded in the head trepanned under chloroform
Having lost my best friends in the atrocious battle
Old and new I know as well as a single man could know them
And this day without being in vexation over the war
Among ourselves and for ourselves my friends
I am critic in that long strife of tradition and creation
            Of Order of Adventure

You whose lips are formed in the image of God's
Lips that are order itself
Will you indulge us when you compare us
With such as were the consummation of order
Us who are eager everywhere for adventure

We are no enemies of yours
We want for our possessions countries vast and strange
Where the secret of flowers beckons any culling
Where there are unbeheld fires colours new to sight
Millings of imponderable shadows
To be manifested into actuality
We would explore the Good the great marches of silence
Remember there is time to hound or to recall
Pity for us fighting still at the frontiers
Of the boundless and all time to come
Pity for our mistaking pity for our sinning

Now in passion comes the summer season
And my youth is as dead as the dead spring
O sun this is the burning hour of Reason
                              and I am waiting
To follow her always the sweet form finely bred
Which she assumes for my undying loving
She comes to my iron heart with a magnet's alluring
                    She has the lure in charming
                    Of a most lovable redhead

Her hair is of gold seen as
A lasting lightning-flash
Or slowly dancing fires
In the fading tea-rose

But laugh laugh at me
Men in all parts but specially you who are here
For there are so many things I dare not say to you
So many things you would not allow me to say
Have pity on me

*[La Jolie rousse]*

## Anna Akhmatova

How lovely here! the rustle, the crunch!
Every morning the frost is stronger.
Flames of white embrace the bush
Where icy roses hang and linger.
Through these sumptuous festive snows
Our ski-tracks silently recall
How in such strange and remote days
Our ways met here, beyond recall.

*['Khorosho zdes' : i shelest, i khrust']*

## Rosalía de Castro

When wind is hard in the north
And fire leaps in the hearth
And they come through my door,
Hungry, like skeletons in rags,
The cold freezes my spirit
As it splits their flesh apart.
And seeing them go comfortless
Shakes my very heart,
Takes it where desolation
And chains and darkness are.

A child, and already a stranger
To the habit of tears:
Misery dries the soul
And the need to weep;
A child, already old
In his gestures and deeds.

Beggar, how you seize life!
Precocious as evil,
Implacable as hatred,
Hard as truth's teeth.

*['Cuando sopla el Norte duro']*


'I in my bed of thistles,
You in your bed of roses and feathers,
He spoke the truth who spoke of an abyss
From your good fortune to me in my wretchedness.
          Yet I would never change
          My bed for your bed,
There are roses that envenom and corrupt,
And thistles on the road to heaven
          Though harsh to the flesh.'

*[' "Yo en mi lecho de abrojos" ']*


The spring does not flow now, the source is exhausted;
No traveller goes now to slake his thirst at its waters.

The grass does not grow there, or the daffodil blow there,
Or the scent of the lilies like a cloud come wafting over.

Only the gravelly bed of the dried-up river
Spells out a memento-mori to appal the thirsty.

And that is all! – Far off another gully murmurs
Where the mild violets breathe and thrive as perfumers,

And foliage of a willow falls to meet its image,
Cascading its coolest shade around the rivulets.

The thirsty traveller who comes along this road
Drenches his lips in that pale clear arroyo
Which the tree with its boughs has overshadowed,
And the spring that has died is forgotten in his joy.

*['Ya no mana la fuente, se agotó el manantial']*

Crows were cawing on the high ground,
The mourners mourned around the dead,
And waves broke with an angry sound
Into the harsh music overhead.

Something ironically rough
Echoed through these symphonic chords;
Some black, fantastic, speechless stuff
That plucked at the soul's anxious cords.

Soon enough the funeral hymns ceased;
The staring crowd shuffled away;
From groans and lamentations released,
The man alone in the earth lay.

And only in the distance, sketched on the haze,
Fringes of the black banner swayed,
As a night-bird's feather sways,
Snatched by the winds, in the swoop they made.

*['En la altura los cuervos graznaban']*


Justice of men! I go in search of you
       And all that I find
Is the *word* your fame gives lustre to;
In the *deed* itself you are stubbornly denied.

– And you: have you too no abiding-place
(With pain I ask), O justice of the skies?
When one sin that was sinned within an instant
Shall linger in its ghastly expiation
       For as long as hell has its fires!

*['¡ Justicia de los hombres!, yo te busco']*

The atmosphere is incandescent;
The fox explores an empty road;
    Sick grow the waters
That sparkled in the clear arroyo,
    Unfluttered stands the pine
Waiting for fickle winds to blow.

    A majesty of silence
    Overpowers the meadow;
Only the hum of an insect troubles
The spreading, dripping forest shadow,
    Relentless and monotonous
As muffled rattle in a dying throat.

In such a summer the hour of midday
    Could as well go
By the name of night, to struggle-weary
    Man who has never known
Greater vexation from the vast cares
Of the soul, or from matter's majestic force.

Would it were winter again! The nights! The cold!
O those old loves of ours so long ago!
Come back to make this fevered blood run fresh,
Bring back your sharp severities and snows
To these intolerable summer sorrows...
Sorrows!...While vine and corn stand thick and gold!

The cold, the heat; the autumn or the spring;
Where, where has delight set up its home?
Beautiful are all seasons to the man
Who shelters happiness within his soul;
But the deserted, orphaned spirit feels
No season smile upon its luckless door.

                *['Candente está la atmósfera']*

Hour after hour and day after day
Between the ever-watchful sky
And earth, life breaks
Like a great headlong river, falls
And streams away.

Restore the perfume to the flower
After it fades;
When waves run up to kiss the sand
And kiss, and die, and kiss, and die – then save
Their plaints, their murmurs, and engrave
On sheets of bronze the harmonies they've made.

Times that are gone, laughter, heartache,
Black afflictions, lies to soothe pain –
Ah, my soul, what track of them remains,
What tokens and truces remain?

['*Hora tras hora, día tras día*']


– I love you . . . Why do you hate me?
– I hate you . . . Why do you love me? –
Saddest, most mysterious
Secret of the spirit is this.
And yet it is a truth, hard
As truth in a torturer's hand!
– You hate me, because I love you;
I love you, because you hate me.

['*– Te amo . . . ¿por qué me odias?*']


Now that the frost
Throws over them its sparkling silver thread,
All the plants stand stiff on a chilled stem,
Stiff as my soul with the cold.

They in these frosts
Take promise of an early-stirring bud;
For me the frosts are silent hands
Promising the fabric of my shroud.

['*Mientras el hielo las cubre*']

I do not even know what it is I am searching for
Through earth and air and sky without rest;
I do not know what my search is for, but
It is for something I lost – I do not know when –
And never find again, though I dream it lives
Unseen in everything I see and sense.

O happiness, shall I never surprise you in hiding
Once more, in sky or air or on earth,
            Even though I know you exist,
            No dream, no idle guess!

                              ['*Ya no sé lo que busco eternamente*']


From the deep measure of the ocean-murmur
            And the moaning of the wind,
From the ambiguous shimmer that plays over
            The wood and the cloud;
From the cheeping as a nameless bird flies past,
From the country smell that goes diffused, untraced,
            Breeze-stolen out of the sierra
            Or out of the valley ground,
From these and from the burden of the world
            That some faint under, there are
            Worlds where haven is found.

                              ['*Del rumor cadencioso de la onda*']


THE BELLS

I love them, I listen to them
As I listen to the wind's whisper,
Or to the fountain's murmur
Or the bleating of the lamb.

The bells are like the birds,
Their cries and echoes welcome
The earliest ray of daybreak
That opens up the skies.

And their notes, pealing out
Across the plains and the peaks,
Keep in them something candid,
Something serene and sweet.

Were their tongues for ever dumb,
What gloom in the air, what cloud!
What silence in every church!
What strangeness among the dead!

*[Las campanas]*


## St Columba


THE MAKER ON HIGH

Ancient exalted seed-scatterer whom time gave no progenitor:
he knew no moment of creation in his primordial foundation
he is and will be all places in all time and all ages
with Christ his first-born only-born and the holy spirit co-borne
throughout the high eternity of glorious divinity:
three gods we do not promulgate one God we state and intimate
salvific faith victorious: three persons very glorious.

Benevolence created angels and all the orders of archangels
thrones and principalities powers virtues qualities
denying otiosity to the excellence and majesty
of the not-inactive trinity in all labours of bounty
when it mustered heavenly creatures whose well devised natures
received its lavish proffer through power-word for ever.

Came down from heaven summit down from angelic limit
dazzling in his brilliance beauty's very likeness
Lucifer downfalling (once woke at heaven's calling)
apostate angels sharing the deadly downfaring
of the author of high arrogance and indurated enviousness
the rest still continuing safe in their dominions.

Dauntingly huge and horrible the dragon ancient and terrible
known as the lubric serpent subtler in his element
than all the beasts and every fierce thing living earthly
dragged a third – so many – stars to his gehenna
down to infernal regions not devoid of dungeons
benighted ones hell's own parasite hurled headlong.

Excellent promethean armoury structuring world harmony
had created earth and heaven and wet acres of ocean
also sprouting vegetation shrubs groves plantations
sun moon stars to ferry fire and all things necessary
birds fish and cattle and every animal imaginable
but lastly the second promethean the protoplast human being.

Fast upon the starry finishing the lights high shimmering
the angels convened and celebrated for the wonders just created
the Lord the only artificer of that enormous vault of matter
with loud and well judged voices unwavering in their praises
an unexampled symphony of gratitude and sympathy
sung not by force of nature but freely lovingly grateful.

Guilty of assault and seduction of our parents in the garden
the devil has a second falling together with his followers
whose faces set in horror and wingbeats whistling hollow
would petrify frail creatures into stricken fearers
but what men perceive bodily must preclude luckily
those now bound and bundled in dungeons of the underworld.

He Zabulus was driven by the Lord from mid heaven
and with him the airy spaces were choked like drains with faeces
as the turbid rump of rebels fell but fell invisible
in case the grossest villains became willy-nilly
with neither walls nor fences preventing curious glances
tempters to sin greatly openly emulatingly.

Irrigating clouds showering wet winter from sea-fountains
from floods of the abysses three-fourths down through fishes
up to the skyey purlieus in deep blue whirlpools
good rain then for cornfields vineyard-bloom and grain-yields
driven by blasts emerging from their airy treasuring
desiccating not the land-marches but the facing sea-marshes.

Kings of the world we live in: their glories are uneven
brittle tyrannies disembodied by a frown from God's forehead:
giants too underwater groaning in great horror
forced to burn like torches cut by painful tortures
pounded in the millstones of underworld maelstroms
roughed rubbed out buried in a frenzy of flints and billows.

Letting the waters be sifted from where the clouds are lifted
the Lord often prevented the flood he once attempted
leaving the conduits utterly full and rich as udders
slowly trickling and panning through the tracts of this planet
freezing if cold was called for warm in the cells of summer
keeping our rivers everywhere running forward for ever.

Magisterial are his powers as the great God poises
the earth ball encircled by the great deep so firmly
supported by an almighty robust nieve so tightly
that you would think pillar and column held it strong and solemn
the capes and cliffs stationed on solidest foundations
fixed uniquely in their place as if on immovable bases.

No one needs to show us: a hell lies deep below us
where there is said to be darkness worms beasts carnage
where there are fires of sulphur burning to make us suffer
where men are gnashing roaring weeping wailing deploring
where terrible gehennas are groaning and groans are never-ending
where parched and fiery horror feeds thirst and hunger.

Often on their knees at prayer are many said to be there
under the earth books tell us they do not repel us
though they found it unavailing the scroll not unrolling
whose fixed seals were seven when Christ warning from heaven
unsealed it with the gesture of a resurrected victor
fulfilling the prophets' foreseeing of his coming and his decreeing.

Paradise was planted primally as God wanted
we read in sublime verses entering into Genesis
its fountain's rich waters feed four flowing rivers
its heart abounds with flowers where the tree of life towers
with foliage never fading for the healing of the nations
and delights indescribable abundantly fruitful.

Quiz sacred Sinai: who is it has climbed so high?
Who has heard the thunder-cracks vast in the sky-tracts?
Who has heard the enormous bullroaring of the war-horns?
Who has seen the lightning flashing round the night-ring?
Who has seen javelins flambeaus a rock-face in shambles?
Only to Moses is this real only to the judge of Israel.

Rue God's day arriving righteous high king's assizing
*dies irae* day of the vindex day of cloud and day of cinders
day of the dumbfoundering day of great thundering
day of lamentation of anguish of confusion
with all the love and yearning of women unreturning
as all men's striving and lust for worldly living.

Standing in fear and trembling with divine judgement assembling
we shall stammer what we expended before our life was ended
faced by rolling videos of our crimes however hideous
forced to read the pages of the conscience book of ages
we shall burst out into weeping sobbing bitter and unceasing
now that all means of action have tholed the last retraction.

The archangelic trumpet-blast is loud and great at every fastness
the hardest vaults spring open the catacombs are broken
the dead of the world are thawing their cold rigor withdrawing
the bones are running and flying to the joints of the undying
their souls hurry to meet them and celestially to greet them
returning both together to be one not one another.

Vagrant Orion driven from the crucial hinge of heaven
leaves the Pleiades receding most splendidly beneath him
tests the ocean boundaries the oriental quandaries
as Vesper circling steadily returns home readily
the rising Lucifer of the morning after two years mourning:
these things are to be taken as type and trope and token.

X spikes and flashes like the Lord's cross marching
down with him from heaven as the last sign is given
moonlight and sunlight are finally murdered
stars fall from dignity like fruits from a fig-tree
the world's whole surface burns like a furnace
armies are crouching in caves in the mountains.

You know then the singing of hymns finely ringing
thousands of angels advancing spring up in sacred dances
quartet of beasts gaze from numberless eyes in praise
two dozen elders as happiness compels them
throw all their crowns down to the Lamb who surmounts them
'Holy holy holy' binds the eternal trinity.

Zabulus burns to ashes all those adversaries
who deny that the Saviour was Son to the Father
but we shall fly to meet him and immediately greet him
and be with him in the dignity of all such diversity
as our deeds make deserved and we without swerve
shall live beyond history in the state of glory.

[*Altus Prosator*]


## Jean Genet

*from* THE FISHERMAN OF THE SUQUET

(i)
A certain complicity,
      a harmony is established
between my mouth and the cock
      (still hidden in his sky-blue shorts)
      of this fisher-boy of eighteen.
All about him – air, weather, countryside
      grew vague. As he lay
on the sand, there was a trembling
in what I could see between the tilted branches
      of his naked legs. The sand kept
track of his feet, kept track of his sex too,
      a heavy packet
moved by the sultry disturbance of evening.
      Every crystal glittered.
– What is your name?
– And yours?

393

In love from that night,
with a boy who was cool who was tricky who was
        fantastic who was
                alive
and where he came you could feel
the shudder his body flung
over waters skies houses
rocks boys girls
and the page my pen's on.
        My patience! –
        a medal on your lapel.
Golden float of dust surrounds him,
        draws him away from me.
With the sun of your face
        you are darker than a gypsy.
His eyes! – in the midst of thistles and blackthorns
        and the misty-robed season, the autumn.
His cock! – my lips drawn back from my teeth.
His hands
        set light to things, then darken them
        bring life to things, destroy them again.
The big toe of his left foot
        with its ingrown nail
sometimes digs at my nostril, or at my mouth.
        Well, it's huge, but
        what about the foot
        and then
        what about the leg –

        .    .    .    .    .    .


(ii)
Hide the night's riches under your feet!
Walk easily on red-hot roads!
Peace goes with you.
Among the whins and nettles, the blackthorns and the forests,
        your step
lays down levels of darkness.
And each of your feet, each jasmine foot
buries me in a porcelain tomb.
You darken the world.


                        394

Riches of that night – Ireland and its rebellions,
musk-rats scurrying across the moors, an arch
of light, wine mounting from your stomach, a
wedding in the valley, a hanged man swaying
in the apple-blossom, and then that place (the heart
knocks madly at the sight of it) in your shorts
protected by hawthorn petals –

O from all parts the pilgrims come down!
tracing the line of your hips in the last sunlight,
panting, climbing the wooded slopes of your thighs
where day becomes night –

By grassy moors, below your unbuckled
belt, with our throats dry and our
feet and shoulders weary, reaching Him.
His is the blaze that even Time is veiled in,
by a crape that perhaps the moon and the sun
and the stars, your eyes, your tears are shining over.
Time lies like a shadow at his feet.
Nothing will grow there but strange purple flowers
from these wrinkled bulbs.
– Our hands clasped at our heart,
our fists at our teeth.

*[Le Pêcheur du Suquet]*


## Ágnes Gergely


CRAZED MAN IN CONCENTRATION-CAMP

All through the march, besides bag and blanket
he carried in his hands two packages of empty boxes,
and when the company halted for a couple of minutes
he laid the two packages of empty boxes neatly at each side,
being careful not to damage or break either of them,
the parcels were of

ornamental boxes
dovetailed by sizes each to each
and tied together with packing-cord,
the top box with a picture on it.
When the truck was about to start, the sergeant
shouted something in sergeant's language,
they sprang up suddenly,
and one of the boxes rolled down to the wheel,
the smallest one, the one with the picture:
'It's fallen' he said and made to go after it,
but the truck moved off
and his companion held his hands
while his hands held the two packages of boxes
and his tears trailed down his jacket
'It's fallen' he said that evening in the queue –
and it meant nothing to him to be shot dead.

*[Bolond munkaszolgálatos]*

## The Greek Anthology
**(In this selection of twenty-six poems, 6th century BC to 5th century AD)**

*Adaios*

For a dishy boy, you must move straight in.
    Tell him what you want. Keep fondling his balls.
It's no use saying: 'I feel like a brother to you':
    shame would hold you shivering at the gates.

(10.20)

*Aischylos*

And black Fate took those stubborn spearmen
    guarding their sheep-rippling acres.
They died but not their fame, their stubbornness.
    Clothed now in dust of Ossa.

(7.255)

*Alpheios*

Where are the birth-places of the heroes?
    The few you see hardly break the plain.
I passed you by, Mycenae, and knew you,
    dead, more desolate than a goat-field,
talked of by goat-herds. 'It stood here' (said
    the old man) 'covered in gold, the giants built it...'

                                                            (9.101)


*Antiphanes*

Man's makeshift days would flash past at the best,
    even if we all reached white hair and stick.
We've scarcely touched our peak when – Oh while it lasts
    pour from the great jug: pour song, love, wine!
Senile tagtail years are waiting. A hundred pounds
    you'd give in vain when the genitals are asleep.

                                                            (10.100)


Piddle-paddling race of critics, rhizome-fanciers
    digging up others' poetry, pusillanimous bookworms
coughing through brambles, aristophobes and Erinnaphils,
    dusty bitter barkers from Callimachus' kennels,
poet's-bane, nightshade of the neophytes,
    bacilli on singing lips: get off, get down, get lost!

                                                            (11.322)


*Hegesippos*

Hang that day with black, that night, sinister, moonless,
    that fearful wind-whipped sea-howl
which threw on shore the ship of gentle Abderion
    as he made unheard vows to the gods.
For out of that utter shipwreck on the sharp rocks
    of Seriphus, all he got was fire
from the city's pious hosts, and a voyage home
    to Abdera, bound in a bronze urn.

                                                            (13.12)

*Herakleitos*

The soil is freshly dug, the half-faded wreaths of leaves
    droop across the face of the tombstone.
What do the letters say, traveller? What can they tell you
    of the smooth bones the slab says it guards?
'Stranger, I am Aratemias of Cnidus. I was the wife
    of Euphro. Labour-pains were not withheld
from me. I left one twin to guide my husband's old age,
    and took the other to remind me of him.'

(7.465)


*Isidoros*

My name is Eteocles. The sea seduced me from my farm
    to be a merchant against my nature.
I was on a voyage across the Tyrrhenian Sea
    when a quick sharp squall tore the ship
from air and sent me down with it. Different winds
    ruffle the threshing-floor and belly the sail.

(7.532)


*Lucian*

Do tell me, Hermes, what was it like when the soul
    of Lollianus went down to Persephone's house?
I can't believe he'd be silent. 'Now listen to me –'
    Good God, to meet that man even when he's dead!

(11.274)


A beard-wagging stick-waving beggarman Cynic
    unlocked his wisdom to us one supper-time.
At first he refused the lentils and radishes:
    'Righteousness is not the slave of the belly.'
But then his eyes popped at some sharp-sauced quivering
    white pork slices that unhooked his prudence,
he quickly asked for a portion, and ate in earnest:
    'Pork slices are no drag on righteousness.'

(11.410)

We were all drunk, and Acindynus was determined to keep sober.
    The fool! To us he was the fuddled man out.

(11.429)


If you really imagine wisdom grows with a beard –
    ask my hairy goat to do a Plato.

(11.430)


I am Priapus. I was put here according to custom
    by Eutachides to guard his scraggy vines,
the idiot. A great cliff round me too. Well,
    all a thief gets here is me.

(16.238)


*Philippos*

Sosicles the farmer dedicated these sheaves
    from the furrows of his few acres to you
Demeter, friend of the wheat; his harvest was good.
    May later reapings also blunt his sickle.

(6.36)


His anchor, seaweed-probing, boat-securing,
his pair of oars that thrust through the swell,
the lead-weights his net soars up from,
his wicker creels marked out by floats,
his showerproof hat with its wide brim,
his evening flint for light at sea –
to you, King Poseidon, he dedicates these,
Archides, ending his beach-wanderings.

(6.90)


The whistling bellows of his furnace,
the sharp-toothed file that burrs the gold,
the fire-tongs with their twin crab claws,
the hare's feet that mop up the scrapings –
dedicated to Hermes by Demophon
the goldsmith, as age silts up his eyes.

(6.92)

A yellow-coated pomegranate, figs like lizards' necks,
    a handful of half-rosy part-ripe grapes,
a quince all delicate-downed and fragrant-fleeced,
    a walnut winking out from its green shell,
a cucumber with the bloom on it pouting from its leaf-bed,
    and a ripe gold-coated olive – dedicated
to Priapus friend of travellers, by Lamon the gardener,
    begging strength for his limbs and his trees.

(6.102)


To Pan the forest ranger, Gelo the hunter
dedicates me, his spear, long-used,
worn-edged, also the tatters of his
ravelled hunting-nets, his throttling nooses,
his trip-snares made of sinews, eager
to snap beasts' legs, his dogs' hard collars –
since time has undermined his stride
and his hill-walking days are dead and gone.

(6.107)


Queen of black-earth Egypt, divine Isis
    in linen robes, accept my well-set offering:
flaky sacrificial cake on the wood-embers;
    two dazzling water-loving geese; nard
crumbled around seed-seething figs; raisins
    like lizard-skins; fragrant frankincense.
But most, great queen: save Damis from poverty
    as you did from the sea, and a gold-horned kid is yours.

(6.231)


Stranger, beware! This terrible tomb
rains verses! The very ashes of Hipponax
have screaming iambics to hurl at Eupalus.
Let sleeping wasps lie. Even in Hades
nothing has soothed his spite. From there
he shoots straight metres in lame bursts for ever.

(7.405)

I am a plane-tree. I was sound and strong when the blasts
    of a stormy sou'wester uprooted me and threw me flat.
Yet a bath of the grape makes me stand again, I breathe
    both summer and winter a rain sweeter than the sky's.
I died to live, and I soak the relaxing liquor
    that makes others bend but only makes me stand straighter.

(9.247)


The sky will extinguish its stars, and the sun
    will appear shining in the folds of night,
and the sea will be a well of fresh water for men,
    and the dead will come back to the land of the living,
before forgetfulness of those ancient lines
    can steal from us the far-famed name of Homer.

(9.575)


You were a pretty boy once, Archestratus, and
    young men burned for your wine-rosy cheeks;
you had no time for me then, on the game with those
    who took your bloom away. Now bristly and black
you push your friendship in my face, holding out
    straw after others have got your harvest.

(11.36)


A long farewell to all you universe-swivelling optics,
    and to all you Aristarchoid acanthologizing bookworms!
What do I care about aphelion or perihelion,
    or the generations of Proteus or Pygmalion?
Clarity, clarity always! and may some tenebrous saga
    wither the bones of the Hypercallimachoids!

(11.347)


*Rufinus*

They used to say I was boy-crazy, but now
    it's girls all the way: for pole, read hole.
It used to be great, those clean clear boys' faces,
    now it's rouge I want, powder, mascara, the lot.

401

Ah well. 'Dolphins will champ the woods of Erymanthus,
   deer run browsing the hoary sea.'

(5.19)

*Thallos*

Now the green plane-tree hides the lovers, hides the lovers'
   rites, its holy leaves are roof and curtain,
its branches are hung around with clusters of vine
   heavy and sweet with pleasures of the season.
Undying plane-tree! long may your rich thick green
   conceal the happy friends of Aphrodite!

(9.220)

## Heinrich Heine

### HOO THE WARLD WAGS

Some hae mickle, and to thaim
Mickle soon sall grow to muckle.
He that hasna but a maik
Sall tine his puckle's hinmaist pickle.

Yince ye've tint the last bawbee,
Ach man, hang yersel on a widdie!
Nane but thaim as has, can hae;
Life, ye gowk, life disna need ye.

[Weltlauf]

*mickle* much; *muckle* a lot; *maik* halfpenny; *tine* lose; *puckle* a little; *hinmaist*
last; *pickle* tiny amount; *widdie* rope; *gowk* fool

## WHAUR?

Whaur sall his ain lang hame be bydan
Yince the wanderer's fordone?
Under lime-beuchs o the Rhinelan?
Under palm-beuchs in the sun?

Sall fremmit hauns in hugger-mugger
Lair my banes in a wilderness?
Or sall I sleep aneath the machair
By the sea-faem and the douce gress?

I carena! Here and aawhere heaven
Rises to Gode and grun to licht;
And here, for caunles sall be hoveran
Starns abune me, in the lang nicht.

*[Wo?]*


I see ye like a flooer
Sae snawy, bonny, and sweet;
I see ye, wi a stoondin
O fear at my hert's beat.

Oh gin my hauns in prayer
Suld sain your heid at aa –
Gode micht shairly keep ye
Sweet and bonny as the snaw.

*['Du bist wie eine Blume . . .']*


The stane wi its runes rises frae the sea.
I sit there, eerie, dreaman.
The wind souchs, the sea-maw skrieks,
The swaws are rinnan and reaman.

*fordone* worn out; *beuchs* boughs; *machair* grassy sandy foreshore; *douce*
pleasant; *grun* ground

*sain* bless; *stoondin* sudden panic

*souchs* sighs; *sea-maw* seagull; *swaws* waves; *reaman* foaming

403

Mony's the braw lass I hae loed,
Mony's the trusty crony –
Whaur are they gane? The wind souchs,
The swaws rin reaman ablow me.

['*Es ragt ins Meer der Runenstein . . .*']


Yonder's a lanely fir-tree
On the Hielan moors sae bare.
It sleeps in the snaw and the cranreuch
Wi a cauld cauld plaid to wear.

It dreams aboot a palm-tree
Murnan alane in the east –
Murnan for aye in the silence
On a desert's clinty breist.

['*Ein Fichtenbaum steht einsam . . .*']


Whit wey is my hert sae eerie?
I speir, but I speir in vain.
An auld auld tale has seized me
And it winna leave my brain.

In the caller air o the gloamin
The Rhine slides lown and quaet;
Westlins the sun gangs rovan
And the hill-taps glint wi't.

There's a ferlie up yonder, a lassie
As fair as the day sits there;
Her gowdie-gauds skimmer and dazzle
As she kaims her gowden hair.

---

*cranreuch* hoarfrost; *clinty* stony

*whit wey* why; *speir* ask; *caller* fresh; *lown* placid; *ferlie* marvel

404

She kaims wi a gowden kaimie,
And whiles she sings a sang;
Its ringan melody dazes
As it echoes lang and lang.

The boatman's taen by her music,
He stoonds to the wild wild notes,
His een are abune in his furie,
He seesna the scaurs whaur he floats.

But I see the chiel at his driftin,
And his boat, baith droont in the swaw.
And this was the end o her liltin,
The Lorelei wan them awa.

*['Ich weiss nicht, was soll es bedeuten']*



**Vera Inber**


*from* THE PULKOVO MERIDIAN

The frosts, the frosts!... The grinding Russian cold,
Our ally, tried and tempered by the past,
Pierces the enemy's soul with iron goad,
Until men lie like fodder, mown and massed,
And by the bodies laid asleep in death
He rolls his icy tank across the earth.

As if from some old ballad, a head looks out
From the turret, a leather-helmeted head
Grey-haired and ruddy-cheeked (*his* health is sound!);
And farther off in that tank-column are led
Blizzards, flurries, drifts of the baffling snow...
Spring is gone, spring will be seen no more!


*kaimie* comb; *stoonds* startles; *scaurs* rocks

405

A crack in the forest! The diamond-armoured world
Flashes with emerald and with ruby fires.
When darkness knocks, and light has scarcely failed,
Our cold and ancient partisan will rise
And raise his killing silvery club for prey
As once he raised it in Napoleon's day.

And here already the enemy's heedless flight
Tries somehow, somewhere to escape his raids.
And a wan German rocket in the night
Soundlessly spatters, shivers, droops, and fades.
It's snow, snow, and neither walls nor gates
All round Olomna and Gorokhovets.

No rustle, and no movement, and no clash.
No stirring of the moon from its high guard
Where one encircling path has met its match
Under the silent sharp attacks of stars.
– And then horizons thunder, leap, go mad...
This, comrades, is the siege of Leningrad!

*[Pul'kovskii Meridian (1943)]*

## Ernst Jandl

### 16 YEARTH

thickthteen yearth
thouth-eatht thtathion
thickthteen yearth
what thall
what thall
he do
thouth-eatht thtathion
thickthteen yearth
what thall
what thall

the boy
what thall
he do
what thall
what thall
he do
thickthteen yearth
thouth-eatht thtathion
what thall
he do
the boy
with hith
thickthteen yearth

*[16 Jahr]*


you were a good girl  to me
    worr o guid gurl ti  ma
you were a good        to me
        o guid gurl     ma
you were              to me
       o guid gurl
you were              to
      gui   gurl
you were

             ti  ma
      good      to
        gurl
    worr  gui      ti
            to
             ma

*['du warst zu mir ...']*

# László Kálnoky

## WHAT AM I?

Piano in a deaf-and-dumb institute,
stone-age transistor,
telescope down a coalmine,
windmill caught in a dead calm,
pointless ticket for a cancelled performance,
bunch of keys to a bombed-out flat,
pair of sunglasses for nighttime viewing,
toupee close-cropped in error,
prodigal son's piggy-bank,
scarecrow scaring the Sahara,
snowman iced in the tropics,
dogfish looking for its doggone dentures,
centipede disqualified from the championship walk,
crocodile wiping off its tears,
tomcat caught in the mousetrap,
leopard running from gazelles,
brown bear in the throes of winter insomnia,
parrot squawking in Etruscan,
hamster sweet as a cooing dove,
firefly cursed with night-blindness,
giraffe strolling under a sofa,
fish gone limp in a drying-out station,
chimney-sweep in a white dinner-jacket,
leaseholder to Jack Landless,
butterfly-hunter at the North Pole,
illiterate polymath,
vegetarian cannibal,
ice-cream man in penguin country,
diver in the depth of the desert,
cellarman afflicted with alcohol allergy,
messenger delivering pure dada,
electrician at the court of King Arthur,
clown in a cortège.

*[Mi vagyok én?]*

## FLAME AND DARKNESS

Without warning you flared up,
a bluish flame burning day and night,
the wind tried in vain to blow you out,
made a beckoning ghost-figure from the dust
of the road – in vain,
you failed to follow it.

Your austere needle had its own target,
nothing deflected it.

What am I now without you?
Ashes sifting from a riddled bucket,
a scrap of paper stuck to a railing,
an animal shadow fading in mist.

The day will come when we search for each other.
You prowl the room as if blind.
Feel a chair, floor, wall.
Touch the cold profile of my life,
and fail to hear me as I try to shout
to you with stretched, silent mouth.
It is useless. You sit alone.
And like a thundering crashing weight
a flake of plaster
drops from the ceiling.

It is for your sake, my make-believe
that I believe the golden legend:
a handhold in the scree of things.

*[Láng és sötétség]*


## THE POSSIBLE VARIATIONS

The possible variations
may be infinite in number, yet no more
than the gradations of grey, the monotonous ticking.
The metronome in our breastbone

slows down, speeds up, stops now and then.
Patterns in ceaseless process
seem to be still as if we knew them
ages back. Present boredoms
equal the catalogue of failures
in years long gone, or what we might expect
in a thinning, shrinking future:
our particle of good,
our proliferating ill. Heads of statues spill dust,
birdshit cakes them. Every twenty years
someone will clean them. Poetry-books too
are taken from the shelf at times. A line
here and there comes clear, the reader pours
his own blood into frozen veins, makes light
steal through smashed eyes. But that is nothing more
than surface, deception, self-harm.
What will our faces be indeed
but a wilderness of sand,
carved into incomprehensible images
by the winds only, only the unresting
endlessly thirsting wasteland winds.

*[A lehetséges változatok]*


## THE FATTIES AT THE BATHS

The sun prowls impatient of its own heat
and kindles the coal deep under ground.
We pant for coolness. But the baths have a weight
of stricken monoliths, stranded slugs, all round

the water's edge, where the heavy fat ones lie;
they sprawl on their backs, growing slowly ripe
like huge fruits in their steam conservatory,
while stubble makes black chins you cannot wipe.

Their chest-hair's thickly matted like dark scrub,
a jungle for the wandering ants to explore;
their belly and their forehead have the daub
of red the summer sun makes roses for.

410

Sweat seeps into the furrows of their fat
and trickles down like greasy, ropy tears,
but gathers in their navel's little vat;
purple apoplexy bulges behind their ears.

The mirage somersaults and shimmers away.
Their heads take a hundred thousand white
steel-rays, reeds like metal in a glittering spray.
The water boils, bursts into flame. Noontide!

Nine angels blow their blistering trumpet-brass,
but the bathers have gone deaf to such appeals,
their vacant watery eyes watch nothing pass,
their consciousness sinks in unfathomed wells.

They lie there peacefully, waiting perhaps
for the sun to suck up their obesity,
and on a light ray, a thread that never snaps,
like indolent balloons, they'd fly away.

*[Kövérek a fürdöben]*


# Lajos Kassák


ABANDONED OBJECTS

I

A chair remembers.
In an empty room
bound tight in a grid of shadows
it can still feel the soft
taste of a woman's thighs
the pawing of a greedy-fingered burglar
a small boy's heavy breathing
as he took his mother-of-pearl penknife
to split the heart of its hardwood frame
it has not forgotten yet

the time it was lent round to the neighbours
but nobody would sit on it there
for they all seemed afraid of it.
Those were the bad times but
its grief found no tears.
It still has no tears.
In silence and with noble unassertiveness
it meets death here
in the empty room.


II

A chilly rumple
the bed sprawls
on four carved legs like a ghastly idol
a body without bones and without skin
it has been mangled through the dark hours
and left as soon as day showed in the sky.
Deaf and dumb
it cannot blab and chatter out whatever
went on in it or around it
a few hours back
accomplice of fury in lust
of nausea twisting in spasms.

It says nothing about the hot roused body scents
the rhythmless agonies of hearts
the great sighs
the gasping assault
the giving ecstasy.

Prostrate in daylight
it faces the open window
like a run-over corpse
abandoned at the kerb by its killers.


III

Look in through the keyhole
through the hole cut out
of the old plank door.

412

Look in just with a glance
and your eyes may light on
the big well-whetted
sharp-pointed blood-draped
knife.
Someone must have thrown it
down on the three-legged table.
Maybe a man betrayed and heart-sick
maybe a woman pregnant and ashamed.
Hard steel
glares in the light
but keeps silent.
Both murderer
and murdered
are safe from its witness.
Only the red smell of blood
shouts for help
from an alien world.


IV

The master has died.
The sculptor's studio is derelict
like an abandoned shed
a chaotic store
an absolute cesspit
hiding mortal exhibits
and hideous dreams and treasures no one has seen.
Finished sculptures in stone and wood
innocence in forms of girls
study for some coat-of-arms
unsmiling bronze of an old woman
masks of gnomes
mythical monsters
and torsos
that the master
for all his pains failed
to animate.
They loll about there mixed with clay-scrapings
under shrouds of stone-powder
and their companions are dead tools and rusty pots.

At times the janitor opens the door on them
fumbles among them
rooting about for something
then breaks into a smile
and once again
leaves them behind closed doors.


V

Waves dash her on the wharf
on the high stone wall,
they rattle
the chain in her bow,
they crack her ribs.
Once
she was very dear to a man and a woman
who used her to measure distance
and made her boards their bridal bed.
Then in a fit of rage
the man stove in her side
the river whirled her away
tugged at her
tore at her
but could not gulp her down.
She lies at the foot of the wharf, dying.
Sometimes children pelt her with stones
sometimes fish spring up from the reeds
to gape at a blue
white red
painted wreck.


VI

In those days
it was greeted by a brass band
at the workshop gates.
Its wheels were garlanded with red paper ribbons.
The mechanical miracle in situ.
500 horse-power at command.
Sometimes it cut up rusty
grumbled and squealed

and renounced all obedience.
And then it got going again.
It lived among the workers for years
just like their brother.
But it came to a standstill at last
and was dumped in a ditch
beyond the board-fence.

Going home in the evenings
the men toss words to it
old crock
drop dead.

From time to time it still sweats out
one
wan
waterlogged
oildrop.

VII

Someone has shut
the fine mahogany casket.
Ripe-coloured – wonderful.
Deep in superb carvings
a gold wedding-ring
lies rolled
in purple velvet.
It was a bride's ring
a virgin's
and before the wedding-night
she killed herself
in a fever of love
shuddering with terror.

Before she took the poison
she shut away the ring –
forgotten ever since that day.

Cast off
it is asleep
perhaps even dead.

It has no ears for the woodworm
crunching patiently
at the wall of the casket.


VIII

A time-expired wall-clock is lying
on the rubbish-dump
its dial
facing the sky like a human face.
Once it measured the river of time.
It comes back in memory
the whole house
the whole village
moved as it dictated
then it developed an unintelligible burr
started to cough like an asthmatic
and died.

Children made it treasure trove.
They smashed up its hands
plucked out its works.
Now worms and spiders
bivouack in its bowels.
Sometimes the dog strolls up
to piss on it.


IX

Who remembers
Vincent van Gogh's clay boots
in front of the door.
What trampled things
they are, downtrodden things.
Life has deserted them
yet they are not dead.
Filled with the breath
of a deranged painter's
soul.
Immortal
finally, and holy.

Today they squirm
in art-dealers' nets.
The market
will quote their value.


X

Greasy and tatty
cards lie scattered
about the house.
Their backs
are nicked and
marked with sharpers' fingerprints.
Some of them have
soaked up women's tears.
They have made men
knife-happy
bottle-happy.

Now they are not worth a look.
When they fulfilled
their beastly office
they died.

The very
broom seems
to sweep away from them
in abhorrence.

*[Elhagyott tárgyak]*



YOUNG HORSEMAN

The horse he sits on is saddleless
and he himself is naked.
Marvellous boy
as his thighs tighten
and his sunburnt chest
heaves up and down.

My mate whom I
can't sing well enough ever.
Burning youth unconscious pride
let me praise you!

[Fiatal lovas]

## I AM WITH YOU

In front of you I go
you in front of me
the early sun's gold chain
jingles on my wrist.

Where are you going – I ask
you answer – how do I know.

I speed up my walk
but you speed all the more.

I in front of you
you in front of me.

But we stop in front of a gate.

I kiss you
you give me a kiss
then without a word you vanish
and spirit my life away.

[Veled vagyok]

## 'AT EVENING WE DIP OUR BANNERS . . .'

At evening we dip our banners we are alone we are wrapped in
    darkness
oh that pithlessness that excludedness
the stars turn round on black iron hoops there are the paths
    stepping over the horizon the flock brought together losing
    its fleece

418

it is reality I am talking about – self-coloured in the heart
I can say No or Yes but the face of things is remade there again
    and again
the blacksmith used to take the air at this time of day under the
    milky moon and turn into a man slowly
but the bakers would stretch stiff over the ovens that broke them
    oblivious of the air with its cold fingers and the long knives
    rasping them in two like objects bound for death
they are all the sons of the mother of men
they are all my brothers
yet my words are not addressed to them as pillars cast in gold
and I leave the soil of their tough boots unkissed
the mists crawl out from the mouths of basements
it is in our first steps we are accomplished
we have left the apathetic hedgerows behind us
we feel that we are living
we are working day and night on the face of our time.

['Esténként lehajtjuk . . .']

TREES ARCH
OVER MR LISPITZ
DUSK   COMBING HIS
    NICE HAIR

but said
that's worth
the least of all
who has
understanding
don't touch the flowers
because your
teeth will fall out
the woman at this point
undid herself for her husband
and uttered

you
he   BRIG

   HTN

then   ESS
it all
strolled across to the straight
and for two days we slept

but this all happened ou-
tside the GOOD folks' shelter

IN VIENNA
then I went onto
the highway and
lifting boulders
stones picked up
bottle eggs 1 2 3 4

GIRLS SING
SING

THE 12 TEENAGERS however
DROVE TO MARK
ET
24 BALLS OF COTTON W
OOL

AND ALREADY we
were all together every one of us
the priest removed his cassock and
announced from then on he'd
only inspect the well at night

DO-WN
WITH
THE
NIGHTCAPS

ON THE
19TH DAY

A  mary clasped her son
L  and blossomed in tears
O  but even this was useless
N  THE BIRDS
G  flew away
   THE FISH
   swam away      & THE BELLR

T                              INGER
H
E  fell asleep
M  on his rope for ever
E  fell asleep
R  poor man
G  above the brilliant
E  cities

420

but this too was
only chickenfeed
we need to know

GOD'S
EYE
OBSERVES
          EVERYTHING

AND i

    TOOK THE OLD W
but people to  OMAN'S BUNDLE
a sea and sa  OVER THE BROOK
taken bridges t
hrough our eyes and someone
daubed uselessly on our brows

→ THE STAR ←

the donkeys with sacks
of salt fear the water

I AM HUNGRY
YOU ARE HUNGRY
HE TOO IS HUNGRY

BESIDES
ON MR SWARTZ'S SCALES
YOU CAN WEIGH DOWN
          EVERYTHING

ALONG
HIGHWAYS
      YELLOW WELLS
          REVOLVE

and on the hills

      CHILDREN

in their palms the
lilies unfold
so the jug smashes
for some today
and for some tomorrow
no who   BROTHER
no mo   BROTHER-IN-LAW
PLUMP GEESE SETTLE BELOW
      THE MOON

OH everyone
OH everyone

OUGHT TO STICK
FUNNELS
INTO HIS H
EAD
we've nothing left
now but a tiny
island BEHIND THE ICE-
BREAKER'S EAR

FOR IT ALL COMES TO ONE

AND
PAIN
PAIN

ANNA
MY DEAR LI
TTLE ANN

THE
LORD
there above the waters

HOVERING
TERRIBLY

HE
CRIES

*['A fák alatt . . .']*

422

# Velimir Khlebnikov

DRAGON TRAIN

*An Escap(ad)e*

We talked about the things that were right,
We lambasted cowardice and vice.
The train ran, guarding its rational freight,

Its dream-rooms breathed-on, dragonized.
A dragon rattled the window-catches,
Shook our foot-soles loose like dice.

The dolls lolled in drowsy snatches,
We were crags of the earth.
Neighbours whispered quietly, matching

The slippery iron dragon's breath.
New terror galvanized me: were these gills
Shining in the dark outside? Worth

A look! He shivered. Both stood still,
Brave enough, peered. Rows of fierce needles,
Wings, a dragon! Death, plague, man-eaters chill

Less than this white-stinged phantom, twitching, needling us.
The phantom sprang and trampled everything –
Great names, highest honour, all peoples.

Seeing this, I remembered the near-nothings
That deities clutch to their grim breasts.
'Why should you,' I cried, 'regenerate the markings

Of victories over the dragon, great fights, great tests?'
Like some monstrous perpetrator of some obscure joke
It took on a subterranean paleness.

Just then, I noticed a toddler's feet poke
Near the relentless switching of the tail.
These moments hit me with such a fearful stroke

That I recall them now and always, without fail.
A tall crest, like peaks in mountain country,
Covered and bridged the broad-backed reptile.

The multifarious massacres of humanity
Flourished like symbols from scale to scale.
Pitiful patterns of ruin and mortality

Threaded its belly like ivy on a wall.
A wide-open book guarded its head
Like a racehorse's forelock-fall.

As the moments passed, the monster's body bent,
Bristled in coils, became horselike, reared like a candle.
Unchaste chains dangled wherever it went.

And its jaws began to gape for the dagger-handle.
But the net of barbs, hung out like stars,
Terrified me; my silent weeping was my scandal.

Reading a hair-like book, one of the passengers
Sat on the reptile, a black raven planked
At the tail-end with a million spines and fissures.

The wing's huge sarafan angered
Someone with its skyey thorn beating, bright dawn
Behind it, thin wound-slits, eye of a tiger.

And my fellow-passenger cried out in sharp pain
But could say nothing, grief-bound. Scary!
My friend looked daggers at me, his reproaches shone.

I thought mankind was the source, but we rushed to the estuary.
And it swung its dragon wing,
Flashing its fangs in grisly array.

And then it was off, racing
To renew its body with flight,
New roll, new movement, new fling.

Murders and dosshouses make its eyes bright,
As a man could read fisticuffs
Behind a yellow curtain's light.

We flickered our glances quickly enough
At our sleepy neighbours on the train
To be bored by their snores and mumbled guff:

The breathed one endless torpid refrain.
I remembered St George and *his* dragon-fight,
How he plunged his sword till the thing was slain.

And the air reeked of the beast, the field dark and bright
With blood, the dumb corpse of the monster at his feet,
The slashed neck of the corpse boiling with blood as black as
    night.

But these were ancient things the heart could not meet.
Yet, after strangest throes and dice-throws a form
Of target was reached: a seat

On its haunches, its neck stretched out, a swarm
Of desires tormenting and maddening it, calling it something:
What rites, what lustrations had come and gone?

It turned back to us – I went rigid, trembling –
Snatched a sleepy neighbour, cracked him open,
Gobbled him up, young lawyer, snake's plaything!

The echoing valley re-echoed with the groaning
And inhuman howling from the lips of the victim.
But those jaws, tight and prickly, slowly

Crunched the doomed man limb by limb.
Sleep still stroked and lulled his neighbours,
And some of them were taken just like him.

'Wake up!' I shouted. 'Wake up! He's gone! Save us!'
But no one heard. Expert snorers
Dug sleep's graveyard.

Then, taking advantage of a halt in the story,
I jumped straight off the train,
Missed being blinded by a fir-spike, poor glory

Of a warrior hiding in a bush, to live and act again.
My comrade followed my example right away.
The fir-tree hid us, gave us a night under the sun.

And we, hidden in the woods like cavemen, could say
We were the dead fire of burnt-out fears,
We carried faith into truth the whole way.

But meanwhile those in whom good sense is scarce
Are food for the dragon as he tears and tears.

*[Zmei poezda]*


Once more, once more
I am your
Star.
No good comes to the seaman
Who takes a false angle of his ship
Or star: he
Will founder on the rocks,
On the unseen sandbanks.
No good will come to you either,
You have taken the heart's false angle on me:
You will founder on the rocks
And the rocks will mock
You
As you mocked
Me.

*['Yeshcho raz, yeshcho raz . . .']*

Song of the lips – bobeóbi,
Song of the eyes – veeómi,
Song of the eyebrows – pieéo,
Song of the look – lieeéi,
Song of the chain – gzi-gzi-gzéo.
So, on the canvas of such correspondences
A Portrait, living in no dimension.

*['Bobeobi pelis' guby . . .']*


When horses die they sigh.
When grasses die they dry.
When suns die they are nothing.
When people die they are singing.

*['Kogda umirayut koni . . .']*


## Michelangelo Buonarroti


THREE SONNETS

With heart and breast of brimstone, flesh of flax,
Bones of inflammable-brittle fuel-timber,
Soul unguided by hand or hampered by bridle,
Quick-whipped desire, will-fever's superflux,

Mind blind and maimed and disendowed of force;
With the world's ill of bait and trap and pitfall –
Little indeed is the wonder of the igniting
Lightning-like at the very first-launched fires!

Art, beauty: which in the divinity shown
Through him who owns them can still vanquish nature
As far as he truly speaks and shapes each scene:

427

If I to them was born neither stock nor stone
But heart-harmonied to whoever plucks me into blazing,
Blame to nature for this doom of fire I assign.

[*'Al cor di zolfo, a la carne di stoppa'*]


The heart through sight accosted flash on flash
Is pierced by all shapes sight-accounted lovely,
And pierced with such vast and facile penetration
That thousands rather than hundreds cross the flesh,

World-range of age and sex; and it is terror I face
Freighted with sorrows, yet weighted more with my envy,
And in all those crowding countenances hopeless of consolation
Complete in one, which living flesh could confess.

Where loveliness in mortal form can enfold
No more than flaring desire, its far-off descending
Soul-friended from heaven is our lie for lust;

But where desire is outvoyaged, to see day poured
Beyond day, 'Amor' it scorns to say, and its trembling
Ends beside love that ends when flesh is sloughed.

[*'Passa per gli occhi al core in un momento'*]


Oh, make me see thy face in every place!
If beauty of flesh can set my feeling burning,
That fire will fade before thy nearing beauty,
And I shall blaze again in thy embrace.

My Lord, my Beloved, to thee alone these prayers,
Cries from my vain and blind tormenting, are turning:
My heart and my life hope only thy renewing –
My poor and halting will, my judgement, my desires.

To space and time thou hast sent the soul, the divine,
And in this body-husk so brittle and long-harassed
Imprisoned it with its raging fate, love's pain;

What power can mine be, Life from life to refine?
Without thee, Lord, all good in me lies perished.
God's doom is for God's hand alone to unchain.

['Deh, fammiti vedere in ogni loco!']


NIGHT

I hug my sleep, and in blocklike rock rejoice,
Insensible of time's ignominies and injustices.
Blind, numb, I win; these are my fastnesses.
O never rouse me with your ringing voice!

['Caro m'e'l sonno, e più l'esser di sasso']


**Nikolai Nekrasov**


THE POOR WANDERER'S SONG

I go by the fields – wind whistles in the fields:
   Cold fit to starve, old stranger-man, to starve!
   Cold fit to starve, dear father, to starve!

I go by the woods – beasts howl in the woods:
   Hungry and starving, old stranger-man, starving!
   Hungry and starving, dear father, starving!

I go by the crops – how are you such thin crops?
   Starved by the cold, old stranger-man, starved!
   Starved by the cold, dear father, starved!

I go by the herds – beasts ready to drop?
   Starved by hunger, old stranger-man, starved!
   Starved by hunger, dear father, starved!

I go to the village: peasant-man, you're kept warm?
   Cold fit to starve, old stranger-man, to starve!
   Cold fit to starve, dear father, to starve!

To another: peasant-man, you're well fed at home?
   Hungry and starving, old stranger-man, starving!
   Hungry and starving, dear father, starving!

And a third: yet you, peasant-man, beat your wife?
   Starved by the cold, old stranger-man, starved!
   Starved by the cold, dear father, starved!

To a fourth: yet the tavern's the half of your life?
   Starved by hunger, old stranger-man, starved!
   Starved by hunger, dear father, starved!

I visit the fields again – wind whistles in the fields:
   Cold fit to starve, old stranger-man, to starve!
   Cold fit to starve, dear father, to starve!

I visit the woods again – beasts howl in the woods:
   Hungry and starving, old stranger-man, starving!
   Hungry and starving, dear father, starving!

*[Pesnya ubogogo strannika]*


## Pablo Neruda


ODE: BOY WITH HARE

In the autumn light
on the roadway
the boy
held up in his hands
not a flower
not a lamp
but a dead hare.

Cars rayed
the cold highway,
faces stayed
rigid
behind glass,
eyes were
iron,
ears
hostile,
teeth flashed
quick as lightning
bolting
towards seas and cities,
and the autumn
boy
with his hare
strange
as a thistle,
hard
as a pebble,
fixed there
lifting
a hand
towards the exhausts
of the drivers.
No one
slowed.

The high ranges
were dusty brown,
ridges
a hunted
puma colour,
the silence
had gone
violet
and the eyes
of the boy with his hare
were like
two embers
of black
diamond,

two sharp
points
like knife-blades,
two little
black knives,
those eyes
of the boy,
lost there,
offering up his hare
in the huge
motorway
autumn.

*[Oda al niño de la liebre]*


ODE: TO MY SOCKS

Maru Mori
brought me a pair
of socks
she had knitted
with her sheep-herding hands,
two socks
gentle as hares.
I put my feet
into them
as if into
two cases
knitted
with threads of
twilight
and sheepskin.
Alarming socks,
my feet were
two fish
of wool,
two lengthy sharks
ultramarine
crisscrossed
with braided gold,

two giant blackbirds,
two cannons:
that is how
my feet
were honoured
by
these
celestial
socks.
They were
so beautiful
that I had a new
experience, my feet
seemed impossible
like a couple of decrepit
firemen, firemen
unworthy
of that embroidered
fire,
those shining
socks.

But still
I resisted
the keen temptation
to lock them away
like schoolboys
keeping
fireflies,
like scholars
amassing
venerable papers,
I resisted
the crazy impulse
to place them
in a golden
cage
and feed them
daily birdseed,
pink melon pulp.
Like explorers
of forests who deliver

the most rare
green deer
to the spit
and eat it
with regret,
I stretched out
my feet
and drew on
those
splendid
socks
then
my shoes.

And the moral of my ode
is this:
beauty is twice
beautiful
and what is good is doubly
good
when we are talking about two socks
of wool
in winter.

*[Oda a los calcetines]*

## Ottó Orbán

THE LADIES OF BYGONE DAYS

Where with their magnetic breasts are Susanna and Martha and
    the Judys of various addresses
time has chewed to pulp Melinda and Vera and Liz my god we
    had breakfast with them bacon and eggs
Gisella what on earth was her last name gone too gone off on a
    Danube steamer

all I know about her is she was a company typist somewhere and she never heard of contraception till I told her and

then it was all amazement under blonde eyebrows and her Iseult-type blue headlights lit up

and I remember Eva too and her caveman-girlfriend the sculptress with her low forehead

and the gold-brown madness that looked for lasting messages among the trembly lacework revives

its search in their Indian laps for New World treasures and the Copernican theory of their hips

over the Babylonian blind the legend ALBERT HECKLER MEN'S TAILOR sings out and our tongues incur damnation by the urgency of one unpostponable kiss

and what's Tonia that wild spinster doing in Paris and where are the adventuresses those Aggies and Cathys and Andreas taking buses to with their bursting shopping-bags

they have split dispersed gone without a message all over the stubble-field of civilization

it makes no odds who did what the spicy details for instance whose husband it was dropped drunk from a New York taxi

they all live somewhere on the earth live well live poor no need to worry energy is conserved

where last year's snow was there's a green of this year's spring

dynasty marked for downfall youth crowned with arrogance the jacket taken out of pawn fitted your royal figure like a glove

ah spirit of heartrending elegies turn your noble eyes to Kertész Street

peeling plaster and whores and pensioners brought down in the world

G.T. the poet reeking of suntan-oil sported a newspaper in his breast-pocket for use as a flying carpet if the right moment came

and two true lovers merged into one body under a world-broad crackle of paper

while on the table Miguel Hernandez was dying in a gaol of laurel-scented terza rimas

and his flashing bones made lightning in the room and lit up the legend tacked to the wall A FRIEND'S FLAT IS NO BROTHEL

and apocalyptic whimpers stole out from the freedom-flavoured stench

on the undying day of the faceless watches when language had still to invent the future tense

435

where the mother of two tempered by shivering fever-fits with
a jug of milk in her hand cycles smash into a lorry
and the three-dimension-clasping limbs are crushed flat into the
sheet of an asphalt-album scrawled with skid-marks
in the happy mother's present time the green blades of the earth
besieged the world's ice
and the scarlet of Viking lips swam on the shoreless sea of a
cushion
and the bodiless starpelt panther lolled and clanked in its planet-
kennel
retracting its workaday claws

Downy creatures dusty earth-chicks your firm flesh and your
elegance
the tongues chirping with 'I says' and 'I don't want none'
but I plan to live for ever on a dilapidated iron bed admiring the
expertise of your professor fingers
with you away sky and memory shiver shudder bleak
but strolling the world on the leash of your arms among the
machinegun-pitted walls was wonderful
wrinkling at the grave my nose picked up immortal scent from
the embers of your bodies
I watched my enchanted ones grunt over the mud of bombs in
the besieged sty
and the wartime Circe had neither chiton nor curls of a goddess
and Greek urn-figures were not her style
nothing is more perilously beautiful than the live mines of your
laps
the history of your hair whispers pleasure in this bomb-crater
rolling round the sun
the spinning-wheel of fate has threaded your arms about my
vertebrae for good
to step from the burning bush of your slips you mutter to me and
it's hoarse GIVE ME A LIGHT
while our shivering cells devour each other in a sweat of honey
and embers of spring of creation-the-destroyer hiss through our
fingers

[*Régmúlt idők hölgyei*]

On this heavenly molehill
where a long-drawn-out war is being waged besides the
    local massacres
and the anonymous heroes of time squatting in the dug-
    outs of their days
know that a smile is only self-deception and joy is death's
    moratorium
for major causes are composed of minor causes
for victory is unreal in a battle where
peasants' huts are bombed with figures
for the business of living is a master sculptor and can twist
    a man's face to a sheep's
and in hunger there is neither poetry nor sense of the
    fundamentals
on this earth where poverty is no news
and no one is fool enough to stammer or cry out in shock
for who has not clambered down from some cross or other
and who has not soaked his nail-stuck feet in a bowl of
    water
what typist has not forgotten her lover's unforgettable
    face
where everybody but everybody has shaken hands with the
    bereaved widow
assuring her of his sympathy gazing deep into her eyes
and has cabled ALL THE BEST on hearing of the resurrection
    of Lazarus
where the idea of endurance was invented to meet the
    torture-chamber
where there is no one who has not seen it all
and who does not have endless opportunities
and who would gladly exchange state affairs for a fishing-
    rod
on the breast of this barren mother
when the stars of cosmic paralysis transfix you to the dust
and you lean on the rail and look down into the valley
you can see the hope of the age the little rickety truck
stuffed with whatever has been salvaged from the fire
sticks of furniture sacks stewpans chickens
like an unkillable bombardier-beetle
like a tin-jowled reptile flashing headlamp-eyes

and lolling out its panting petrol-tongue like a child
while in front of the flames embossed on its jolting flanks
the nickel trade-mark shines:
Gaiety and Good Heart

*[Derü és vidámság]*


TO BE POOR

To be poor, even just relatively poor, means that a man lacks the
brashness to decorate his speech with Christmas-tree baubles
and hold forth to the fighters of a war on the whistling wings of
gorse. To be poor is to have an irresistible wish to answer yes or
no if we are questioned. To be poor is to wade barefoot through
the splintered-glass sea of technology and hand-feed a lion
equipped with every modern convenience. To learn an upside-
down ethics, to discover everything about the concealed dun-
geons of a sky-bound earthscraper; to crawl backwards along the
narrowing corridors of the cavern of history into that primordial
workshop where blood and wretchedness are pounded into the
enchanted form of humanity. To be poor in a world where Romeo
is a car and Juliet a cosmetic may be an embarrassing merit but it
is also a happy embarrassment, for the poor man lives in the
besieged stronghold of thought without relying on any possible
safe-conduct, and instead he gallops bareback on an earth with
its mane flying and he uses his patient anger to spur it on its way.

*[Szegények lenni]*


CHILE

The patrol came down without having found anything.
'The third time they've been,' said the woman, 'and found
        nothing.'
'Cheerio, kid,' the lieutenant said to the child. 'We won't be here
        again.'
'Why, did you find daddy in the attic?', the child asked.

438

'We did,' said the lieutenant and went back into the house and
     brought the man down and shot him dead in the yard in
     front of the child and the woman.
Pupils stare like great worlds: the Earth, in its green dress, tells
     lies about sea and spring, surrounded by the searing stars.


REPORT ON THE POEM

From now on, the Earth. Test of Earth's gravity. Ferroconcrete sea.
Pro boxer grows old. Passions too raw for poetry
in the empty harbour, where no one wipes off tears:
          'It's time!' It is too, and the decent poet

inscribes on wood-free paper: 'Age of Manhood',
and noble emotion and restrained tears shake in his voice,
like a condom thrown in a puddle. Enough of that.
          It's the old girl's cosmetics that bore me. Let her

tame panthers on her cloudlike walks or wag her hips
in angel-feathers under the stagy moon. She can hold out
her tricksy salvation, thick arias for thickheads: I know what it's
     worth.
          From now on, the story is more important.

The It-Happens-To-Us-All. The Only-To-Me. The Don't-Turn-
     Back.
The fact that won't be changed by star-soaring composition.
The fate that from unseen motives aims at a single goal
          may be smalltime, yet a matter of life and death.

From now on, the logistics-poetry of polar exploration. Foxhole
     letters.
In place of magic ear-and-eye enchantment: stout boots, warm
     clothes.
Head-clutching verse, a circus stunt,
          flight of fancy with head-in-sand.

439

That's how it is. Sad that our concepts of God are always man-
    faced.
Better to fly on wings of pity, but the interrogator comes from the
    interrogated.
To smoke cigarettes with spine-sized tobacco-stalks to ashes,
      anger and love, give me a light!

*[Jelentés a versröl]*

## THE APPARITION

Yes, an angel has summoned me too,
though not just like Blake or Weöres:
kindling a freemasonic burning bush in my room
or dictating lines to me over the phone.
'Come on,' the voice said, 'there's no one at home.'
The shoddy victory among ancient furniture
was outlined sharply in the cigarette-smoke:
there we lay on the World War I family bed,
like monumental sculptures bathed in sweat.
My mouth was chapped, wine
after vodka isn't good.

The apparition kept me waiting till morning.

The wizened face and the black hair-tangles –
that's what I saw. Enough
for some nameless secret distress
opening lashless eyes in my cells
to sense the ray-scarred huntsman camouflaging his trap.
Not that I can say he told me anything,
in advance, I mean, the metaphysical messenger.
The hospital, the dying, the 'Daddy Orbán',
the pedestrian Odyssey from shilling to shilling,
the holed socks, the outgrown shoes, the 'Who's going to say
    hello?',
in a word the whole piss- and blood-smelling novel
which Central Europe works up
from the Verona balcony-scene,
and even the guerrilla raids of more universal bad luck,

the biological mines, planted in the loam of pleasure,
detonating and detonating
in heart and stomach – all that remained hidden.
Only – the curtain went up on an ancient puppet-show,
and around us so-called destiny:
a theatrical Danube, shores scarred by industry,
a Tom Thumb country with the stolidity of a giant
darkening the sky with smoke and poverty.
How should I know whether fire scared me or deadly cold?
In some murderous medium, flashing up and down,
the butterfly-creature was in terror;
no doubt about it, already drawn to the lamp
men usually call: love.

I smoked a cigarette: modern film-hero.
But later, as the siege and the orphanage
only made a little savage of me, yet not so humourless
as to pluck a verse-harp at that crucial moment:
'O shaggy mustang, O fiery youth!',
plunging in Professor Piccard's live bathyscaphe
into the abyssal wheezing I again fell asleep.

[A jelenés]

## Jacques Prévert

DUNCE

Na, na, says he wi his heid
But his hert aye says Ay.
Whitever he fancies gets Ay
Sae his dominie gets Na. Deed
Ay. Aince he's on his feet
They speir at him and speir
Till he's mair deaved nor sweirt

speir ask; deaved deafened; sweirt reluctant

441

And wow! but he's no feart
For then he lauchs like a loonie
And rubs oot aa their lear –
The ready-ma-deazies and the wee bit sums,
The grammaticals and the flimflams and the pons-asinorums –
And the dominie canna daunton him
And the wheengean clypes cannae dere him
As he taks up the cauks o the renbow
And scrieves ower the board's black Wae's-me
The lauchan phisog o his Leeze-me.

[Le cancre]


## Aleksandr Pushkin


DESIRE FOR FAME

Swept into silence by delight, advancing
Into love, kneeling before you, glancing
Upon you, I thought: here you are mine indeed, –
And you know, my darling, whether fame was then my need;
You knew me: a roamer from a world too restless,
A poet whom the title sickened as too senseless,
Tired of the long tempests, I did not miss
The distant buzz, the public hiss or kiss.
What voice awarding glory would but evade me,
When you with your lover's looks would overshade me
And lay your hand lightly where my head lay
And whisper: You love me? You are happy? Say
If you will ever love someone else like me – will you?
Me you will never forget, my dear friend – will you?
While I kept silent, and what could I reply,
Filled with that brimming rapture, what thoughts had I
Of any future, of the terrible day that might sever us


*lear* learning; *ready-me-deazies* reading-books; *daunton* intimidate; *clypes*
informers; *dere* hurt; *cauks* chalks; *scrieves* writes; *Leeze-me* I'm very pleased

Arriving – ever! But later? Tears and slanderous
Tormentings and betrayals fell suddenly intermixed
Upon my head ... What am I, where am I? Transfixed,
A traveller in a desert struck by lightning,
I stand in a huge darkness. It is brightening
Now under a new wish, my hard desire to have fame,
So that you will be for ever aware of my name
Ringing in your ears, for ever by me be surrounded,
Hear me in all things, all things on earth resounded
About you by loud-voiced renown, so too
That when in the stillness my true words come to you
You will remember the last prayers I once started
In a garden, in the darkness of night, at the moment we parted.

*[Zhelanie slavy]*


## WINTER MORNING

Sunshine and frost – a day of days!
My friend, my charmer sleeps as I gaze:
But wake up now, my beauty, rise,
Lift those drowsy lids, and watch
Aurora's northern presence match
Your open northern starry eyes!

Remember last night, how the sleet hissed,
The sullen sky was thick with mist,
The yellow moon in the swirling gloom
Showed like a wan stain; in the room
You sat, and sighed the hours away –
But now ... look through the pane today:

Sparkling under the blue blue skies
There in the sunlight the snow lies,
A dazzling carpet without dust;
Only the light-pierced wood shows black;
Frost vies with green on firs, the slack
Stream shines beneath its icy crust.

443

The whole room swims in amber, glows
And flickers, crackles to the throes
Of the lit stove as it spits and sings.
Lovely to lounge there, thinking things...
But look, why not call for our sleigh,
Harness the brown mare, and away!

Gliding across the morning snow,
Dear friend, let us race forward so
That the keen horse may gallop free,
And let us see the empty fields,
The bare woods autumn so soon yields,
The river-bank so dear to me.

*[Zimnee utro]*


## THE CAUCASUS

The Caucasus, below. I stand on the peak
Alone at the edge of the cliff and the snow.
An eagle that far-off crags must know
Comes hovering evenly here – to a bleak
Birthplace of mountain-stream and storm
Where awesome avalanches form.

Floating at my feet, quiet clouds
Are threaded by throaty waterfalls;
Below the falls, bare boulder-walls;
And lower, dry scrub, mossy shrouds;
And at last the green shade of a grove
Where birds twitter and deer rove.

Men's huts crouch there in the hills,
And the sheep drift on the grassy slopes,
And the shepherd goes down to the valley of his hopes,
The dark banks where the Aragva spills,
And the starving rider hides in the pass,
And the Terek rolls in a wild glad mass –

444

Rolling and roaring, a young beast at play,
Eyeing the food from its iron cage,
Lashing its shores in useless rage,
Licking its boulders with hungry spray...
Vain play! It finds no food, no rest,
Its guards dumb, its will suppressed.

*[Kavkaz]*


## THE AVALANCHE

Crashing against the gloomy rocks
The water brawls and froths and breaks;
Above my head the eagle shrieks,
    The pine-wood sighs,
And white through swirling mists the peaks
    Of mountains rise.

I see where once the avalanche
Lurched loose and fell with its gruff crash
To choke the rocky pass and stanch
    In one dead mass
The river Terek – strike and crush
    Great waves like glass:

Till all at once, O Terek, you
Ceased roaring, and crawled tame and slow;
But baffled waves broke through the snow
    In anger still...
The cold and shattered fetters show
    Your furious will!

And long the landslide debris lay
In mounds and heaps, without a thaw;
The snarling Terek ran below,
    Splashing its waves
And hissing its fine spume and spray
    Through icy caves.

445

And here a road led, a broad road,
The horse galloped, and the ox groaned,
The merchant of the steppes went round
    With camel and cries,
Where winds unlock the only ground
    Now in these skies.

*[Obval]*


## THE UPAS-TREE

Deep in the withering desert wastes,
On ground the sun has scorched and blistered,
The upas stands on guard, its face
To the whole unpeopled world, pitiless.

In a day of wrath it was conceived,
Nature from her parching steppe-land
Leaned to envenom roots and leaves;
Grim is its green, and its sap deadly.

The poison surges and melts at noon,
Trickling through where the bark will suffer it,
And evening congeals this resinous bloom
To ropy glittering beads and gutterings.

Bird's wing never touched this tree,
Nor tiger's paw – only the tornado
Darkens the dreaded trunk and receives
Its venom even in whirling to evade it.

And if a cloud should wander by,
And water these rank leaves in passing,
The rain, to sand that burns like fire,
Drops poisoned from the burning branches.

And yet a man by a man was sent
To the upas-tree; a glance was an order;
He bowed, and went on his way, and fetched
The poison back with the coming of morning.

446

He came back with the ooze, the seepage, the death,
Carrying a branch of that blighted foliage,
And down from his blanched brow the sweat
Was pouring in streams, appallingly, coldly;

He came back – and collapsed, and fell, and lay
On the floor of bast in the tent in the desert
And died the helpless death of a slave
At the feet of his lord whose power was perfect.

And this prince took the poison, and fed
With that his unrepentant arrows
And with those arrows sent out death
To multiply his neighbours' sorrows.

*[Anchar]*

I loed ye. Mibbe yit intil my breist
Thon is a lowe that blaws on its ain gleeds.
But noo, I'd hae ye o that fash disseised;
I want your hert's remeid – that nae drap bleeds.
I loed ye wordlesslie and wanlesslie,
Noo jealouslie, noo thievelesslie fordone;
I loed ye sae gentlie, sae allutterlie –
God gie the lave loe ye as I hae done!

*['Ya vas lyubil . . .']*

*lowe* fire; *gleeds* embers; *fash* trouble; *disseised* released; *wanlesslie* hopelessly;
*thievelesslie* listlessly; *fordone* exhausted; *lave* rest

**Miklós Radnóti**

AN ESKIMO THINKS OF DEATH

I am happy only at the time
when the mists of early morning rise
and I am dandled in them, half-awake,
while the great sun, drowsy too,
pads slowly up into the blue.

For night brings terror: worms thread through me,
I lie here awake, their swarms undo me,
I feel their cold flesh in my flesh,
and along the tingling bones of my leg
the well-knit splinter cracks again.

I lie awake here and I wonder:
is there a harder life to live under?
Winter is cold and rags are few,
a bear's weight of cares leans now at my back,
warm skins, boot-skins, skins of care too.

And I stood and stood on the smooth ice-floe,
no food, no skins in my igloo,
fat fish flicked clear of my hook,
my net swung emptily to and fro,
new cares worse than old cares took

root, as they do today! and in summer thaws,
when I hunt for tasty hide and paws,
pursuing my fugitive supper bite,
even then care thaws underneath
and the worn-out mind sleeps with cares all night.

I am happy only at the time
when the mists of early morning rise
and I am dandled in them, half-awake,
while the great sun, drowsy too,
pads slowly up into the blue.

*[Egy Eszkimó a halálra gondol]*

448

## LETTER TO MY WIFE

In the depths there are worlds listening, silent,
the stillness wails in my ears and I cry out,
but no one can answer it from far
Serbia sunk fainting in war
and you are not near. Your voice is braided
with my sleep, I find it again in daytime
in my heart, I listen, and around me the song
of cold-feeling stately ferns floats up and on.

I know nothing of when I might see you again,
you who were strong as a psalm and sure as stone,
and beautiful as light and beautiful as shadow,
to whom in blindness, dumbness I'd still travel,
you're exiled in these fields and so you flare
inward upon my sight, mind-projected there:
you were reality, now again you're dream,
and I back in my teenage lumber-room

jealously pound my question, Do you love me?
and whether at the peak of my youth you will some day,
one day become my wife, – my hopes revive
and dropping back into my waking life
I know you have. My wife and friend, only
so far away. Three savage frontiers. Slowly
it is autumn. Will even autumn forget me here?
The recollection of our kisses is sharper.

Miracles? I believed in them and forgot their days,
bomber squadrons fly over me, I gazed
at the miraculous blue of your eyes in the sky
but it clouded over and the bombs were dying
to fall from the plane. I live in spite of them, –
and am their captive. What I have sized up then
is all my hopes and still I can return to you,
the soul knows how I have dived down for you, –

and so do lands and frontiers! Reddest embers,
plunging flames fakir-like I'll encounter
if I must, but still I will come back;
if I must I'll take the toughness of tree-bark,

and in these endless dangers I am appeased
by peace of mind worth all the shouts and spears
of wild men living turbulently, and the grave
2 x 2 of reason claims me in one cool wave.

Lager Heideman, in the mountains
above Žagubica, Yugoslavia,
August-September 1944.

*[Levél a hitveshez]*

FORCED MARCH

Crazy when safe on the ground    to get up and walk again –
the man stirs knees and ankles    like some galvanized thing of pain,
but still he follows the road,    you'd think he'd wings to lift him,
and the ditch is not his friend,    he daren't be a drifter,
and if you ask why not,    he'll maybe tell you yet
he has a wife in wait for him    and a less mad, ugly death.
What a crazy piety    when yonder now for ages
hearth and home have blistered    to the dry wind raging,
house-walls struck flat,    the plum-tree bare,
and night on the homestead    crawling with fear.
O if I could believe it –    not only my heart
holding what I must hold to,    but a home, waiting late:
could it be yet! as once    on the old cool porch
the bees of peace hummed    while plum jam grew rich,
and late summer stillness    baked in the sleepy garden,
fruits rocked naked    in the leaves, and Fanni
stood with her fair hair    by the tawny hedgerow,
and the slow morning    slowly tracked by its shadow –
but this can still be!    the moon is so round tonight!
Stay, wait, my friend,    shout at me! I'm on my feet!

Bor, 15 September 1944.

*[Erőltetett menet]*

# PICTURE POSTCARDS

## (1)

Bulgarian guns rumble gruff and wild,
pound the mountain ridge, stutter, go mild;
what a mash of men and beasts and carts and thoughts,
the road rears and whinnies, the maned sky trots.
You live unchanging within me, through this restless chaos,
you shine deep in my consciousness, forever motionless
and silent, like the angel marvelling at desolation
or an insect burying itself in rotting vegetation.

## (2)

Six miles away, everything is on fire,
every house and haystack,
and peasant folk sit silent at the field's edge
smoking, stiff with fear.
One little shepherd-girl ruffles the water in the lake,
leading her ruffled flock
into the water where they drink the clouds
as they bend in their walk.

## (3)

Oxen are dribbling their blood-flecked saliva.
Everyone passes blood-stained urine.
The stinking battalion stands in ragged crowds.
Disgusting death drives its fetor through the clouds.

## (4)

I fell beside him, his body flipped over
as tense already as a string about to snap.
Shot in the back of the neck. – You'll end like that, –
I whispered to myself, – just lie still and quiet.
Patience spreads a flower-head into death. –
*Der springt noch auf*, – voice above me, angry breath.
My ear stuffed with dried blood, with filthy earth.

*[Razglednicak (1944)]*

451

**Rainer Maria Rilke**

LONELINESS

Loneliness is like a rain.
Towards dusk it leaves the sea where it has lain;
It mounts to skies unslaked by all they gain,
From far-off plains, unvisited retreats.
Soon from the sky it drops on city streets.

It rains down here in those ambiguous hours
When all the lanes wind onward into morning,
And saddened bodies, emptied of their powers,
Unlink in disenchantment, lords of nothing;
And couples who are couples in their loathing
Must search in one bed for their warring dreams:

Then loneliness flows with the streams...

*[Einsamkeit]*

**Viktor Sosnora**

DOLPHINS

I have no confidence in dolphins.
All that playfulness comes from fish-fat.
From the fact that
so many flabby herring are out of play.
Dolphins' blood
flows sluggishly
through sclerotic veins.
All that joy of living
comes from others' guts and roes.

452

This is the exuberance of a glutton.
No: you can keep dolphins
with their gambols of grace
and their grand pearly paunch.
This is pure corps-de-ballet.
This snorting,
these splashings and cavortings are for films,
for artists
who want to turn a prudent talent
into handclaps of colours.

Then: dolphins as music-lovers.
Well –
what's good about listening to the odd clarinet
at the end of a week's furious feeding?
kicking up your heels in a dance pour épater?
There they are housed in the sea,
but no fish.
They fly, yes,
but with what hope of becoming birds?
Dolphin-ballerinas,
long-beaked creatures
with wicked crooked teeth.

*[Del'finy]*

## Three Spanish Ballads

ROMANCE OF DURANDARTE

At the foot of a huge mountain, Durandarte lies dead,
His pillow is a stone, a green beech overhead,
In the air about him all the mountain birds collect,
Montesinos who saw him die cried out his lament,
At the grave he had made for him in a hard rocky bed,
He was prising off the helmet, he had got the sword unbelted,
He was tearing off the breastplate, he was plucking from the breast

453

The heart of Durandarte which he'd promised him to send
To Belerma, and plucking it, he laid his cheek to the dead
And cried so terribly in the dead man's face, and fainted again
    and again,
And at last came to himself, and these are the words he said:
'Durandarte, Durandarte, may God in mercy accept
Your soul, and pluck me from this earth to join my friend!'

*[Romance de Durandarte]* .


ROMANCE OF ALORA

Alora, besieged and surrounded, Alora by the riverside,
You that the Governor invested, on a Sunday, by early light,
The field thick with men on foot and thick with knights,
His big artillery had breached an entrance in your side:
You'd see the Moors all hurrying to the fort, taking in their flight
The flour and wheat, their women clutching clothes, their spry
Young sons loaded with raisins and figs, and a tribe
Of girls of fifteen lifting fine gold safely by.
They had unfurled their banner where the rampart met the sky.
Between the battlements there, a Moorish youth had climbed,
Armed with a crossbow, the crossbow with an arrow, and he
    cried
With a ringing voice, and everyone listened to his cry:
'A truce, a truce, Governor! The fort gives up the fight!'
He raises up his vizor to see who has spoken. Right
Through his head went the arrow, aimed between his eyes.
Little Jacobo took his hand, Pablo held the reins tight –
Those two he had brought up in his house since each was a child.
They carried him to the doctors – wondering if he might survive.
His last will and testament were the first words he sighed.

*[Romance de Alora, la bien cercada]*

## ROMANCE OF COUNT ARNALDOS

Who ever saw such a happening on the sea and its waters
As happened to Count Arnaldos on the morning of St John!
Out hunting for game, and on his hand a falcon,
He saw a galley coming in and making for the shore.
He saw its sails were of silk, and its rigging soft and costly,
And the sailor at the helm came in singing a song
That made the sea go peaceful and the winds blow softly,
That made the fish swim up from the deep parts they haunt,
That made birds settle on the mast out of their wanderings.
And then Count Arnaldos spoke, and you shall hear his voice:
'Tell me for God's sake, sailor – O tell me that song now!'
The sailor gave him his answer, and this is the answer he got:
'Only the man who comes and follows me learns this song!'

*[Romance del Conde Arnaldos]*


## Dezsö Tandori

### THE GREETING

Only the possible exists. Go down
into your deepest channels, take a chance: lie low.
Light filters down through the quiet water,
the foot stumbles on the shingle of the future –

the light stumbles: merely penetrating its water-bed
it has already run off with it, throwing branches out like flames –
– you know this was still, all this was still inside,
in those that are whole. So great still. Only

the possible exists.
Wait for it all. Your still-untraced life
opens inside you. Think how the veins of light

in the stream are not tracked either, yet the stream
scatters its colours, and – how often, often – returns
under the leaf that falls on its skin.

[*Az üdvözlet*]

THE BUSH FLOWN AWAY

You, who for all these years have been
the nest of the restless waters, growing
on the bank with your little grey companions,
huddling together, shivering, blowing –
now that the river has shrunk away
its caved-in bed is a track where
a single root points after you,
a single root, and you not there.

I wish I could have seen the moment
your foliage flapped into the sky,
when a poor grey willow grew
into a wonder, *impossibility*:
oh, how the thick loosened rigging
of your branches must have whipped and snapped
as if you were some parachute
tumbling bizarrely out and up.

Let other trees fall leaf by leaf,
or moulder from below, go dry,
but you went whole, knowing yourself,
choosing the place you'd go to die.
We know now your body was a bird,
its willow-incarnation pained it,
lonely among its friends, until
it learned the truth and so disowned it.

And you had the power to disown
– they themselves let you leave the land –
the anchors of your willow-life
which hooked you down into the ground;
for every pain withdraws there, deep

into the roots, collects there, ties
its knots and knarls there, where they keep
alliance with the earth they prise.

Now you are light as air in air,
and trembling for yourself, and glad
because you cannot know you unfold
for the last time if you unfold;
you swing and sway in the unknown,
a rapture unaware of rapture,
until the unknown breaks you down
with laws of air, an alien capture.

Sometime the water will come back,
the bushes on the shore will hang
branches above your vacant place,
the new shoots cover all your tracks:
the sky rejects you, the bank hides you,
and yet you have those gnarled roots,
as long as they have life, to guard you –
your living seal, stamped in the ooze.

*[Az elrepült bokor]*

## Marina Tsvetayeva

August – asters,
August – stars,
August – stacks
of grapes and rust-red
rowan-berries – August!

Play on, play on like a child
with your royal apples, August,
with such full, sweet-tempered fruit.
Smooth the heart with your palm,
August, in your royal name:
August! – The heart!

Let us kiss the month of late things,
late roses and late lightnings!
Meteor-showers –
August! – Month
of meteor-showers!

['Avgust – astry . . .']

## THE RETURN OF THE CHIEF

Horse – limp,
Sword – rust.
This – who?
Crowd's chief.

Step – hour,
Sigh – age,
Glance – down.
All – there.

Friend. – Foe.
Thorns. – Bays.
All – dream . . .
– Him. – Horse.

Horse – limp.
Sword – rust.
Cloak – old.
Shape – straight.

[Vozvrashchenie vozhdya]

## DIALOGUE OF HAMLET AND HIS CONSCIENCE

'She's on the bottom, with mud
and weeds . . . She went down there
to sleep – there's no sleep yet.'
'But she had all my love

that forty thousand brothers
could never match!'
                    'Hamlet!

She's on the bottom, with mud:
mud!... And her last wreath
swam with the logs on the river...'
'But she had all my love
that forty thousand...'
                    'Worth
less, really, than one lover's.

She's on the bottom, with mud.'
'But she had all my –
                    (*had she*)
                              – love?'

                    *[Dialog Gamleta s sovest'yu]*


## 13 Tuscan Folk-Songs


I staun at the winnock, the sea-faem blinds my een,
And aa I see's hertseikness frae lang syne,
And I cry oot the name o my luve – but och, in vain!

                    *['M'affaccio alla finestra e vedo l'onde']*


Stravaigin galliard laudie, gang your gate!
Braw ye may be, but my sang's no for you, lad.
The sang I sing's for my ain luve that later
Gaed by, mair braw, mair sprig, mair true, lad!

                    *['Giovanottin che passi per la via']*


*staun* stand; *winnock* window; *syne* since; *stravaigin* wandering; *galliard laudie*
gallant lad; *gang your gate* go your way

459

Flooer o the rye.
We'll aye be friens, but mair sae frae this day.
Mair friens we'll be – this is a sair guidbye!

['*Fiore di grano*']


Thon bird, thon rossignel – ye hear its sang?
Its liltin notes are eerie-wilfu, hurt-like.
Sic sangs are mine gin I daur ettle sing –
Sangs i my mou, but naethin liltin hert-like.
Sangs i my mou, my hert is liltin nane:
My luve that loed me leavit me my lane.

['*Vedete là quel rusignol che canta*']


Flooer o the cypress-tree.
Bleeze up, daurk caunle, ower thon daurker brae,
Licht for my luve wha comes this nicht tae me!

['*Fior di cipresso*']


I staun at the winnock, my een are on thon sea.
My thocht's o daith, that gies aa things ae day.
The best-loed hopes hae but slee tenandry.

['*M'affaccio alla finestra e veggo il mare*']


Glisk o the burn.
Wi you my luve in Januar and in June,
In life, in daith, tae you dear luve I turn.

['*Acqua di rio*']


*rossignel* nightingale; *thon* that; *sic* such; *gin* if; *ettle* try; *slee tenandry* precarious
status; *glisk* flash

460

I maun tae the sea, gang doon I maun tae the sea.
Doon by the sea my luve I micht meet.
Gin we suld meet, he'se nae mair weet his ee.

['*Alla marina me ne voglio andare*']


Gin ye but kent the wecht o dule in prief –
O eerie memorie o guid days gane!
When I think o't, I trimmle mair nor leaf –
What aince I was, what-like I hae became.
When I think o't, I shak like leaf in shaw –
What time noo gars me see, what aince I saw.

['*Se tù sapessi ancor quanto l'è doglia*']


I staun at the winnock, the sea liggs ootby.
The boats come nebbin in, nebbin this wey.
Lang, lang taks the boat o my luve tae gang by!

['*M'affaccio alla finestra e vedo il mare*']


Whit wee wee things o the yerth, yet nane sae bonny!
Whit wee wee things o the yerth, yet nane sae dear!
Tak noo the perl: the perl's a puir body,
A perl is peerie, but it buys great gear.
Tak noo the olive: whit a scrunty tree,
A peerie tree, but fruits sae bien and free.
Tak noo the rose: a warld's ee michtna see't,
The flooer sae peerie – but the smell sae sweet.

['*Le cose piccoline son pur belle*']


Tanger-orange, squeeshit sherp.
Laudie, I dinna greet tae loss your hert!
I greet I gied my ain hert's benmaist pairt.

['*Melangolo, melangolo spremuto*']


*maun* must; *he'se* he shall; *kent* knew; *dule* misery; *prief* proof; *shaw* grove;
*gars* makes; *liggs* lies; *peerie* small; *bien* fine; *benmaist* innermost

461

Faur oot i the sea-faem a wee bird keepit.
Ye'se hear nae sang but ane, ane cry, ane threep
Warld-faur: *Och, trechour hert,* he weepit, weepit.

[*''Ndel mezzo al mare che c'è un uccellino'*]

## Fyodor Tyutchev

The night sky hung so menacingly...
Clouding over from east to west,
Yet there was no mind, no menace there –
Only a troubled, sullen rest,
And flashes of the summer lightning
Flaring in and out of sight
Like hands of deaf-mute demons signing
Their conversations down the night:

But then! as if at a cordial signal,
Light blazing through a rift of sky –
Fields and far-off woods transfigured
Against the gloom they clarify –
And everything gone dark again, held
Tranquil in that dark, fine air –
As if some problem had been settled
Incomprehensibly – up there.

[*'Nochnoye nebo tak ugryumo'*]

*threep* repeated cry

**Mihály Váci**

THE MOST-AGE

See how we produce
with the most modern technology
for the most varied purposes
our most identical products,
in the most varied assortments – but within these
keeping a most eagle eye
on the most similar measurements
most understandably, surely, for within each group
the most minute variation
would cause the most massive confusion, this alone
must be most clearly
most understandable, must it not.

Following the most international interests
the most individual requirements
must be the most universally satisfied. Today
the most individual is what
is the most ubiquitous, and
the most original is what
is the most such-like as
the most absolutely
non-like. Everyone
would most preferably be like what today
mostly everyone is. The
most individual individual is
the most similar to everyone and the one
we can most readily be similar to. The
most original is what
most can
most readily attain. Today the
most dissident is the one who's
the most readily acceptable. The
most dissenting, to whom
most people
most readily
give assent in most things. The
most revolutionary, whatever

463

can be played with most safely
with the most innocuous aim
with the most meaninglessness
for the most people.
Today the
most
is the
mere.

This perhaps is
the most understandable
even for the most few
and the most futile too, is it not.

*[A leg-korszak]*

**István Vas**

PEST ELEGY

A what a town! Mud spurts up bursting with dirt.
February is busy laying slush on purple crape for the dead.
Soot sifts down ceaselessly thickened by sleet.

The compost-heaps of snow grow dark with grime.
The racked, hacked body of the town shudders in its mire.
Even deep in mud that body is one with mine.

Fog like poor wartime cottonwool hides the wounds of the
    Boulevard.
No more smoke from the Royal, the Emke, black and charred.
The New York's brand-new neons quiver by bombed-out shards.

This town has challenged the town-murdering fever,
its tortured gaieties are rekindled, it struggles to its feet,
declines again to drown in running mud, mortar, and fear.

464

Ten o'clock. The neons of life are quivering yet – just.
Despair, a helpless drunk, vomits in the mud.
Night cringes on Pest; sporadic car-revs thrust.

But oh what voices rose over the streets of the town!
Impossible hope with its fresh whistling sound,
utmost purity showering bright arguments around.

We flash eyes at each other and still remember its lights –
and it's everything we remember, my poor friends, am I right?
The dicky brickheart town beats to our own time.

The dicky brickheart misses beats but never stops,
and if fate should someday strip the town of stones,
it would rise again in time by the right it stores.

Its stones and beams and walls are not what make it,
a hundred demolitions could not break it:
its eternity is redeemed when death would take it.

The town has redeemed itself and it has redeemed me:
there my sins go swimming, in filth of February.
It was the time of the great Shriving, now and here.

And hell slips from my heart, repentance marked by solitude:
the town has redeemed itself, redeemed me for its good.
A strange forgiveness glimmers at me from its wounds.

Now every light is out; faith dawns through misty air.
I know this will be put on record, somehow, somewhere:
I lived here and never wished to live any place but here.

[*Pesti elégìa*]

# Paul Verlaine

STRAINS OF FORGETFULNESS – VIII

Shining like sand on the lea
Lies the snow,
Brokenly powdering all the monotonous
Levelness.

Bronze sleeps the sky,
Glimmerless,
And the life of the moon
Might be death.

Like clouds are the oak-trees
Afloat in the near woods;
Grey are they,
Grey in the night-mists.

Bronze sleeps the sky,
Glimmerless,
And the life of the moon
Might be death.

What do you do then,
O hoarse-throated rooks,
And you, hungering wolves,
Caught in the bitter blasts?

Shining like sand on the lea
Lies the snow,
Brokenly powdering all the monotonous
Levelness.

*[Ariettes oubliées VIII]*

466

## Théophile de Viau

ODE

Ahead of me a grey crow croaks,
Shade of a ghost is cast on my face;
I see moving across this place
Weasel with weasel, fox with fox;
My horse is stumbling where he trots,
My epileptic lackey drops,
Thunder cracks into a roar,
Charon stands by my body, calls
My soul to his ferry that no man recalls;
The earth lies open to its core.

This river runs back to its source,
A bull clings where the bells clang,
The blood is trickling from this crag,
She-bear and asp have intercourse;
High on a tower the vulture's beak
Stabs in vain at strangling snake,
The fire inside the ice is red,
The sun is mantled by a shade;
As the moon slides to fall and fade
This tree has moved from where it spread.

*[Ode: Un corbeau devant moy croasse]*

## Andrei Voznesensky

(Untitled poem from sequence 'The Ditch')

   – The grey ones the brown ones the living ones the enquiring
ones the childish ones the girlish ones the womanly ones the
short-sighted ones the angelic ones the oil-yielding ones the risible
ones the black ones the burning ones the passionate ones the

beautiful ones the all-seeing ones the unforgiving ones the mad ones the holy ones the pale blue ones the unbearable ones the happy ones the highest ones the dark blue ones –

(the golden ones the cold ones the commission-paid ones the rich red ones the faceted ones the greek ones the turkish ones the showcase ones the big ones the fake ones the emerald ones the pre-nuptial ones the chilly ones the gifted ones the crazed ones the clothed ones the warmed ones the family ones the carried ones the kissed ones)

– the frightened ones the arrested ones the distracted ones the despairing ones the pitiful ones the humble ones the persecuted ones –

(the hidden ones the sewn-up ones the self-concealing ones the family ones the warm ones)

– the weeping ones the terrible ones the uncomprehending ones the blind ones the comprehending ones the angry ones the praying ones the dead ones –

(the buried ones the ice-cold ones the forgotten ones)

– the grey ones the brown ones the insolent ones the appraising ones –

(the purified ones the golden ones the shopfront ones the sparkling ones the accounted ones the hundred-rouble ones)

– the heavenly ones the enquiring ones the eternal ones

*['Serye karie zhivye...']*

Sándor Weöres

HOMEWARD BOUND

At the city-limits market
dark-green wreaths in a basket:
it is All Souls' Day today.
My life and death lie elsewhere,
the poem flies me home there,
to Csönge hamlet far away.

There, death is a dear relative:
a crypt stands as the family grave,
a guardsman, vigilant, steadfast.
A cool wind ruffles its grass-hair –
and its angles and its door
have ivy coats thickly massed.

The gathered clan of that one blood
floats with the plenum-seeking flood
like a galley in the moonlight:
my poor uncle Géza, and my
grandfather: men of mild eye
who nursed their trees up to the light.

What a crowd of layered coffins,
set down each on each, crosswise,
short or long, but in repose,
my stillborn younger brother who
had neither name nor life to rue,
my grandmother, my aunt Rose.

And great-grandparents and who knows
how many dowagers, airy girls,
ladies, artless child-angels –
under the vaulted stone they float
on their lovely backs as in a boat,
facing the sky's wide ranges.

Oh the minutes I stand here now,
oh the years I shall sleep below.

and I have never entered yet.
Here my millenniums will be spent,
here I must lie till the Judgement,
unloosed, dissolved, dispersed.

With an outsider's blood I escape,
but the omphalos is my trap,
back into the family pit.
All our breaths go down to it,
the living send root after root
into the chill, the inert.

I feel the steady breath of the crypt:
no ego, only family unit,
no individual judgement-throne,
and I am moved to recognize
ancestral habits as they revive
in the body I thought my own.

Pang of a moment in my fate:
what good is it for heart to beat
or morning blaze so dazzlingly?
The merely passing being goes,
I sing a happy song with those
hosts of the at-one-with-me:

'The space-stuff peeled off from us,
our being was gone, reason, like gas
from a puny puffed-up burner.
But what we have of interdependence
was born with eternity and is endless
through past present and future.

Here the "I, you, he" are one,
our sacred flock is mass-undone,
no walled-round being, everything streaming.
Our past deeds leave a churning wake
down through the years without a break
in a world left dreaming.

We walked once on forbidden ground
and yet our trespass still praised God,

470

everything was from him, for him.
O Will that spurns a crude restraint,
forgive yourself in our old taint,
as your son promised when he came.'

My wishes are: when I am dead
you must lay me in the bed
of our vault, just as of old.
Let some far descendant plough
my loamy knot of bones right through
dear Csönge's furrow and fold.

*[Hazaszálló]*


FOR MY MOTHER

Rich teeming branch, you,
mother of mine,
my life's very first
woman,

big warm flower-bed,
soft pillow,
goblet brimming with
dawn-dew,

within you I found my
first nest,
my breast beat with
your breast,

between I and not-I no
barrier hung,
within you I and the world
were one.

My dream noses back into your
creeks and bays –
my dream noses back into your
creeks and bays!

Idol of alabaster,
mother of mine,
my life's titanic
woman,

your eyes gleam Isis-emeralded,
clear and fine,
your hair is bronze, Pallas-helmeted,
with pristine shine,

only on your face all shadows
grew hard,
like the hard afternoon sky
kestrel-barred.

My first beautiful toy,
mother of mine,
my childhood's opulent
woman,

The adolescence you gave me
got me mixed,
my eyes sidled from yours
unfixed.

I wondered: 'Why did she give me
life and love
with nothing to be the eternal
life of?

I make her kill and bury
so much, I know!
Why did she not expose me
in the snow!'

The adolescence you gave me
got me mixed,
my man's heart found you again,
steady, fixed,

my man's heart found your heart,
your breast,

grateful now for minutes, years
and death.

My dream drifts back into
your arms,
my dream drifts back into
your arms ...

Strong home, beautiful flag,
mother of mine,
my fate's unshakable
woman.

Once this whole life is squeezed in me
right through,
I will die into the all-in-all
as into you.

*[Anyámnak]*


DE PROFUNDIS

Whatever my origin, driven out into the earth,
my clothes will always carry the sheepfold stench
    of things here below.
This is the place where God's every plant and beast
pullulates through its appalling feast,
    chewing its neighbours raw.

I confess it was not good I expected to find,
but such a freight of misery was far from my mind:
    a son of a different star,
if he had even one minute's taste of our pain,
plunged into molten ore with sparks like rain,
    would soon be steam and air.

We swing from keen to glum, from gloom to joy,
up and down, up and down in our seesaw,
    swung without a say,
like someone forced by torturers to watch

473

a strobe of light and dark until they hatch
  his madness in that way.

Any reason in this world is a poor by-blow of Reason,
scrabbling at the mere shell of things, seizing
  nothing near the bone.
Half-asleep in half-darkness we slump,
wrestling through our fray in the deep swamp,
  our prison and our home:

for what are we but cannibals of each other,
buying our own life with the death of a brother:
  earth's law, earth's fee.
What are brothers but stone, tree, beast, man,
I eat my brother with gut-slithering pain,
  and my brother eats me.

An alley cat laps a young chick's blood:
one twists in death, one fights for food:
  I suffer both the same.
Rocks are crushed, earth's flesh punctured, cut:
neither stone nor earth knows any hurt,
  but I have the pain.

When anything is killed, I am killed,
the earth with all its miseries and ills
  gapes me its jaws.
A fly hits a flame: I'm writhing there,
I'm dying a thousand times every hour
  and without a pause.

Split the veil into the next existence,
and I shall still look shivering down the vistas
  and pits of this world.
There would be no assuaging even in heaven:
God's own light will build no haven,
  nor my lament grow cold.

SELF-PORTRAIT

My friend, you who claim to know me,
look round my room: nothing of its decoration
was my own choosing; open my wardrobe:
it has nothing to show you that is specially me.

My lover and my dog know how I caress them,
but I remain unknown to them. My old instrument
is well aware of my hand's contours;
it too cannot sing about me.

Yet I am not in hiding – simply, I do not exist.
I act, I suffer, as all men do,
but my essential core is non-existence itself.

My friend, you must not regard me as having secrets.
I am as transparent as glass – how then
do you imagine you can really see me?

['Barátom, ki azt mondod . . .']


'ETERNAL DARKNESS CLINGS . . .'

Eternal darkness clings to the concave of the surface.
That is the ingrown frame
of things; that is hell. Uniform the night-face,
uninterruptedly stony, black, unflickering flame.

That is hell: life tilts out from it, the
scatterer, out from this stillness! Clod, grass, man, animal,
all spring from it, all that hurt and kiss each other,
from hell, all those on whom sun-rays fall!

The outer and the inner arch of things –
is it obverse or reverse that rings?
is there a third arch: light without dark?

From soil to heart, all things sing;
not with intellect: they respond with their being,
like a woman, a poem, just as they are.

[*Örök sötétség . . .'*]


ARS POETICA

Memory cannot make your song everlasting.
Glory is not to be hoped from the evanescences:
how could it glorify you, when its glitterings are not essences?
Your song may flaunt a few embers from eternal things
while those who face them take fire as a minute passes.

Sages suggest: only individuals are in their senses.
All right; but to get more, be more than individual:
slip off your great-poet status, your lumbering galoshes,
serve genius, give it your human decencies
which are point and infinity: neither big nor small.

Catch the hot words that shine in the soul's estuaries:
they feed and sustain countless earth-centuries
and only migrate into your transient song,
their destiny is eternity as your destiny is,
they are friends who hug you and hasten soaring on.


THE OLD ONES

They are so derelict, the old ones.

I watch them sometimes through the window
as they trudge home in an icy wind
with a back-load of firewood –
or in a panting summer
as they sit in the sunny porch –
or on winter evenings by the stove
slumped in deep sleep –
they stand in front of the church
with palms stretched out in sadness, downcast,
like faded autumn leaves
in the yellow dust.

And when they stutter through the street
with a stick, even the sunshine looks askance at them,
and everyone makes it sound odd to say:
'How goes it, old man?'

The summer Sun,
the winter snow,
autumn leaf,
crisp spring flower
all pour an endless song in their ears:
'Life-cauldronful of old meat,
life-cartful of old hay,
life-candleful of guttered wax:
you are eaten up,
you are thrown away,
you are burnt to nothing,
you can sleep now...'

They are like someone
ready for a journey
and starting to pack.

And sometimes, when their gnarled hands
caress the blond head of a child,
it must surely hurt them to sense
that these two hands,
hard-working hands,
blessing hands
are needed now by no one any more.

And they are already prisoners,
prisoners in chains, drowsy, apathetic:
seventy heavy years shackle their wrists,
seventy years of sin and grief and trouble,
seventy heavy years have chained them to wait
for a kindly hand,
a dreadful hand,
an unarguable hand
to give its command:

'Time now, lay it down.'

[Öregek]

477

## LE JOURNAL

a mare ran into the yard
a cedar caught her sight
virginal phenomena paired
'its image is my spirited spirit'

O to sing in Horsish
bitted and bridled by the Muse
the saddle receiving Orpheus
ode psalm hymn in my jaws

Chung-kuo Hellas France Mizraim
would marvel at my hoofs of porcelain
my white lamp my socks prim
beyond the lasts of our understanding

a spherical breviary would come
up gratis sogar
I'd need no honorarium
only heavenly fire

I'd lift into the light of the sun
I'd fall into the dew of the moon
with sweet fruit pouring in
the hieroglyphics of my skeleton

anthropoid heaven-dwellers by the score
would be houyhnhnmized in my horsehood
and Xenophons' belief be proved
if I sang to my horsely score

the apehead is an evil pitcher
heavenly sparks prance there
and sink back to cinders in matter
as soon as they are music and picture

on the plain the bacchanalia
on the peaks King Zeus in the abyss
Aphrodite Pelagia
coral-reef in purple darkness

Helen's brothers in the skies
far flame no spit can sting
your groin-spasm in heavenly fires
you've as much domestique orang

your hand creates no more
than a fold on Diotima's robe
and she smooths it on her breast
to shine where it was pressed

thinking about the authority
of Attica of Italia
a stoa of babblers actually
serenade for Garufalia

one morning I get up early
look stomachly footly handly
my loving Garufalia
is in love with Garufalia

I gaze at you O Garufalia
mirror-wall of my being
I sniff my own snout finally
self reconciles everything

but life-like side by side
shepherd shouts sheep graze
man and worm forage
on woman horse and other gods

orang komm her look around
no mango palm liana sandalwood
your country dreams in other images
concrete bulks steel stretches

on the shore of the city's man-din
the field's girl-body lies
with stripped hills the victim
of shuddering technologies

Danube gets the gull's droppings
the swallows shit on the porches

a Hittite king goes jigging
under Lajos Kossuth's portrait

balsam for all the inhabitants
to make the limb sweet as a violet
mummies shut in mastabas
you're a Hittite don't deny it

the Hittite the Hittite
a strange race is the Hittite
it's believed by every Hittite
everybody else is a Hittite

an odd bird is the gull
it's believed by every gull
that whenever he meets a gull
it is never really a gull

let your dreams revolve your potential
it grows light over the city
the dustman starts up early
his nag no Pegasus after all

in the fading whirlpool of stars
his dagger-point stabs flying paper
while Debrecen wakens on the shores
of the Ganges where palm-trees waver

Sárika goes in her sarong
by the Déri Museum for a stroll
musk-smells drift along
by the six-footed Golden Bull

endless dreams of the plains
painted on mirage-soft seas
Aurengzebe's mosque raised
above Hindu temple-cornices

waves from Debrecen's Great Wood
flood a sleek barber's shop
snails octopuses are whirled up
mirrors lose their drowsy mood

attentive assistants in white
stand in water to their brows
customers in the muddy pit
foam infusoria on their scowls

patch on patch the sea grows
Golgotha is drenched Csokonai
hangs on a giant cross
Tóth and Gulyás by his side

oh I need no foolscap to write
for if I should shed my skin
the same dumb witness would rise
from the hieroglyphics of my skeleton

what I don't know let me say
what I do know let me hide
and when tomorrow flies and I stay
I am asked and my skeleton replies

what I don't think let me declare
and what I do think let me conceal
shut up the truth the fake is shrill
the rest must be clawed from its lair

in chinks between lines of verse
angels and prophets clutter
the paper's whitest space
worth more than any letter

creation never bettered a stroll
blessed trackless periplum
but the pyramid's no joke at all
clinging to each minute-long millennium

the sewer clogs you with weed
to keep you here in the world
Homo Esothericus and your fellows
droves of Homo Bestialis

the sisterhood of Narcissa
recommend a solitary love-in

481

and the goat-breeders's synod
adopts the puny faun

Hellene eye and Hebrew sight
have their lines crossed in such a state
that hell-egg and heaven-fruit
make pining-apple omelette

orang geh weg give no sign
you are a useless oracle
all this is natural miracle
says Franz Kafka the divine

already both sides of our moustache
hold little bubbles in a net
and there is a rout of goldfish
from jaws now wide and wet

the whole aquarium wakes
to a throbbing panicky stir
the old cupboard shakes
and even the thermometer

but the dingy family faces
look blankly down from the walls
winking no come-ye-alls
either to us or the fishes

marvel rather at the charger
it knows indescribable things
its smile in its soul is larger
than any its lips could bring

its harness and saddle are alien
yet it bears them if laid on
all it shuns is the muddy fountain
and the fallow field is its domain

what it accomplishes the many tasks
are not for it to meditate
by the time it has its questions asked
its hide squeaks on our feet.

**Pedro Xisto**

SEAWEED

coldgreenishwaterscoldgreenish
waterscoldgreenishcoldgreenish
coldgreenishwaterswaterswaters
waterswaterswaterscoldgreenish
waterscoldcoldgreenishgreenish
waterscoldgreenishcoldgreenish
coldgreenishwaters coldcoldcold

*[Algas]*



**Yevgeny Yevtushenko**

Poetry smoulders
without being extinguished.
Poetry's moulders
are fun to distinguish.

That fellow's no dunce,
chewing his librium,
briefcase in equilibrium,
with boiled carrot lunch.
He'd give it all for a rousse
and rum babas, but
the Muse –

      and what a Muse! –
zaps his lapels –

        hup!
And thoughts drill his forehead,

and he forgets about his spoon,
he goes up like Goliath!
                        Socrates!
... in his Oblomov balloon.
He's no Apollo either –
scrawny, plain as a scone.
Like a mushroom, he teeters
transparent and forlorn.
But suddenly his ears
whistle –
            full stop!
Or the age takes a boxer's swipe
on the snout –
                a line appears!
And look –
            a crazy little bird
staggers – down –
a ragpicker, a clown –
a drawing-room drunkard.
But let her hear the command
and –
        like branches in winter
God
    rings
            within her
and –
        her eyelids are marblebound.
And see that
            slob,
                    shaman,
absol-
    ute babbler:
give him champagne,
hot mommas
                not rum babas –
and the order from within
strides fast and severe,
he's the people's clarion,
Savonarola's here!

Poetry's moulders
are fun to distinguish,

but poetry cold-shoulders
us, patents our souls.
What sort of judge d'you wish?
Well,
        to the biedermeier we're 'trash',
but to ourselves all of us
are, what are we but –
                                saviours!

                        *['Poeziya chadit...']*


INCANTATION

Think of me in the spring night
and think of me in the summer night,
think of me in the autumn night
and think of me in the winter night.
If I am nowhere near your side,
if I am travelling far and wide –
lie flat beneath your long cool sheet
and float in waves from head to feet,
lost in the easy slow sea-beat
with none but me or seas to meet.

You must not think during the day.
The day must take its random way,
make wine run red and smoke spread grey.
Well, think of anything but me.
Think of anything by day –
at night it's me and only me.

Hear me through the whistling trains,
through the cloud-cut weathervanes,
when I'm racked by ruthless pains,
take me back to those dark rooms
where you brooded joys and glooms
and pressed your temples into tombs.

I beg you – in the quietest quiet,
or at the hissing rainstorm's height,
or by the snow-bright window-light,
eyes half open, dreams in flight –
think of me in the spring night
and think of me in the summer night,
think of me in the autumn night
and think of me in the winter night.

*[Zaklinanie]*

# INDEX OF POETS

Endre Ady (1877-1919)
pp.373-8
Gennady Aigi (b.1934)
pp.364-9
Guillaume Apollinaire (1880-1918)
pp.379-82
Anna Akhmatova (1889-1967)
p.383
Pierre Albert-Birot (1876-1967)
pp.378-9

Aleksandr Blok (1880-1921)
p.335
Edgard Braga (1897-1985)
pp.302-5
Bertolt Brecht (1898-1956)
pp.43-6, 282-3

Haroldo de Campos (b.1929)
pp.286-92
Rosalía de Castro (1837-1885)
pp.383-9
Luis Cernuda (1902-1963)
p.268
Claudian (c.370-404)
p.325
St Columba (c.520-597)
pp.389-93

Hans Magnus Enzensberger (b.1929)
pp.283-6

Garcilaso de la Vega (1501-1536)
pp.176-9
Jean Genet (1910-1986)
pp.393-5
Ágnes Gergely (b.1933)
p.395
Eugen Gomringer (b.1925)
pp.293-300
[Eugène] Guillevic (b.1907)
pp.222-5

Heinrich Heine (1797-1856)
pp.402-5
Friedrich Hölderlin (1770-1843)
pp.256-61

Vera Inber (1890-1972)
pp.405-6

Ernst Jandl (b.1925)
pp.406-7
Attila József (1905-1937)
pp.340-64

László Kálnoky (1912-1985)
pp.408-11
Lajos Kassák (1887-1967)
pp.411-22
Velimir Khlebnikov (1885-1922)
pp.335-7, 423-7

Giacomo Leopardi (1798-1837)
pp.229-44, 326-30
Federico García Lorca (1898-1936)
pp.262-7

Giambattista Marino (1569-1625)
pp.181-2
Leonid Martynov (1905-1980)
pp.51-2, 269-72
Vladimir Mayakovsky (1894-1930)
pp.37-41, 114-55, 337
Henri Michaux (1899-1984)
pp.273-9
Michelangelo Buonarroti (1475-1564)
pp.326, 427-9
Eugenio Montale (1896-1981)
pp.6-24, 225-7, 338-40

Nikolai Nekrasov (1821-1877)
pp.429-30
Pablo Neruda (1904-1973)
pp.46-51, 430-4

Ottó Orbán (b.1936)
pp.434-41

Yury Pankratov (b.1933)
p.301
Boris Pasternak (1890-1960)
pp.32-5, 204-11
Francesco Petrarca (1304-1374)
pp.164-6

August Graf von Platen (1796-1835)
pp.309-21
Ezra Pound (1885-1972)
p.370
Jacques Prévert (1900-1977)
pp.272-3, 441-2
Aleksandr Pushkin (1799-1837)
pp.330-4, 442-7

Salvatore Quasimodo (1901-1968)
pp.212-21

Miklós Radnóti (1909-1944)
pp.448-51
Rainer Maria Rilke (1875-1926)
p.452
Robert Rozhdestvensky (1932-1994)
pp.280-2

Maurice Scève (c.1500-1560)
pp.166-76
William Shakespeare (1564-1616)
pp.227-8
Vladimir Solovyov (1853-1900)
pp.334-5
Viktor Sosnora (b.1936)
pp.452-3

Dezsö Tandori (b.1938)
pp.455-7

Torquato Tasso (1544-1595)
pp.179-81
Nikolai Tikhonov (1896-1979)
pp.41-2
Marina Tsvetayeva (1892-1941)
pp.36, 457-9
Fyodor Tyutchev (1803-1873)
p.462

Mihály Váci (1924-1970)
pp.463-4
István Vas (1910-1991)
pp.464-5
Paul Verlaine (1844-1896)
p.466
Théophile de Viau (1590-1626)
p.467
Yevgeny Vinokurov (b.1929)
p.212
Andrei Voznesensky (b.1933)
pp.186-201, 467-8

Sándor Weöres (1913-1989)
pp.63-101, 469-82

Pedro Xisto (1901-1987)
p.483

Yevgeny Yevtushenko (b.1933)
pp.53-5, 201-4, 483-6